IMAGES
of Aviation

YEAGER AIRPORT
AND
CHARLESTON AVIATION

On the Cover: A Capital Airlines DC-4, the *Capitaliner Atlanta*, sits on the ramp in front of the new administration building of Kanawha Airport in the early 1950s. (Courtesy of Charleston Newspapers.)

IMAGES
of Aviation

YEAGER AIRPORT AND CHARLESTON AVIATION

Nicholas Keller on behalf of the Central
West Virginia Regional Airpot Authority
Foreword by W. Kent Carper

ARCADIA
PUBLISHING

ISBN 978-1-4671-2541-3

Published by Arcadia Publishing
Charleston, South Carolina

Printed in the United States of America

Library of Congress Control Number: 2016958675

For all general information, please contact Arcadia Publishing:
Telephone 843-853-2070
Fax 843-853-0044
E-mail sales@arcadiapublishing.com
For customer service and orders:
Toll-Free 1-888-313-2665

Visit us on the Internet at www.arcadiapublishing.com

To my late father, Thomas Wayne Keller, who encouraged a love of aviation in me during my childhood

Contents

FOREWORD

Kanawha Airport is a story of smoothing out mountains and, where they once impeded movement, making of them an airport from which one might go with speed wherever his inclination or his need required.

—Carl Calvert

The words of Kanawha County Court president Carl Calvert in 1947 still hold true 70 years after the opening of Kanawha Airport. Today, Yeager Airport provides the public with convenient access to almost any city in the world with only one or two stops, making it West Virginia's gateway to the world. Indeed, today, Yeager Airport is West Virginia's busiest commercial airport, serving more than half a million passengers a year.

As president of the Kanawha County Commission, I am proud to have led the fight against an ill-advised scheme to close the airport in favor of a new "Transpark"—a move the Federal Aviation Administration deemed economically unfeasible because the new airport's costs would exceed its benefits. I was also honored to work with Sen. Robert C. Byrd and Maj. Gen. Allen Tackett to overturn the Pentagon's Base Realignment and Closure Commission initial recommendation to close the 130th Airlift Wing of the Air National Guard in 2005. The Air National Guard, which has operated at Yeager since 1947, has played a critical role in the Global War on Terror and continues to be a source of pride for West Virginia and the National Guard community.

Today, the airport is one of the largest economic development engines in the region and responsible for creating over 1,800 jobs and $174 million per year in economic output. Carl Calvert and the visionaries who helped lead the drive to undertake one of the largest earth moving projects of its time in order to create this airport could have scarcely imagined how wildly successful their efforts would be. In this 70th anniversary year of Yeager Airport, it is altogether fitting and proper that the success of commercial aviation in the region be chronicled in this outstanding book.

—W. Kent Carper
President, Kanawha County Commission

Acknowledgments

I am grateful to many people who have encouraged me to write a book about the aviation history of the Charleston area, especially my friend Tim Abraham. Among those to whom I owe a special debt of gratitude is Terry Sayre, a mentor of 10 years and current airport director. Additionally, I would like to thank Kanawha County Commission president W. Kent Carper; without his visionary leadership, Yeager Airport as we know it would not exist today. Former commissioner and current West Virginia secretary of revenue David Hardy and commissioner Henry Shores have steadfastly supported the airport over the years and recognize its importance to the economic vitality of the county. I am thankful to the Board of Members of the Central West Virginia Regional Airport Authority who offer excellent vision and support to airport management. I am grateful to Trip Shumate, who assisted me in finding several wonderful photographs from the newspaper archives. Retired colonel Bill Peters provided me with a wealth of information for captions and several historical Air National Guard photographs. Special thanks are also given to my great friend Mike Plante and the following members of airport staff who assisted me in searching for photographs and conducting research: Paige Butcher, Alex Ellis, Roger Hill, Chris Keyser, Nathan Koepsel, April Payne, and Travis Ryan. Many of the Yeager Airport photographs that appear in these pages were taken by Kimberly Lewis and Brenda Thomas during their airport careers.

Finally, a special debt of gratitude is also owed to my wife, Allison, who advised me, corrected many errors, and endured me working on the book during many evenings and weekends.

Unless otherwise noted, all images appear courtesy of the Central West Virginia Regional Airport Authority.

Airport Directors of Kanawha Airport and Yeager Airport

1947–1959	Fred C. Alley
1959–1976	Calvin F. Wilson
1976–1981	Ralph R. Cowgill
1981–1996	Jeffrey D. Bubar
1996–1999	Danny C. Huffman
1999–2015	Richard A. Atkinson III
2015–present	Terry D. Sayre

INTRODUCTION

Charleston's first glimpse of aviation occurred June 25–27, 1912, when three aviators held a meet at a South Charleston ball field. Just days afterward, the first seaplane was flown in West Virginia on the Kanawha River from Wilson's Island to Blaine Island. In the 1920s, a small airfield existed in Kanawha City near the present-day intersection of MacCorkle Avenue and Thirty-Fifth Street. Recognizing the need for airmail and commercial passenger service, the City of Charleston commissioned the building of Wertz Field in Institute, West Virginia. Opening in 1930, Wertz Field became the first public airport in the Kanawha Valley, which led to the first commercial passenger service in October 1933 on American Airlines. Wertz Field became host to trainees from the West Virginia State College Civilian Pilot Training Program in 1939. This program was integrated in 1940, which helped pave the way for later civil rights advances. Approximately 30 of the African American trainees would later become Tuskegee Airmen in World War II. In the late 1930s, it became clear that newer and larger aircraft, such as the DC-3, would make Wertz Field inadequate.

A search for a new airport site was held, and ground was broken for the Kanawha Airport in 1944. During construction, over nine million cubic yards of dirt and rock were moved using over two million pounds of explosives. Opening in November 1947, the Kanawha Airport was conveniently situated north of downtown Charleston, West Virginia, and provided ample space for aircraft operations. Also in 1947, the 167th Fighter Squadron of the West Virginia Air National Guard was formed at Kanawha Airport. Expanding over the years to keep up with advances in air travel, the airport was renamed Yeager Airport in 1985 in honor of Brig. Gen. Charles "Chuck" Yeager. Today, Yeager Airport meets the needs of the region by providing convenient and cost-effective transportation options to the traveling public.

One

Early Aviation and Seaplanes

Charleston saw its first airplane flight on June 25, 1912, during an aviation meet that was heavily promoted in the press. Local department stores featured aviation sales, and one store displayed one of the aircraft that would later fly. During the third day of the meet, former Charleston resident Paul Peck flew around the dome of the West Virginia capitol, which was then located on Capitol Street in downtown Charleston. In the 1920s, an airfield was established in Kanawha City near the Thirty-Fifth Street and MacCorkle Avenue intersection. Most notably, United States Army Air Service bombers operated at the airfield for potential use against protesting coal miners during the Battle of Blair Mountain in 1921.

In the 1930s, seaplanes became popular and bases were established on the Kanawha River in Charleston, Institute, Montgomery, and South Charleston. The first seaplane was owned by O.R. "Shorty" Hayes, who stored it on the Elk River in a hangar behind Morgan Lumber Company, near the present-day location of Pennsylvania Avenue and Lee Street. The most popular seaplane base was the Kanawha Flying Club, operated by Glenn Clark at the downtown Charleston levee for much of its existence.

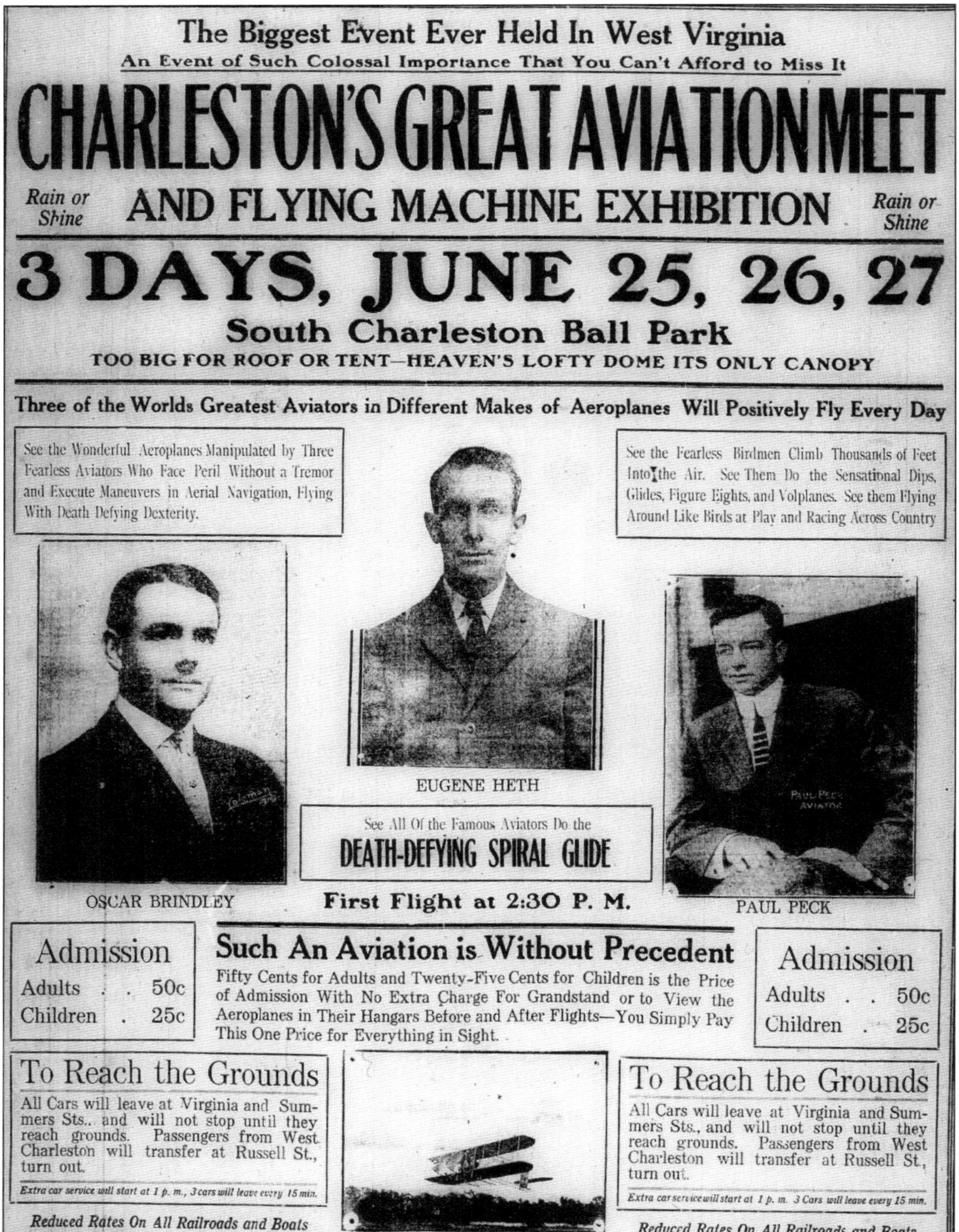

The Biggest Event Ever Held In West Virginia

An Event of Such Colossal Importance That You Can't Afford to Miss It

CHARLESTON'S GREAT AVIATION MEET

Rain or Shine AND FLYING MACHINE EXHIBITION *Rain or Shine*

3 DAYS, JUNE 25, 26, 27

South Charleston Ball Park

TOO BIG FOR ROOF OR TENT—HEAVEN'S LOFTY DOME ITS ONLY CANOPY

Three of the Worlds Greatest Aviators in Different Makes of Aeroplanes Will Positively Fly Every Day

See the Wonderful Aeroplanes Manipulated by Three Fearless Aviators Who Face Peril Without a Tremor and Execute Maneuvers in Aerial Navigation, Flying With Death Defying Dexterity.

See the Fearless Birdmen Climb Thousands of Feet Into the Air. See Them Do the Sensational Dips, Glides, Figure Eights, and Volplanes. See them Flying Around Like Birds at Play and Racing Across Country

OSCAR BRINDLEY

EUGENE HETH

PAUL PECK

See All Of the Famous Aviators Do the

DEATH-DEFYING SPIRAL GLIDE

First Flight at 2:30 P. M.

Admission
Adults . . 50c
Children . 25c

Such An Aviation is Without Precedent

Fifty Cents for Adults and Twenty-Five Cents for Children is the Price of Admission With No Extra Charge For Grandstand or to View the Aeroplanes in Their Hangars Before and After Flights—You Simply Pay This One Price for Everything in Sight.

Admission
Adults . . 50c
Children . 25c

To Reach the Grounds

All Cars will leave at Virginia and Summers Sts., and will not stop until they reach grounds. Passengers from West Charleston will transfer at Russell St., turn out.

Extra car service will start at 1 p. m., 3 cars will leave every 15 min.

Reduced Rates On All Railroads and Boats

To Reach the Grounds

All Cars will leave at Virginia and Summers Sts., and will not stop until they reach grounds. Passengers from West Charleston will transfer at Russell St., turn out.

Extra car service will start at 1 p. m. 3 Cars will leave every 15 min.

Reduced Rates On All Railroads and Boats

This advertisement in the *Charleston Gazette* promotes an aviation meet to be held on June 25–27, 1912, with Oscar Brindley, Eugene Heth, and Paul Peck from the Berger Aviation Company. Four biplanes and one monoplane were brought to the ball field in South Charleston. The meet marked the first time in West Virginia history that three pilots and aircraft flew on the same day in the same location. Each pilot was scheduled to fly two flights each day of the meet.

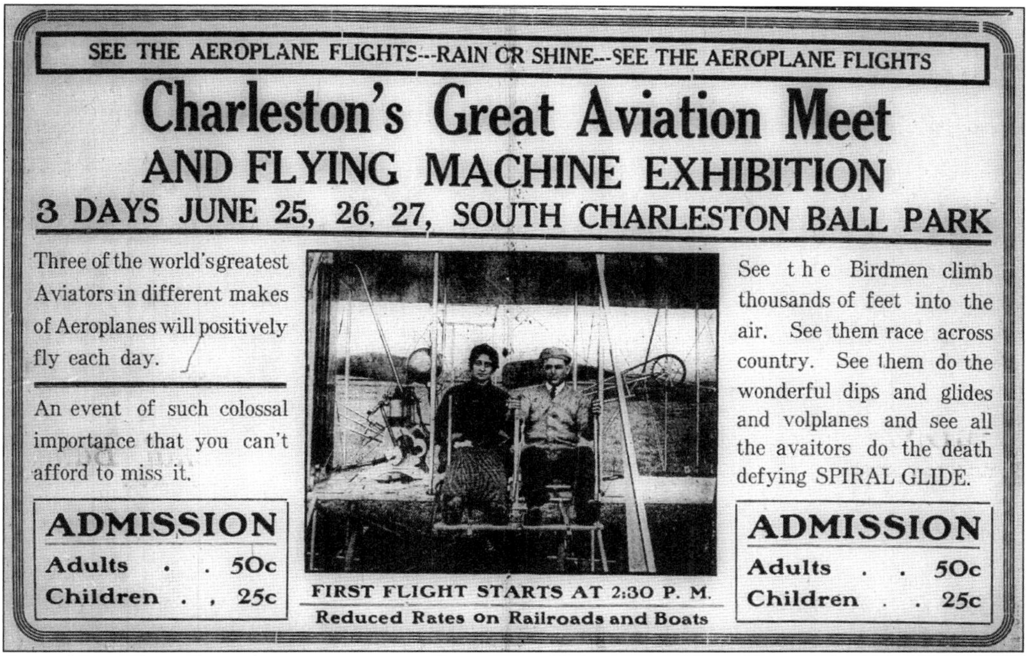
SEE THE AEROPLANE FLIGHTS--RAIN OR SHINE--SEE THE AEROPLANE FLIGHTS

Charleston's Great Aviation Meet

AND FLYING MACHINE EXHIBITION

3 DAYS JUNE 25, 26, 27, SOUTH CHARLESTON BALL PARK

Three of the world's greatest Aviators in different makes of Aeroplanes will positively fly each day.

An event of such colossal importance that you can't afford to miss it.

ADMISSION

Adults	50c
Children	25c

FIRST FLIGHT STARTS AT 2:30 P. M.

Reduced Rates on Railroads and Boats

See the Birdmen climb thousands of feet into the air. See them race across country. See them do the wonderful dips and glides and volplanes and see all the avaitors do the death defying SPIRAL GLIDE.

ADMISSION

Adults	50c
Children	25c

June 25, 1912, marked the first time in history that an airplane flew over the Kanawha Valley. The first flight was piloted by Oscar Brindley, who took off at 2:45 p.m. and stayed airborne for 10 minutes. The second flight was by Eugene Heth, who stayed airborne for seven minutes in a Wright biplane. The third flight was by Paul Peck, who flew his Columbia biplane at speeds of 70 miles per hour at an altitude of 1,200 feet.

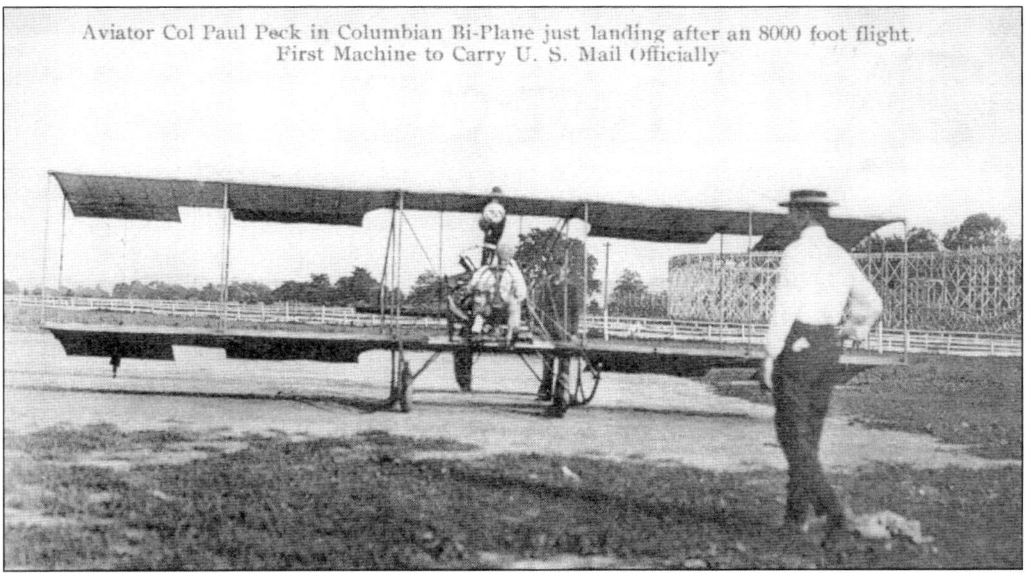

Ansted, West Virginia–born Paul Peck is seen here with his custom-built Columbia biplane. Peck lived in Charleston during his youth and began flying in 1911 at the age of 22 under the instruction of Glenn Curtiss. Peck was one of the first West Virginians to receive a pilot's license. He set many records, including being the first person to fly over the Capitol and the first person to carry airmail for hire. Unfortunately, Peck's life was cut short when he died in an airplane crash on September 12, 1912.

GAZETTE. WEDNESDAY, JUNE 19, 1912.

Flying! Flying! Flying!

The Biggest Outdoor Event Ever Held in West Virginia.

Charleston's Gigantic Aviation Meet

And Flying Machine Exhibition

RAIN OR SHINE

3 Days--June 25, 26, 27, South Charleston's BALL PARK

3 of the World's Greatest Aviators in Different Makes of Aeroplanes Will Positively Fly Every Day.

NOTE You must Take Cars at Virginia and Summers Streets

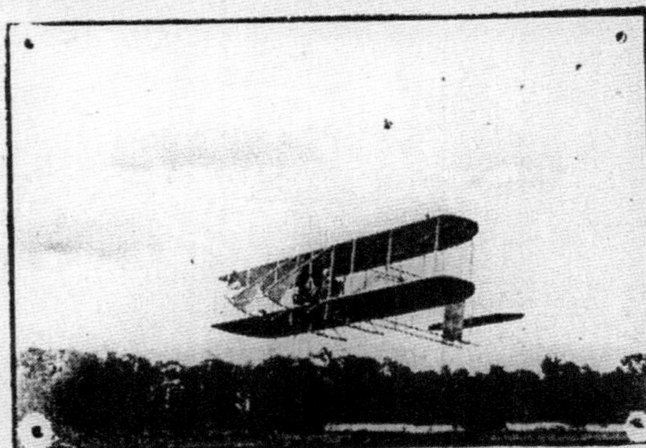

All Cars Will Leave at This Point and Go Through Without a Stop

See the wonderful birdmen in their sensational dips, glides, and volplanes. See them climb thousands of feet into the heavens. See them race across country and see them do the death defying Spiral Glide.

FIRST FLIGHT AT 2:30 P. M.

ADMISSION		Rates on all railroads and boats	ADMISSION	
Adults	50c		Adults	50c
Children	25c		Children	25c

The second day of the aviation meet was June 26, 1912, and included one close call after Oscar Brindley encountered a storm. Reaching speeds of 100 miles per hour flying with the wind, Brindley turned toward the field, cut his engine, and landed after barely clearing a fence and the grandstand. On June 27, 1912, Paul Peck departed South Charleston, flying against a strong wind toward Charleston. Reaching Capitol Street in downtown Charleston, Peck circled the dome of the state capitol and flew back to South Charleston reaching speeds of 70–75 miles per hour.

The first hydro-aeroplane, or seaplane, flight in West Virginia occurred on June 30, 1912, on the Kanawha River. Eugene Heth took off from the river near Lock 6 in North Charleston, flew down the river to Wilson's Island in Dunbar (under the current Interstate 64 bridges), upriver to Blaine Island in South Charleston, and back to the Lock 6 area of North Charleston.

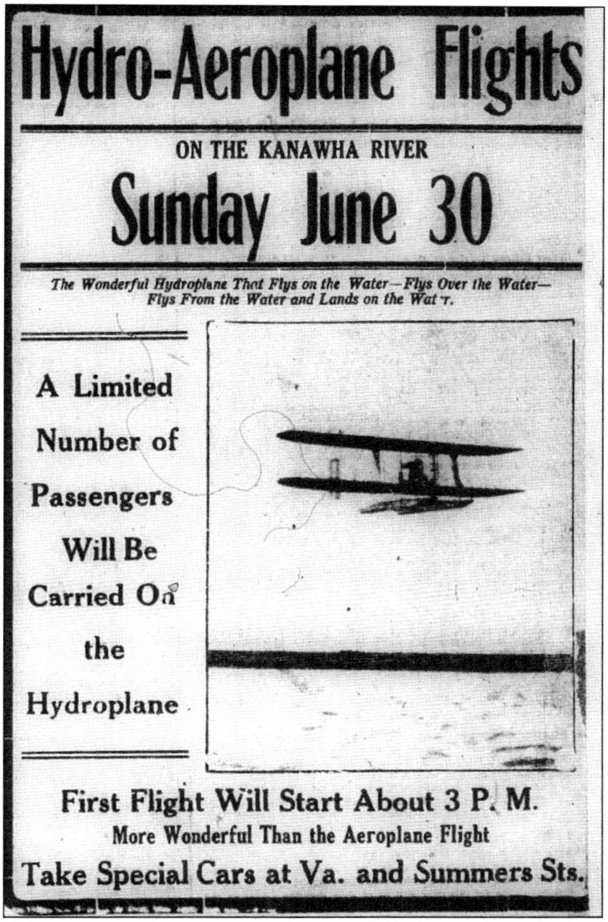

George Delforge (second from left), age 25, and Edgar O. Michaux (seated on the right) are pictured with an unidentified airplane in South Charleston, West Virginia, around 1920. (Courtesy of the West Virginia State Archives, Margaret Delforge Collection.)

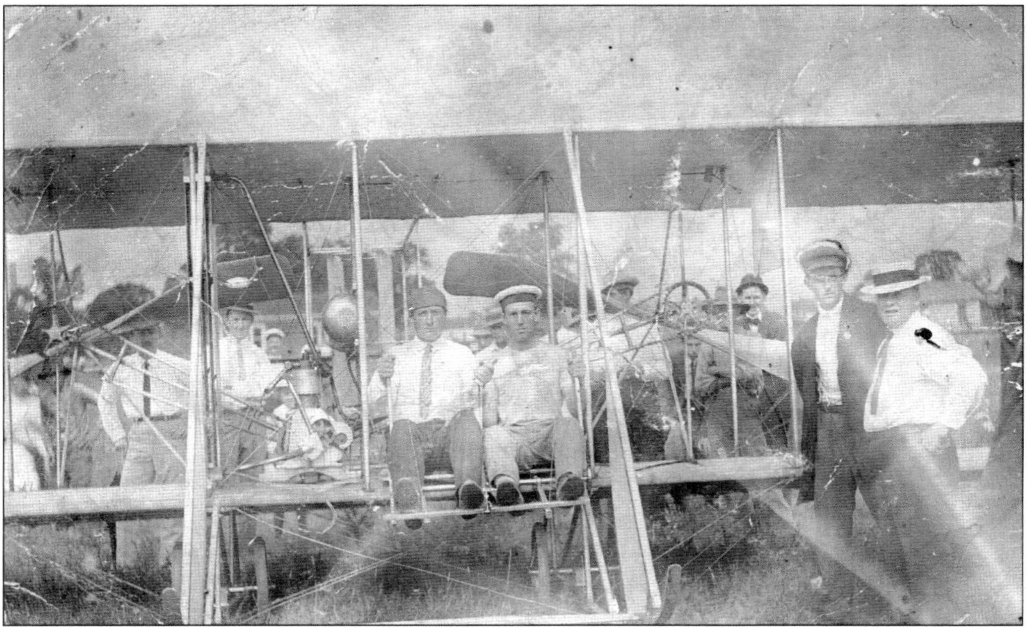

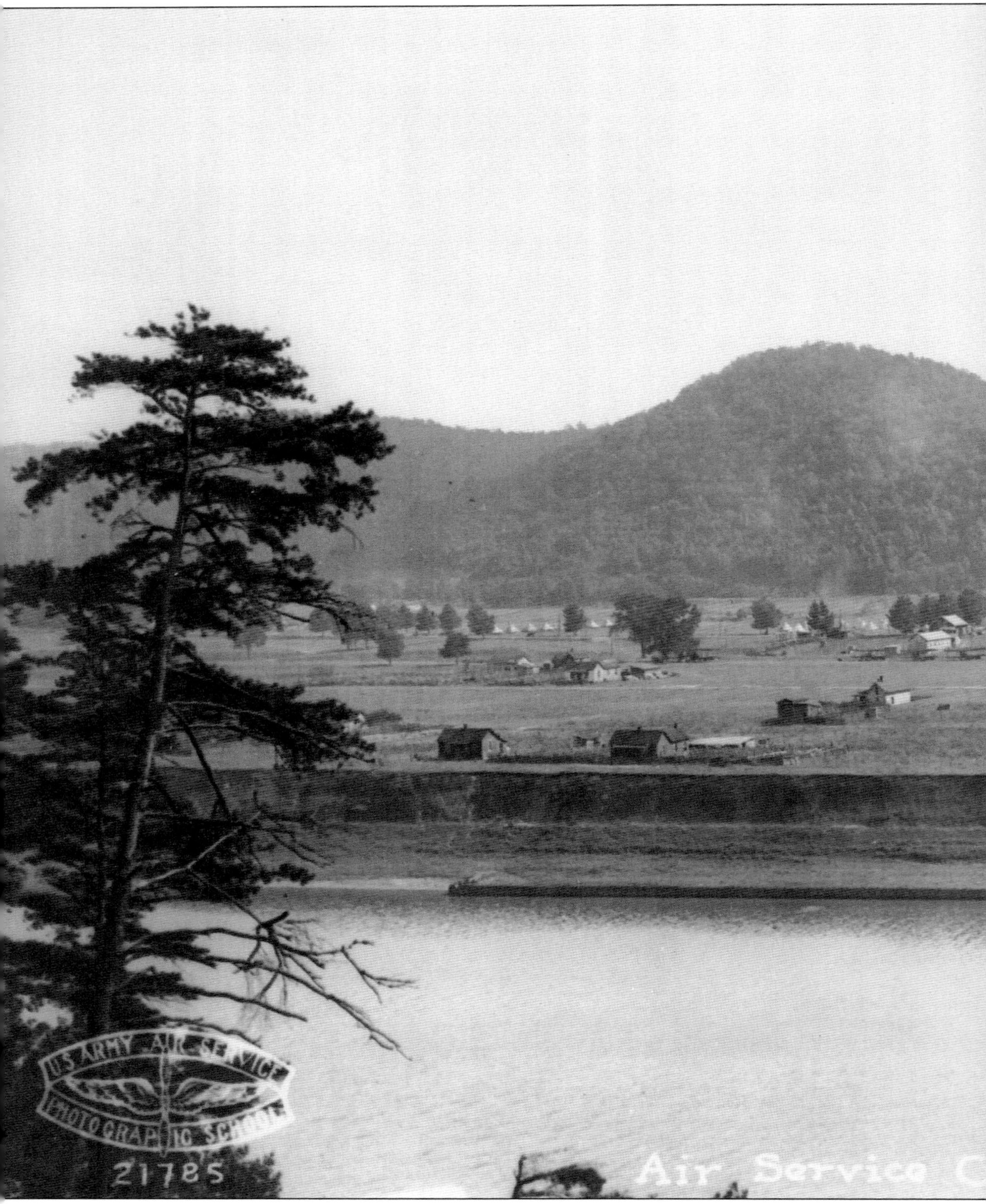

During the Battle of Blair Mountain in 1921, US Army Air Service bombers were brought to West Virginia to assist federal troops. On August 26, 1921, Brig. Gen. Billy Mitchell led an expedition of three bombers to the Kanawha City airfield to scout it for suitability as a base of aircraft operations. This Army photograph from September 1921 shows one Martin MB-2 twin-engine

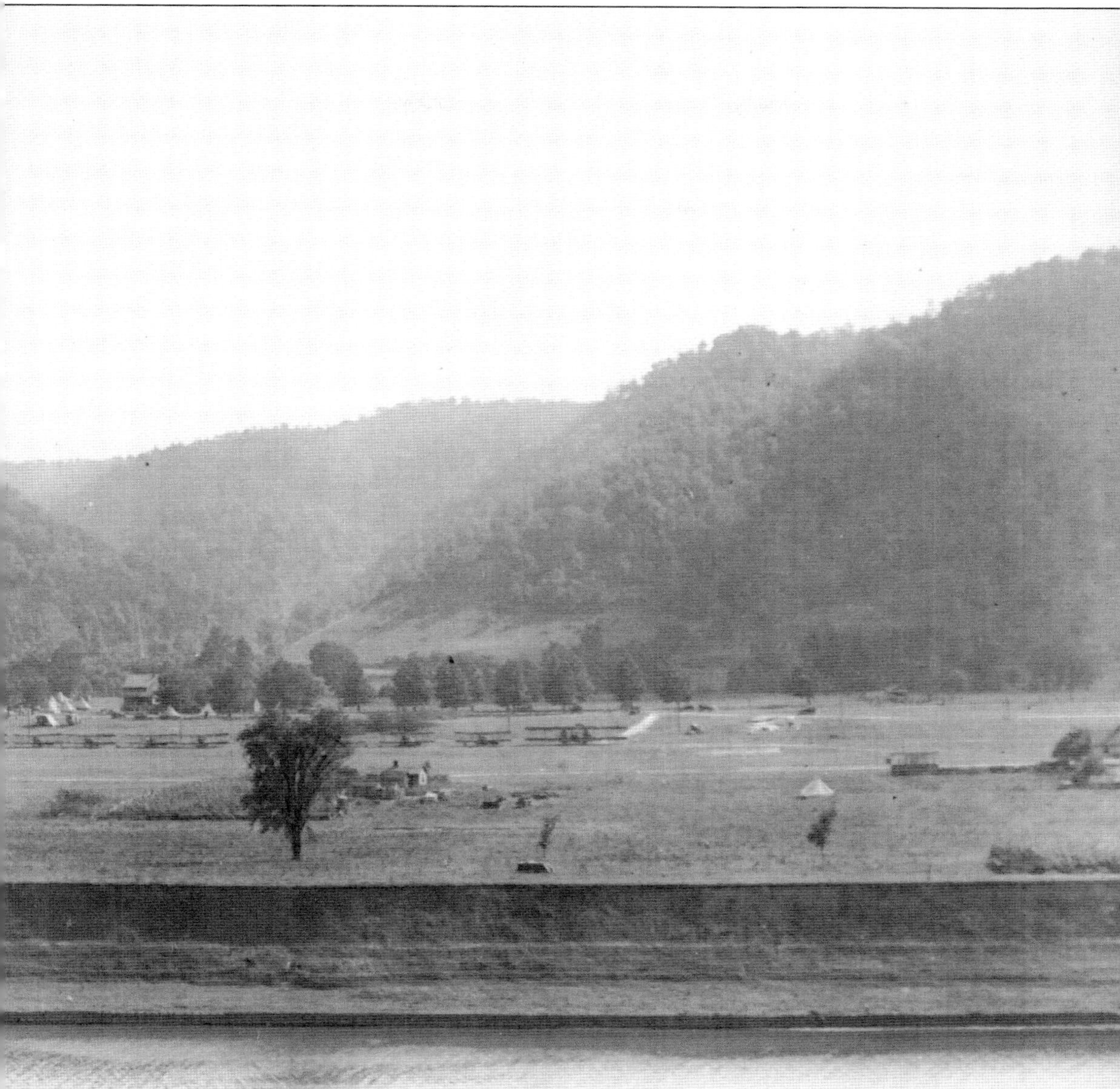

bomber on the right, next to a row of 11 DH-4B bombers near the present-day MacCorkle Avenue and Thirty-Fifth Street intersection. Armed with machine guns, fragmentation bombs, and tear gas, the bombers' weapons were not used. (Courtesy of the Library of Congress.)

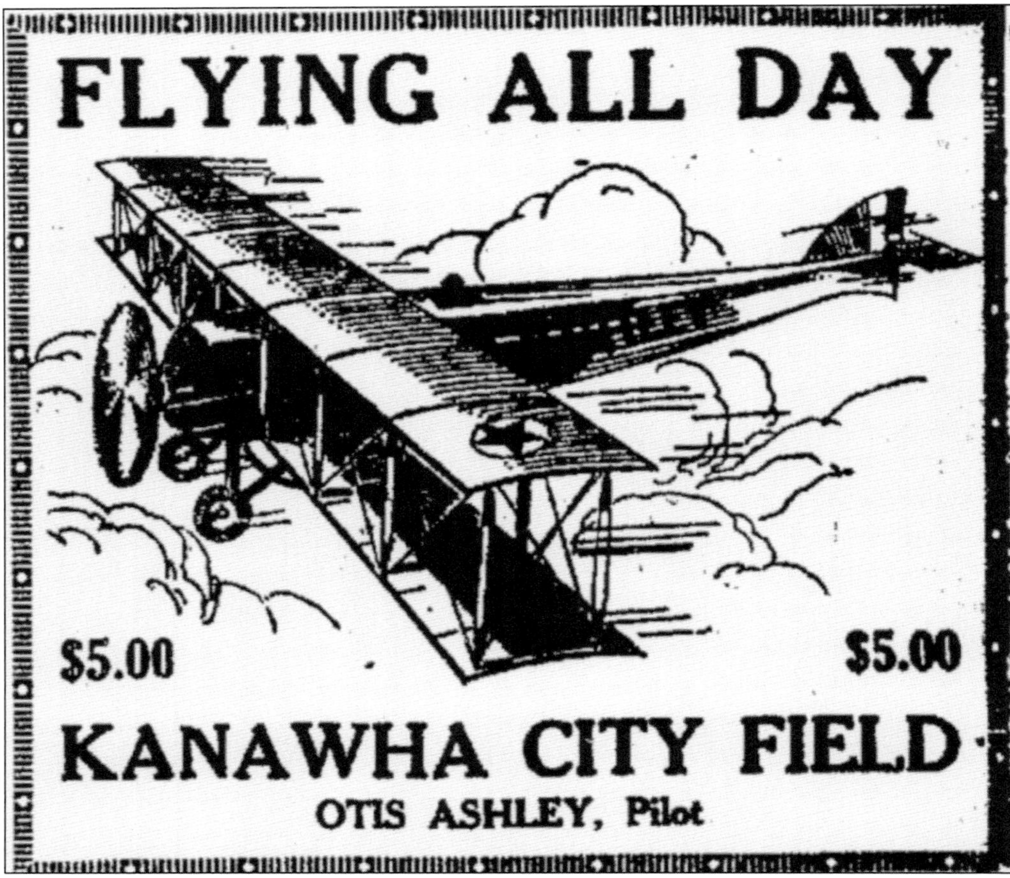

The Kanawha City airfield was located near the current intersection of Thirty-Fifth Street and MacCorkle Avenue in Charleston. This advertisement from the *Charleston Gazette* on July 5, 1925, offers flights for $5 ($68.76 in today's dollars) by pilot Otis Ashley.

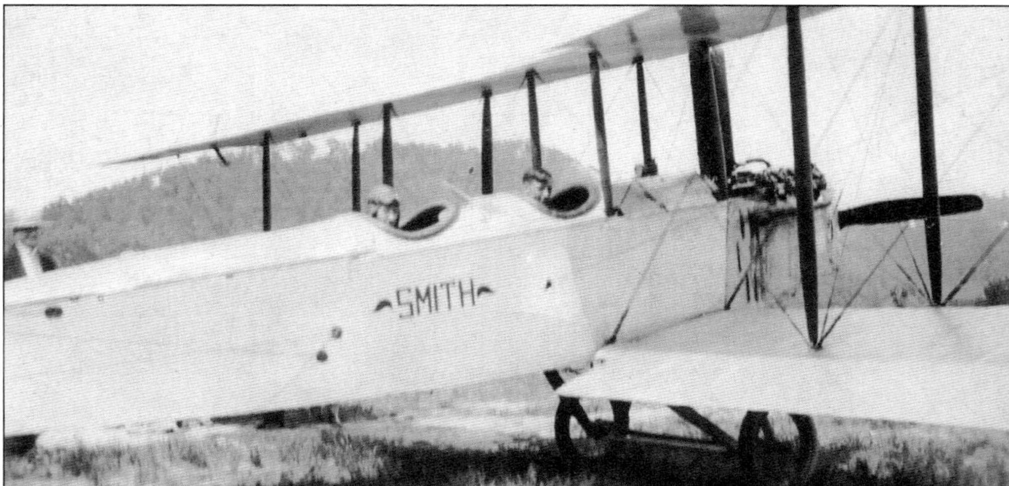

Omar Crim sits in the cockpit of a Curtiss JN-1 Jenny in Kanawha City in 1927. Crim was a well-known pilot in the Kanawha Valley, serving in the Civil Air Patrol during World War II.

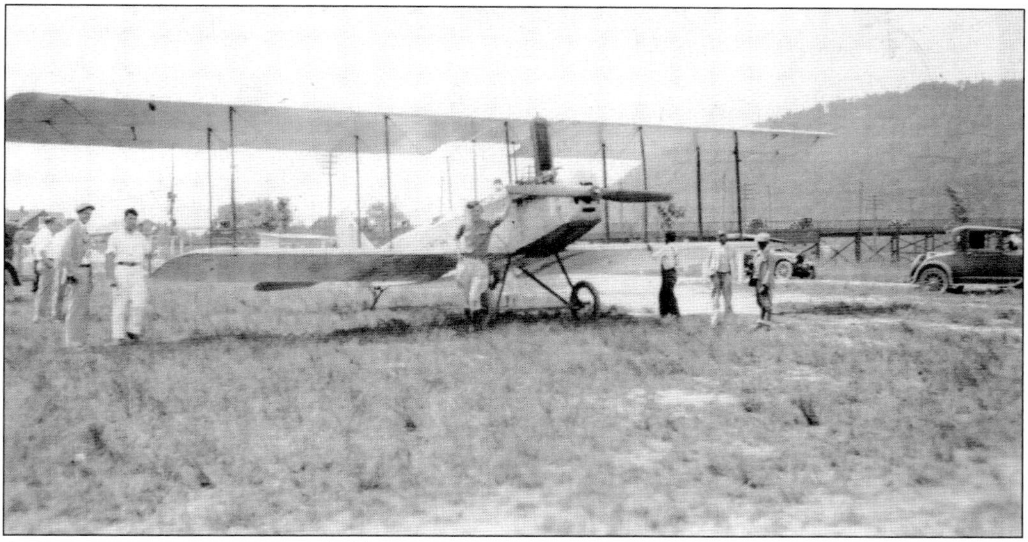

A Curtiss JN-1 Jenny sits in a field in Kanawha City in 1927. The Jenny was used in World War I and became a popular aircraft of the 1920s, with over 6,000 being built.

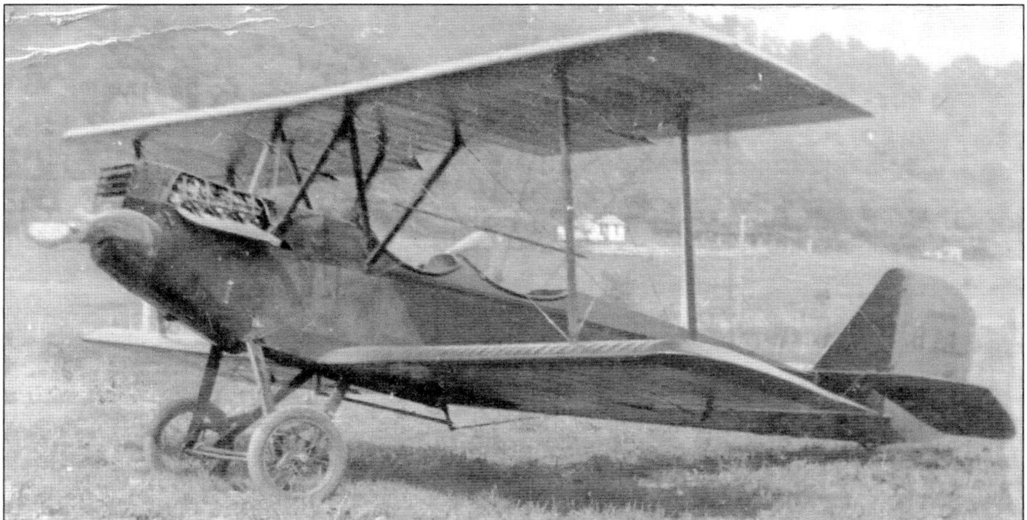

A Swallow TP (registration NC 8733) sits in a Kanawha City field in 1927. The Swallow TP was a two-seat trainer aircraft with a cruising speed of 75 miles per hour and a wingspan of 30 feet 11 inches.

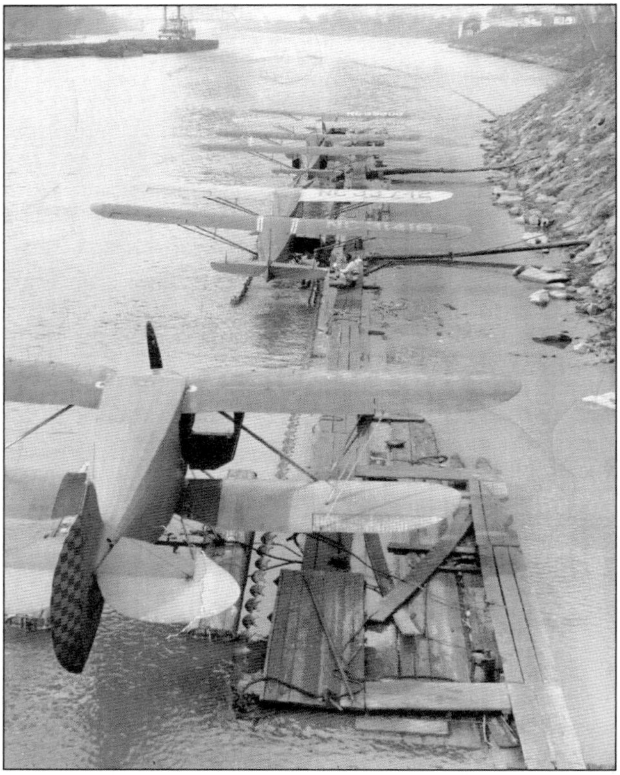

Seven seaplanes sit at the dock of Glenn Clark's Kanawha Flying School in the 1930s. The base was located at the foot of Summers Street next to the levee in downtown Charleston, West Virginia. Two people appear to be working on the second aircraft. The seaplane base operated on the levee until 1946, when it moved across the river to the south side.

Three unidentified men pose with a Fairchild seaplane on the Kanawha River. Throughout the 1930s and 1940s, seaplane bases were located in Charleston, Institute, Montgomery, and South Charleston.

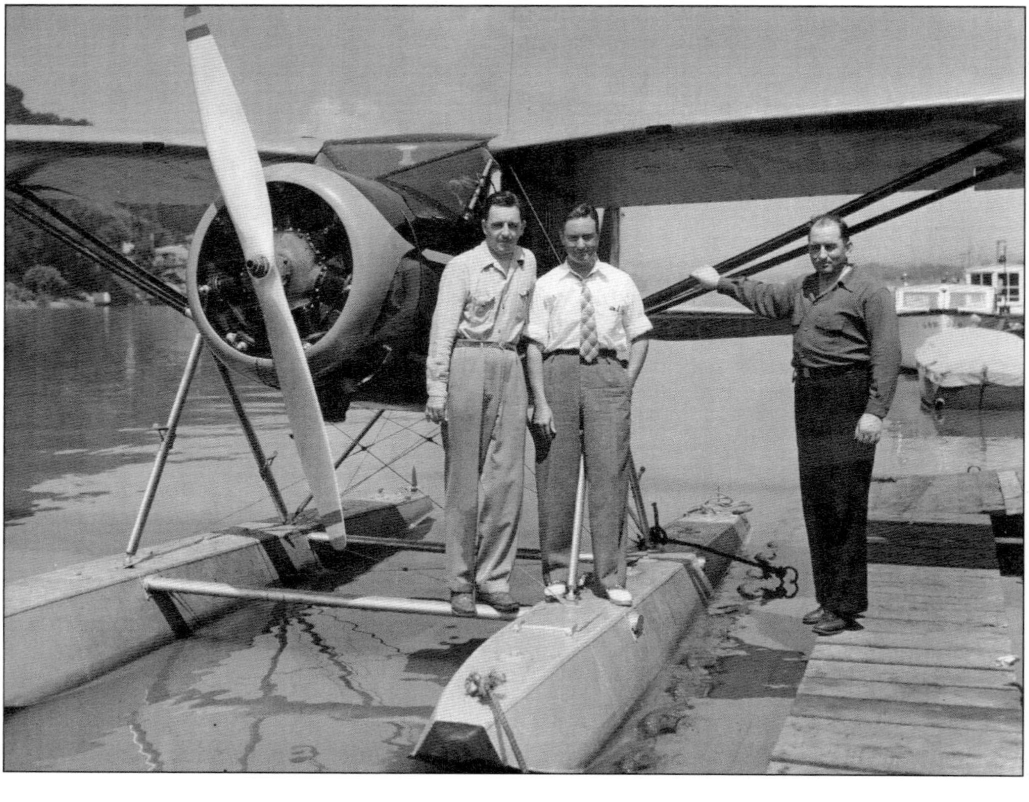

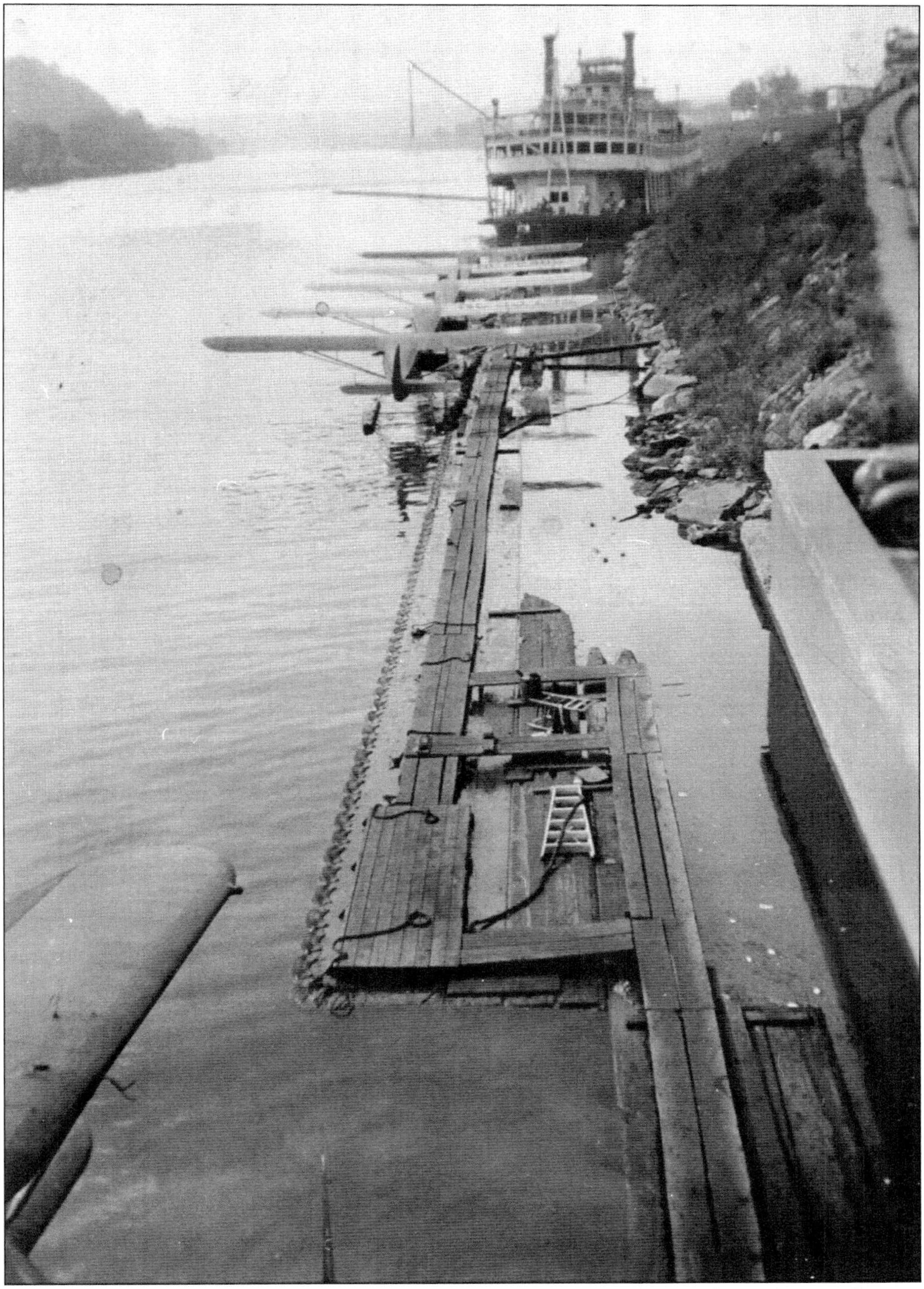

Seaplanes sit on the Kanawha River in the 1930s. Between 1932 and 1935, almost 200 people were given seaplane flight instruction by the Kanawha Flying Club and 85 had completed solo flights on the Kanawha River. The club received its first Aeronca seaplane in March 1932. (Courtesy of the West Virginia State Archives, Judy Escue Collection.)

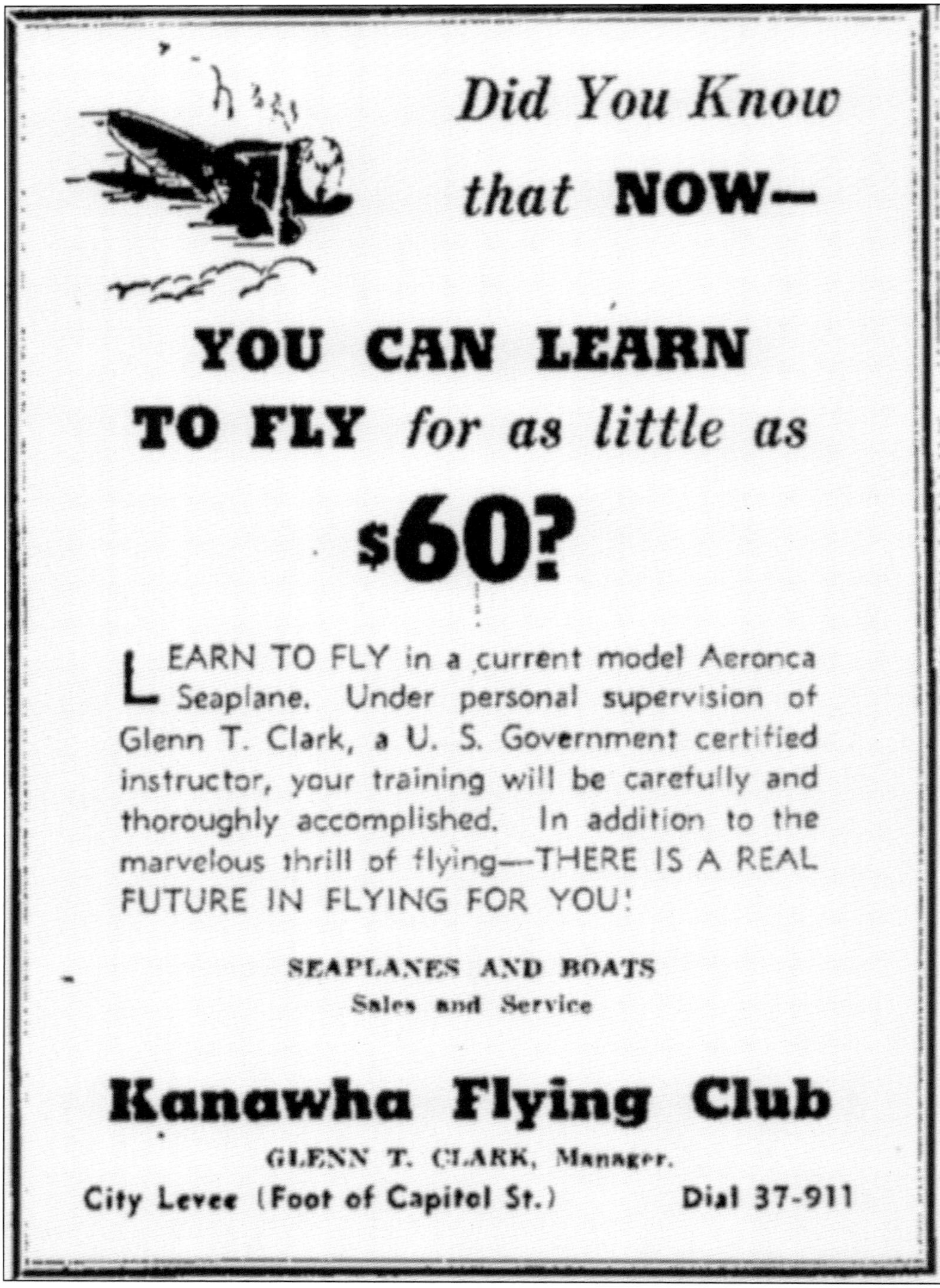

This *Charleston Daily Mail* advertisement from June 4, 1939, was run by the Kanawha Flying Club, which operated Aeronca seaplanes at the Charleston, West Virginia, levee. The advertisement states Glenn Clark is the manager and instructor.

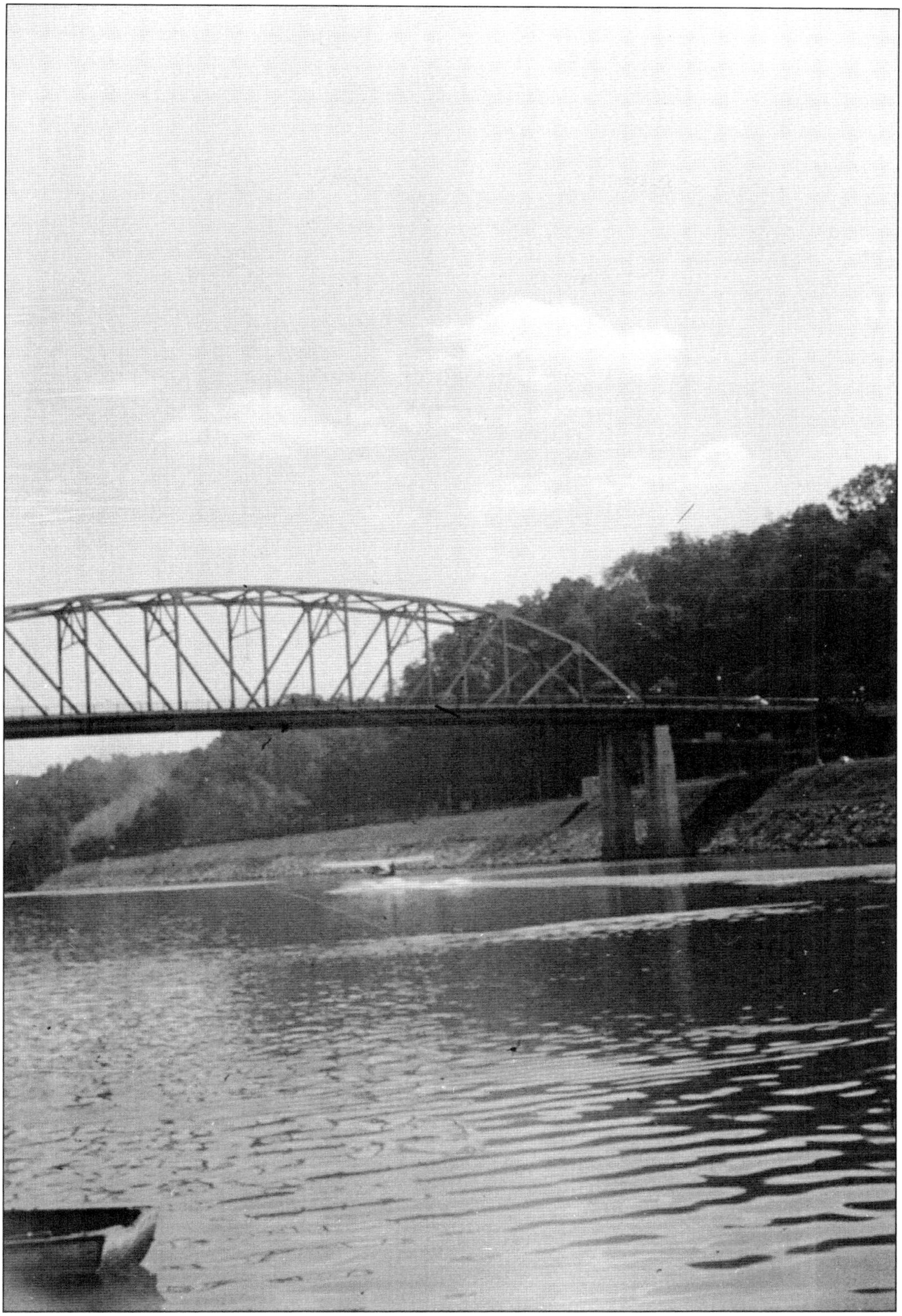

A seaplane takes off under the South Side Bridge in downtown Charleston, West Virginia, on September 22, 1941. (Courtesy of the West Virginia State Archives, James Bowling Collection.)

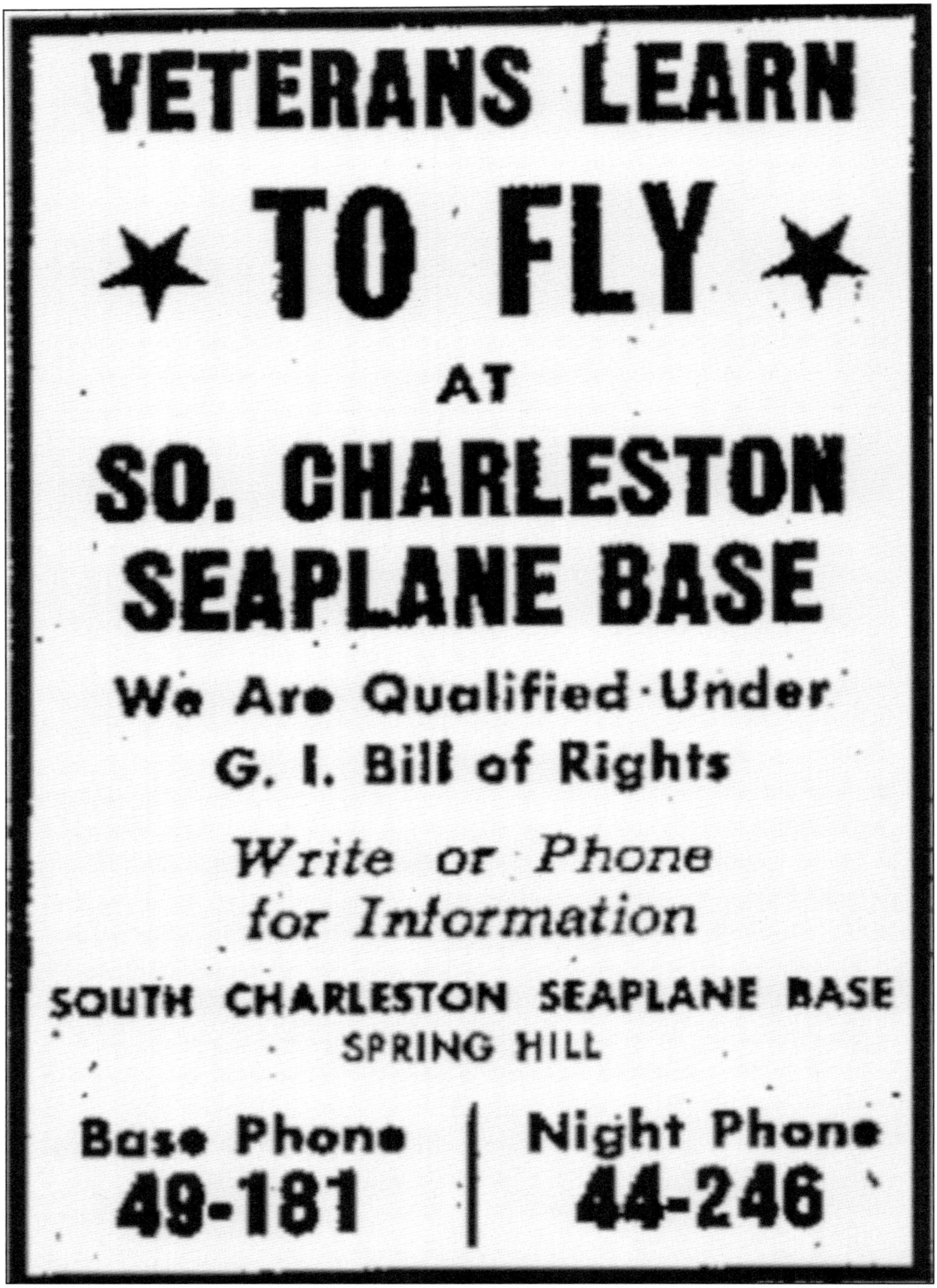

The South Charleston seaplane base was located in the Spring Hill area of South Charleston, West Virginia. The base advertised in the *Charleston Daily Mail* on June 22, 1947, that veterans could learn to fly under the Servicemen's Readjustment Act of 1944 (commonly called the GI Bill). In 1939, the National Youth Administration, a federal agency during the Great Depression, built new hangars for seaplane bases in Montgomery and South Charleston. Each city contributed supplies, and youth working at the naval ordnance plant in South Charleston built the hangars for work experience.

Two

Wertz Field and the Civilian Pilot Training Program

Recognizing the growth of aviation and the need to connect Charleston with airmail and passenger service, city officials began plans for a municipal airport. Land was purchased in nearby Institute, West Virginia, in 1929, but the City of Charleston did not have necessary funding to develop and operate the airport. A group of business leaders formed West Virginia Airways, Inc., which leased the site from the city and began airport operations. Opening on July 4, 1930, Wertz Field became Charleston's first municipal airport. American Airlines introduced the first passenger service using Ford Trimotor aircraft in October 1933. Pennsylvania Central Airlines began service to Wertz Field in April 1937, giving travelers more route options.

In 1939, the Civilian Pilot Training Program began at West Virginia State College. The program primarily trained African American students to become pilots and was integrated without problems in 1940. Approximately 30 African American graduates from the program at West Virginia State College would become Tuskegee Airmen during World War II. By the late 1930s, it was becoming clear the newer and larger passenger aircraft being produced would have problems operating at Wertz Field due to the constrained area. A search was begun for a new airport that could accommodate future growth. Wertz Field would continue to operate until May 12, 1942, when the construction of a government synthetic rubber plant blocked flight approaches. Charleston would be without an airport until the opening of Kanawha Airport in November 1947.

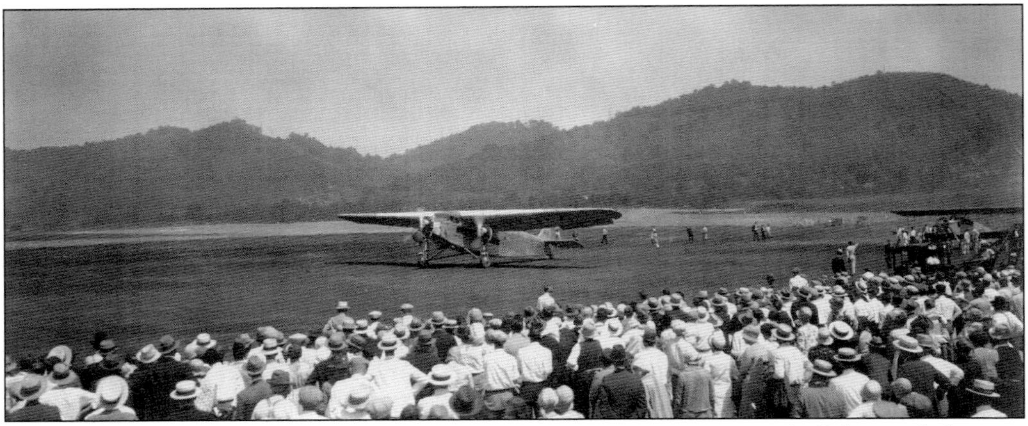

A large crowd watches a Ford 4-AT-B Trimotor flown by Capt. O.M. Goodsell during dedication ceremonies of Wertz Field. Flights over Charleston were offered to the public by Ford Motor Air Tours. Ford produced 199 Trimotors before ending production in 1933.

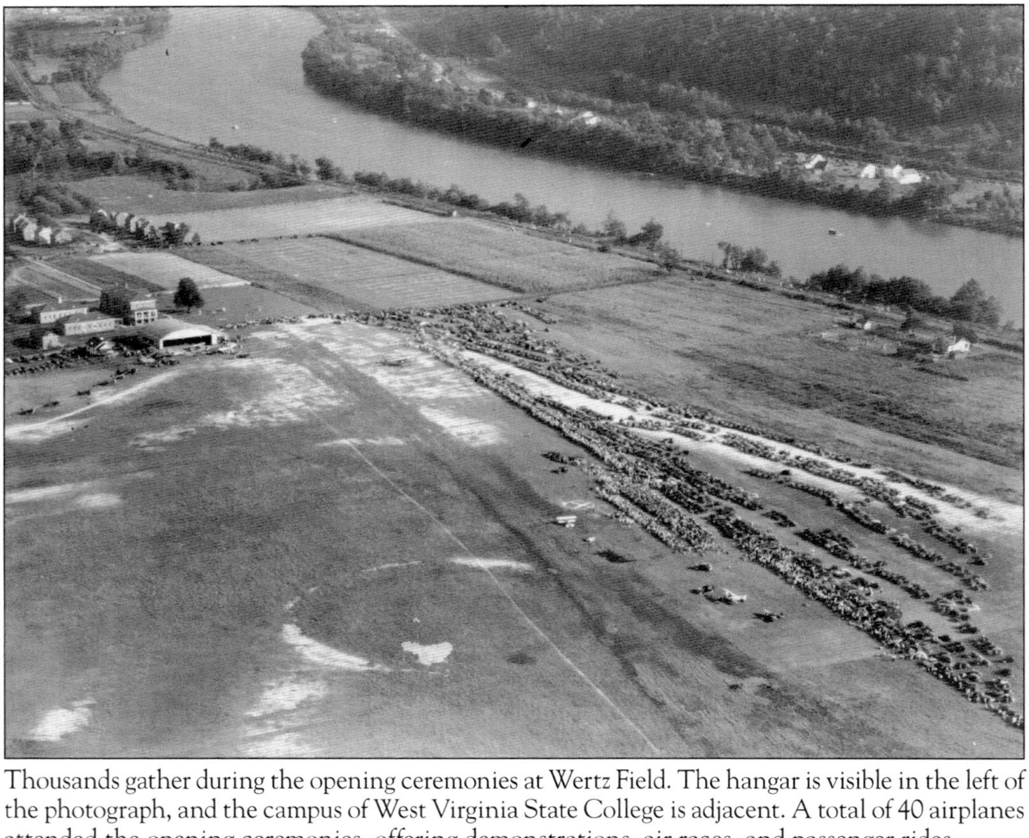

Thousands gather during the opening ceremonies at Wertz Field. The hangar is visible in the left of the photograph, and the campus of West Virginia State College is adjacent. A total of 40 airplanes attended the opening ceremonies, offering demonstrations, air races, and passenger rides.

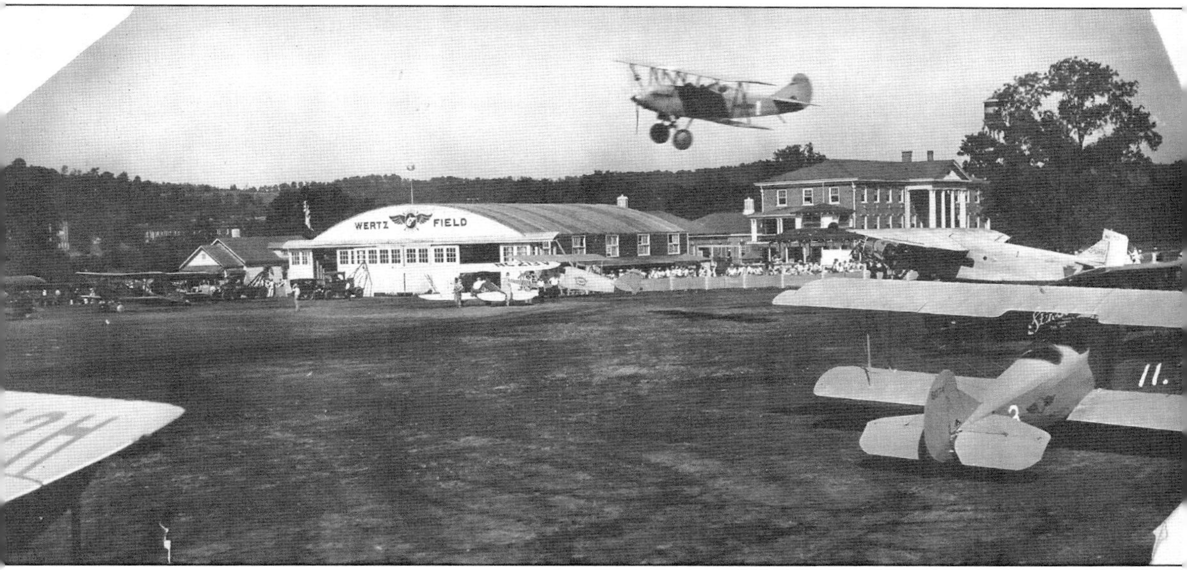

Several aircraft sit on display around the field as a crowd watches a Travel Air biplane fly during opening ceremonies on July 4, 1930. The opening of Wertz Field was commemorated from July 4 to 6, 1930, with special flying exhibitions each day.

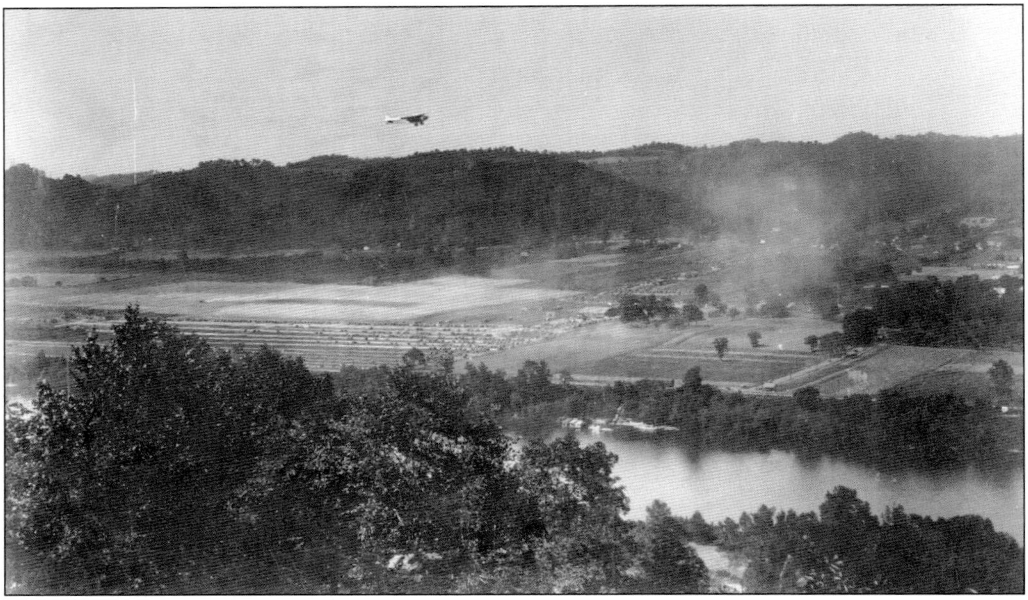

A Ford Trimotor flies over Wertz Field during opening ceremonies. The 200 acres of land that encompassed Wertz Field was purchased by the City of Charleston for $200,000 ($2,816,994 in today's dollars).

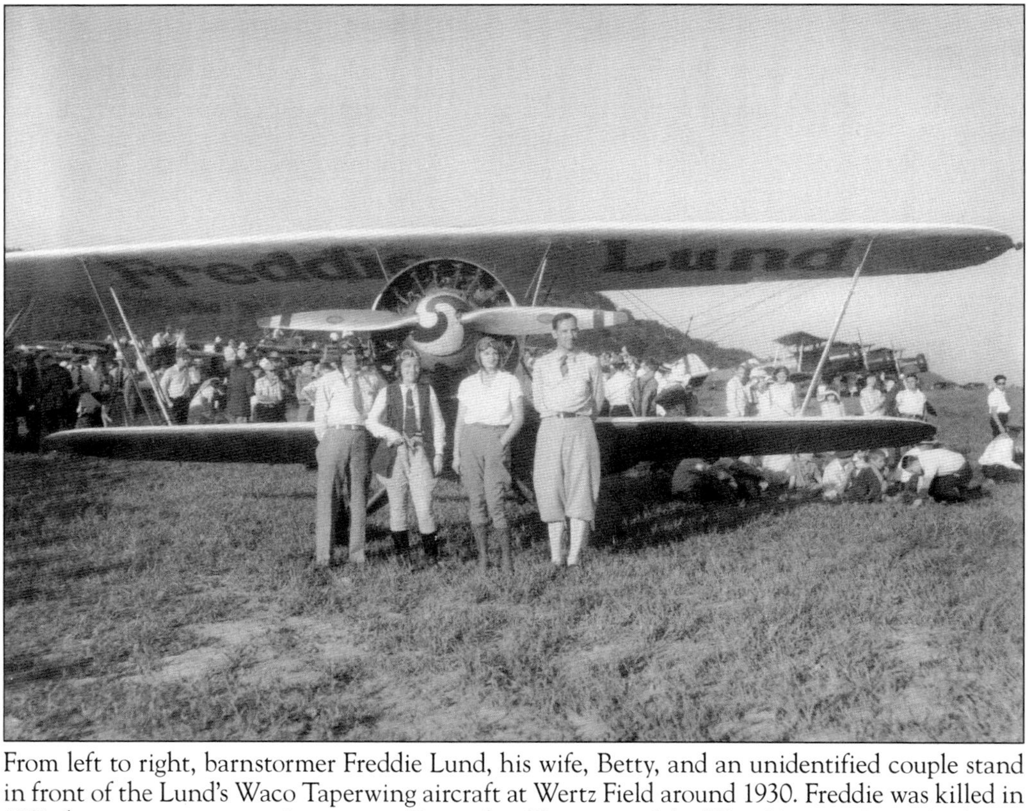

From left to right, barnstormer Freddie Lund, his wife, Betty, and an unidentified couple stand in front of the Lund's Waco Taperwing aircraft at Wertz Field around 1930. Freddie was killed in 1931 during an air race in Lexington, Kentucky. (Courtesy of the West Virginia State Archives, Warren Woomer Collection.)

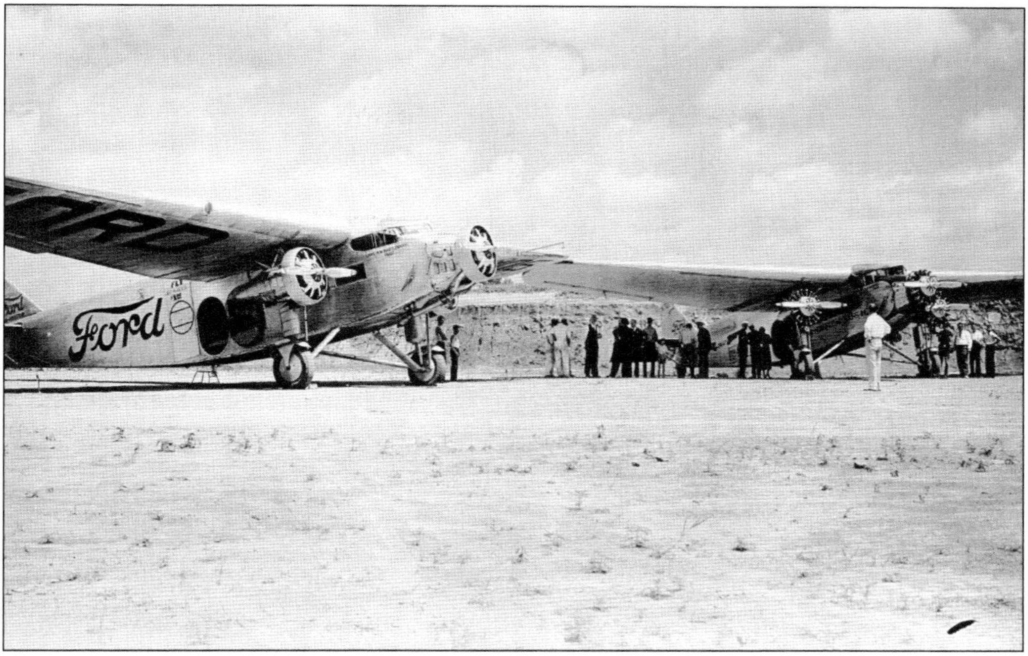

A pair of Ford Trimotor aircraft sit at Wertz Field in this undated photograph. The Ford Trimotor was the largest passenger aircraft when it entered commercial service in September 1926. (Courtesy of the West Virginia State Archives, Julia Holt Coyle Collection.)

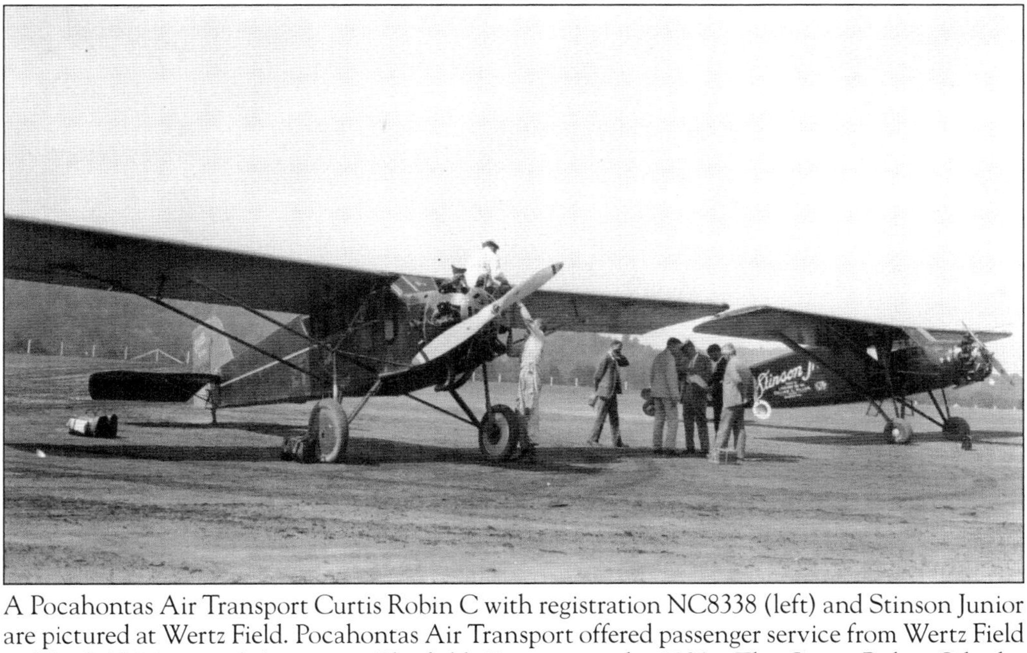

A Pocahontas Air Transport Curtis Robin C with registration NC8338 (left) and Stinson Junior are pictured at Wertz Field. Pocahontas Air Transport offered passenger service from Wertz Field to Bluefield Municipal Airport in Bluefield, Virginia, in the 1930s. The Curtis Robin C had a cruising speed of 102 miles per hour and range of 300 miles.

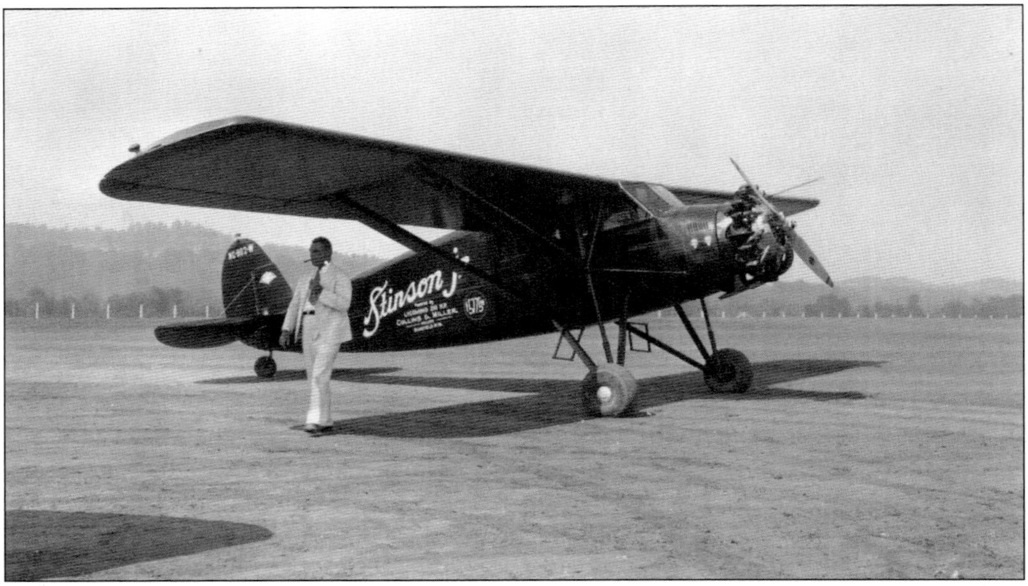

An unidentified man walks from a Stinson Junior while smoking a cigar. Stenciling on the side of the aircraft reads, "Stinson Jr powered by Lycoming 210 H.P. Collins & Miller dealers Bluefield W.Va. $5775.00." Stinson produced several variants of this aircraft, which offered a fully enclosed cabin and choice of three or four seats.

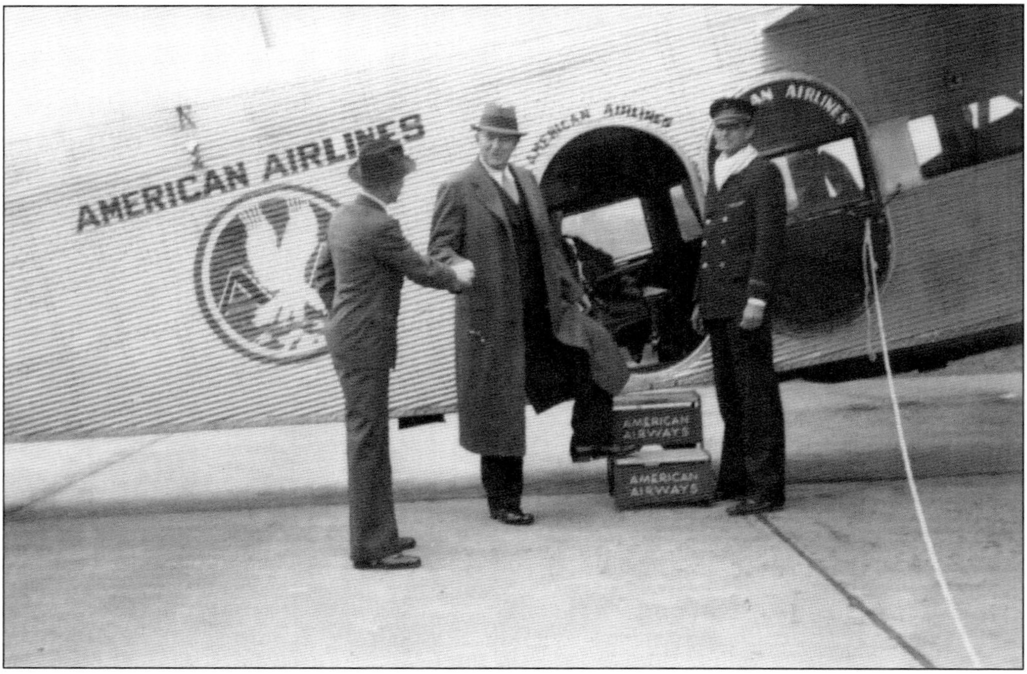

An unidentified man prepares to board an American Airlines Ford Trimotor, a three-engine 10-seat plane also known as the "Tin Goose." American Airlines began passenger service from Wertz Field on October 18, 1933, to Washington National Airport using a Trimotor. In 1933, nonstop service was offered once daily from Charleston to Cincinnati and Washington. A stop in Huntington, West Virginia, was added on the flight to Cincinnati in 1934. A round-trip ticket from Charleston to Washington in 1934 cost $28.84 ($517.93 in today's dollars).

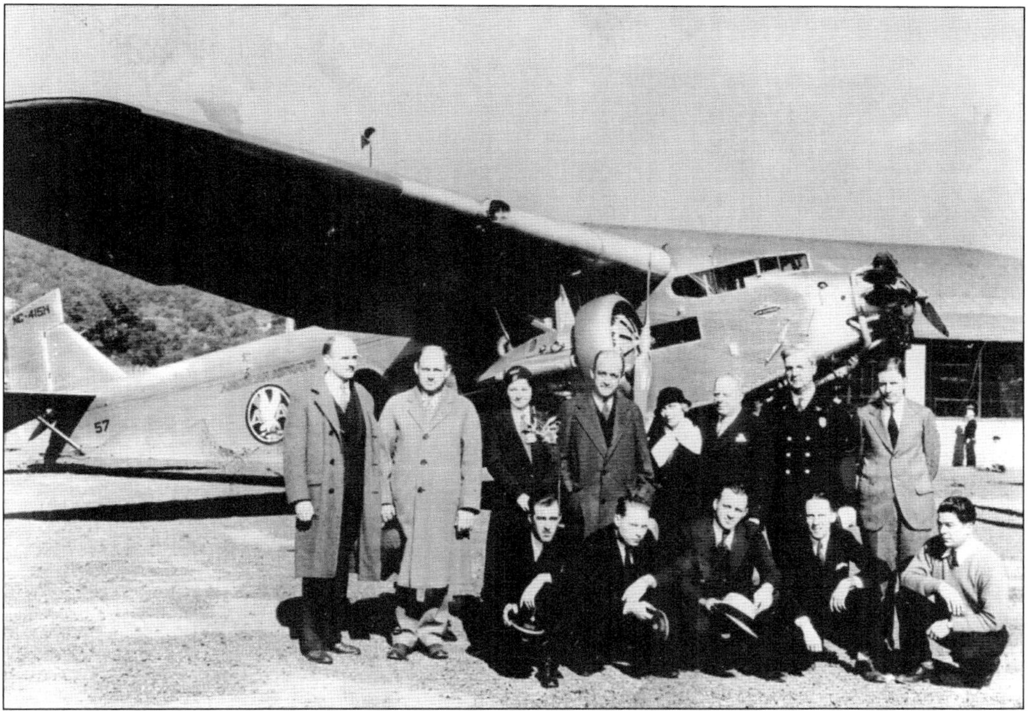

An American Airways Ford Trimotor sits at Wertz Field in October 1933. American Airways operated in 72 cities across the country in 1933. (Courtesy of the West Virginia State Archives, Hubert and Beulah Stark Collection.)

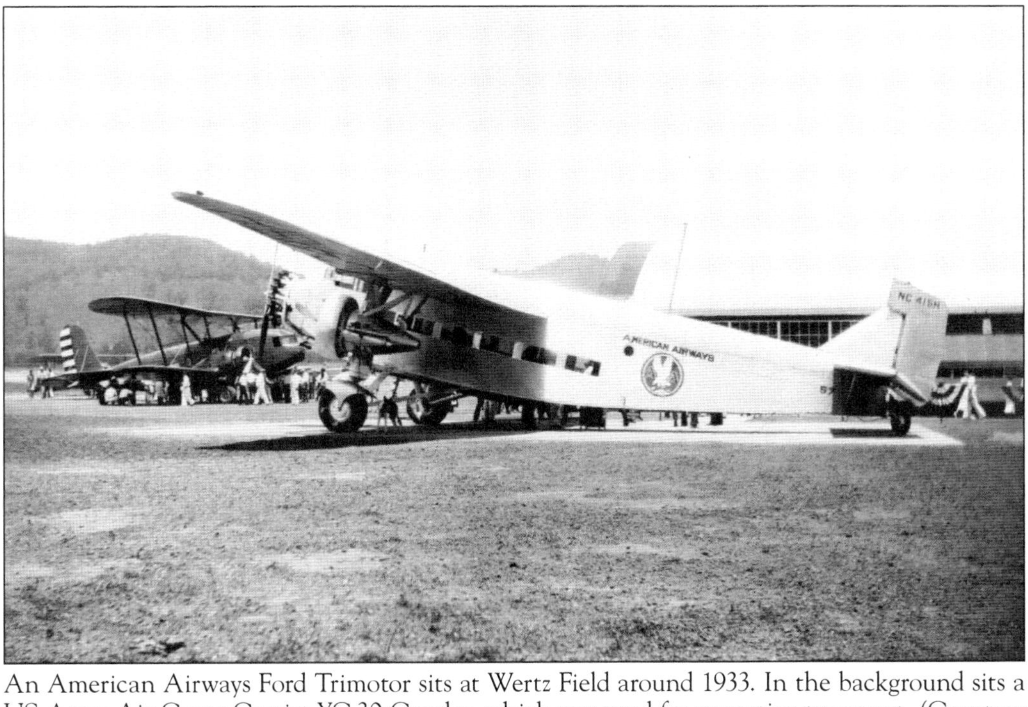

An American Airways Ford Trimotor sits at Wertz Field around 1933. In the background sits a US Army Air Corps Curtiss YC-30 Condor, which was used for executive transport. (Courtesy of the West Virginia State Archives, Beulah Stark Collection.)

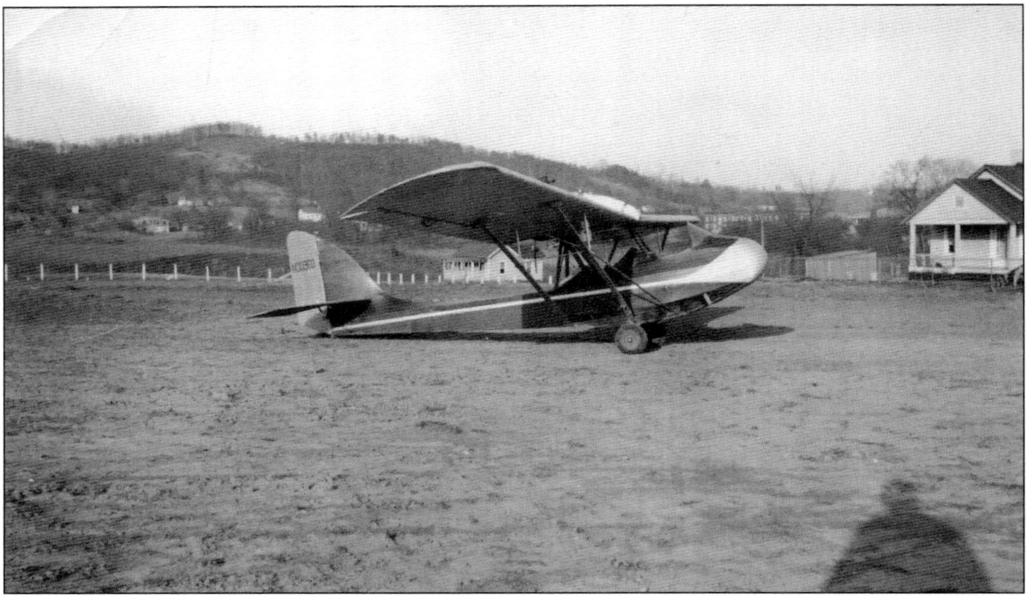

This Curtiss-Wright CW-1 Junior (registration NC 10960) is seen at Wertz Field in 1935. The Junior was advertised as an affordable sport aircraft that could carry one passenger at a speed of 80 miles per hour.

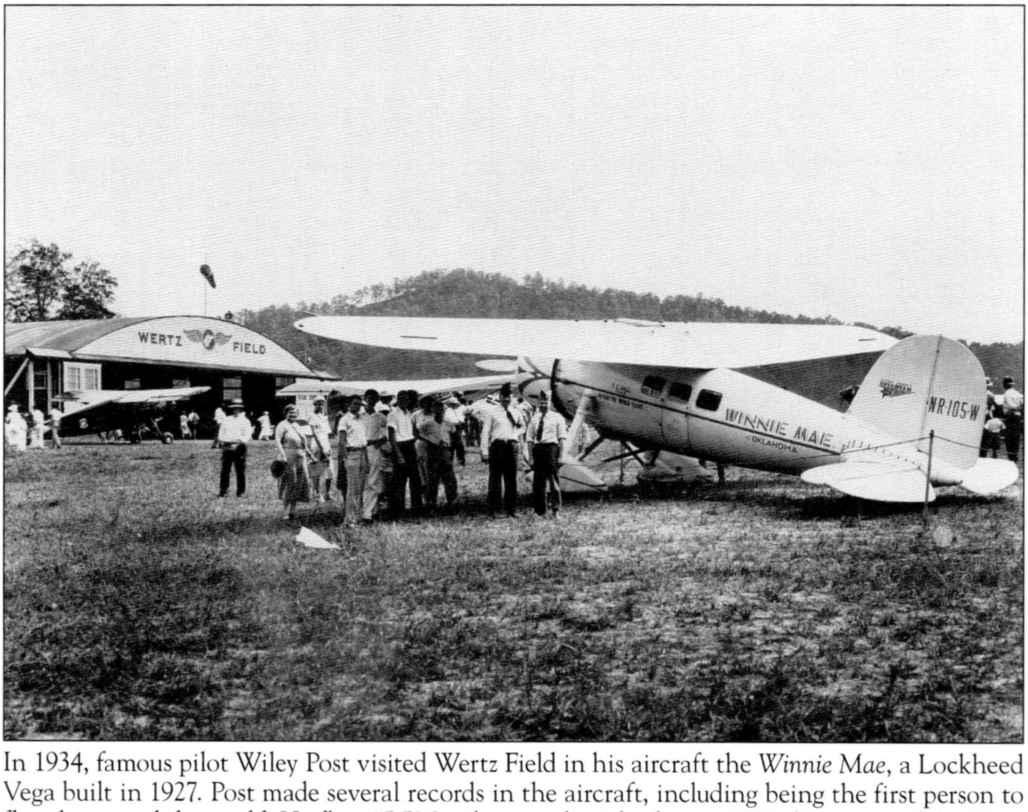

In 1934, famous pilot Wiley Post visited Wertz Field in his aircraft the *Winnie Mae*, a Lockheed Vega built in 1927. Post made several records in the aircraft, including being the first person to fly solo around the world. He flew 15,596 miles in only eight days in 1933. (Courtesy of the West Virginia State Archives, Beulah Stark Collection.)

Pilot Wiley Post is seen getting into the cockpit of the *Winnie Mae*. Post was killed in an aircraft accident in Alaska on August 15, 1935. The *Winnie Mae* is on public display at the Smithsonian Institution's National Air and Space Museum in Washington, DC.

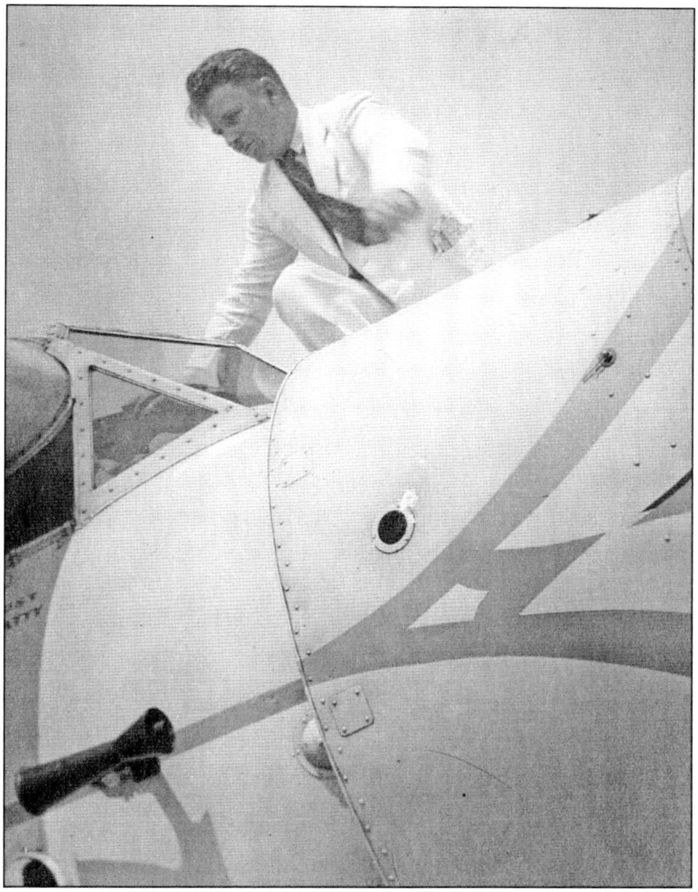

An American Airlines Curtiss Condor sits behind a fence at Wertz Field in 1935. American advertised service between Washington, DC, and Chicago, Illinois, with stops in Charleston and three other cities using the Condor, which featured a "club luncheon aloft" in a sound-proofed cabin and cruising at 170 miles per hour.

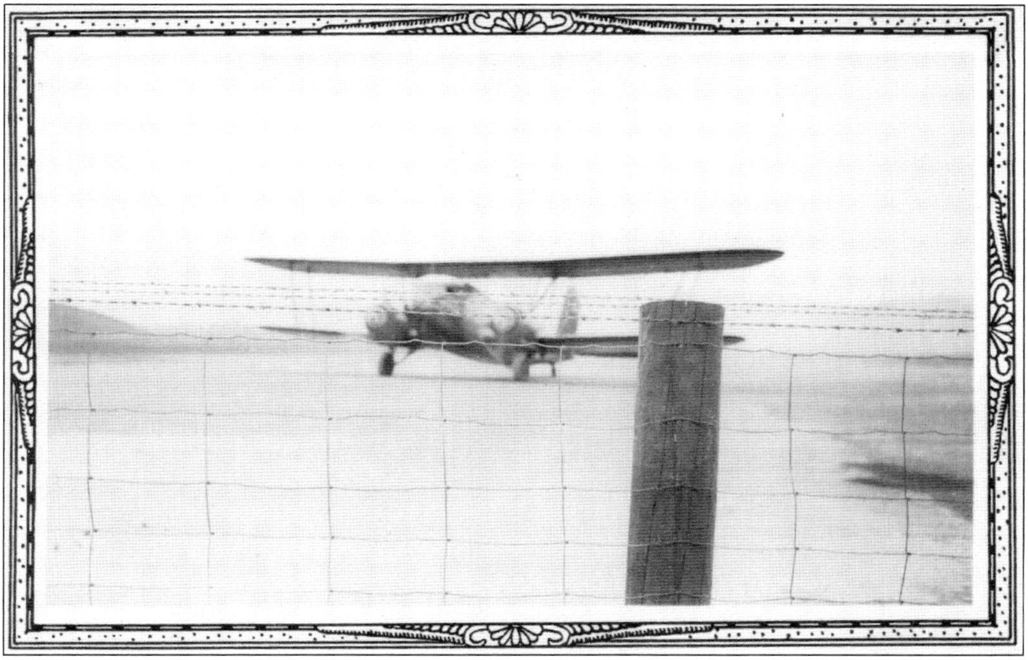

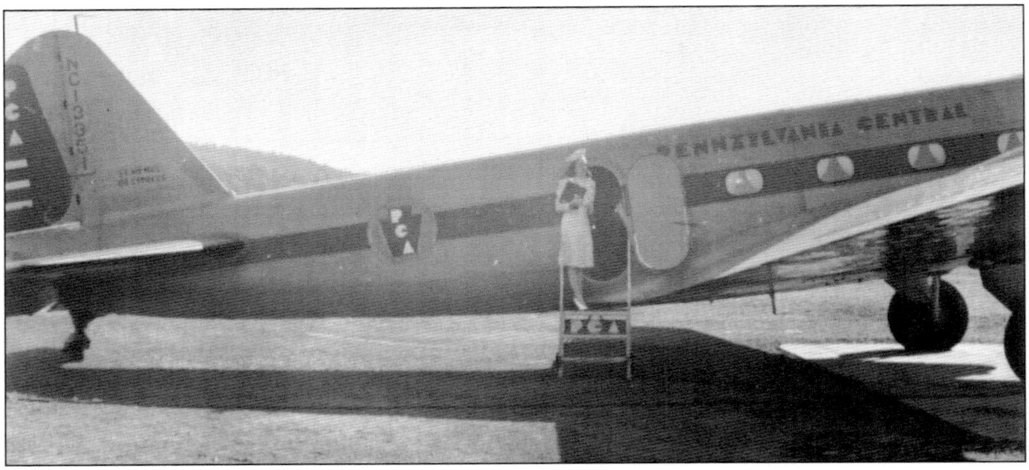

An air hostess stands in the door of a Pennsylvania Central Airlines (PCA) Boeing 247-D (registration NC13351). PCA began scheduled passenger service to Wertz Field on April 8, 1937, serving Pittsburgh, Pennsylvania, with a stop in Parkersburg, West Virginia. By 1941, a stop was added in Clarksburg, West Virginia, on the route to Pittsburgh. A southbound flight was also added to Tri-Cities Airport, which served the Tennessee cities of Bristol, Johnson City, and Kingsport, and terminated in Knoxville, Tennessee.

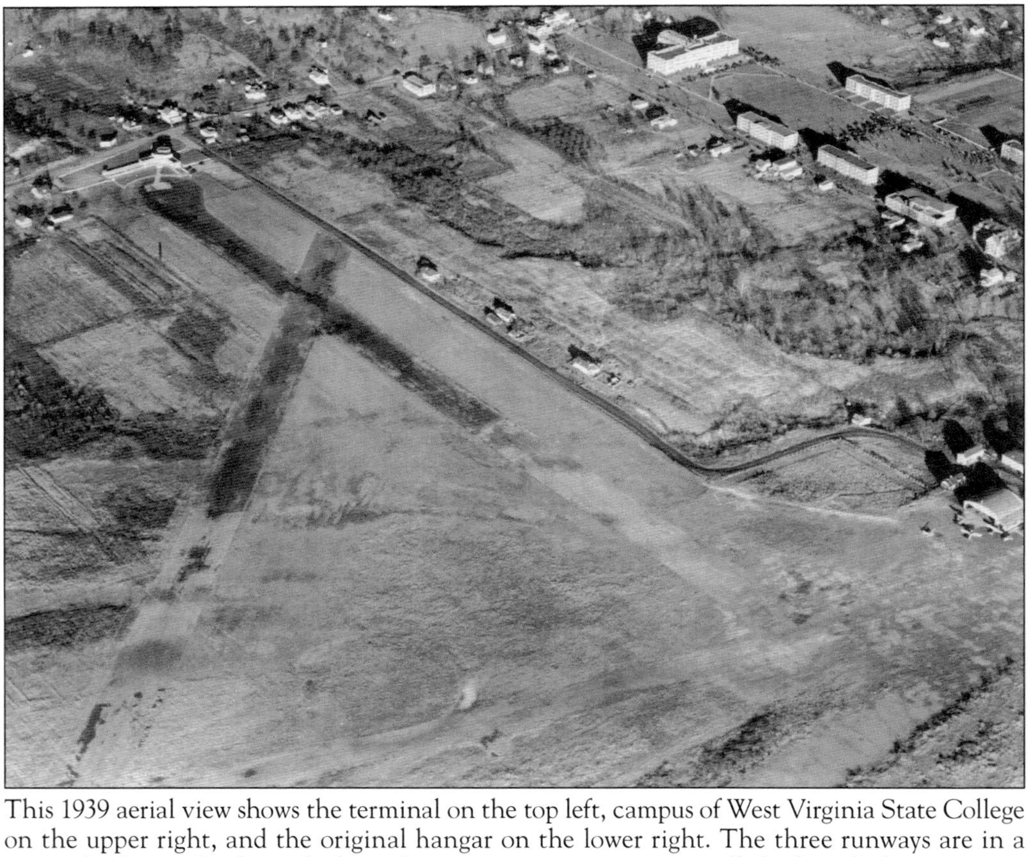

This 1939 aerial view shows the terminal on the top left, campus of West Virginia State College on the upper right, and the original hangar on the lower right. The three runways are in a triangular layout. In the early days of aviation, airports were normally built with three runways in this configuration to give pilots more options to land and takeoff into the wind.

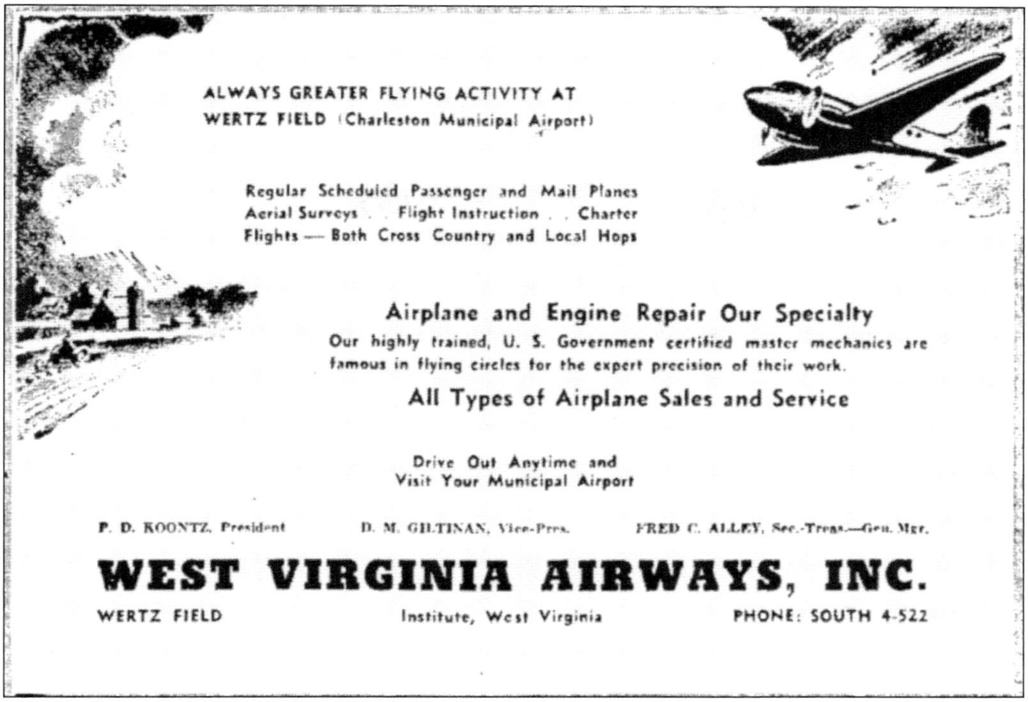

West Virginia Airways, Inc. was the operator of Wertz Field and ran this advertisement in the *Charleston Daily Mail* in 1939. Fred C. Alley was the manager of Wertz Field and would become the first manager of Kanawha Airport.

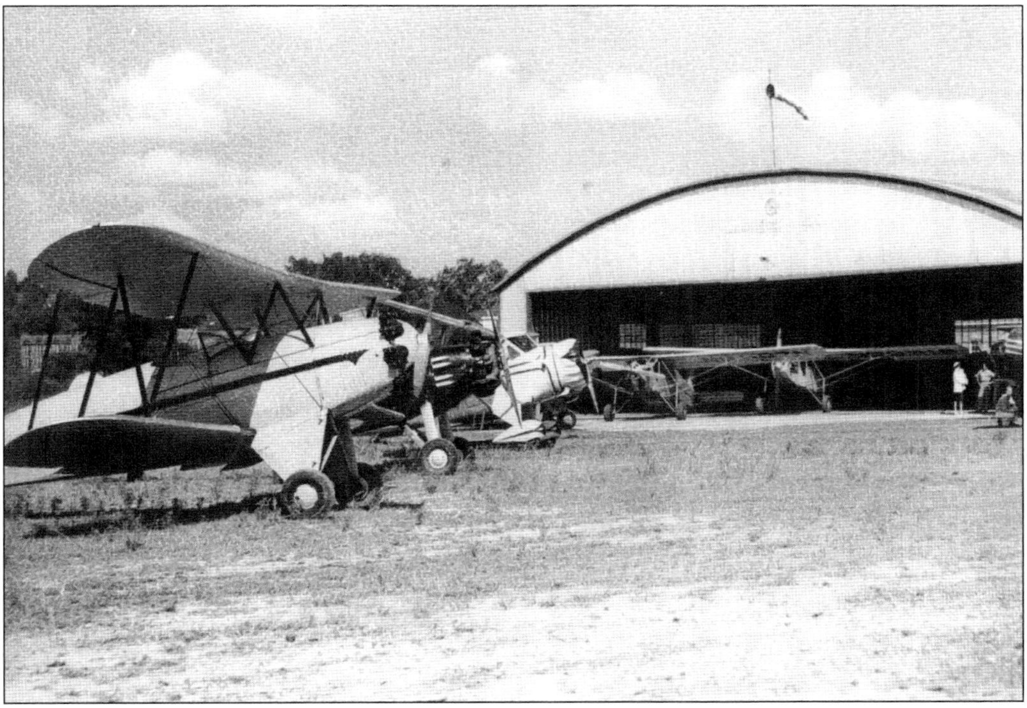

A biplane and four other aircraft sit near the hangar at Wertz Field. Before the terminal building opened in 1935, passenger operations and airport offices were located in the hangar.

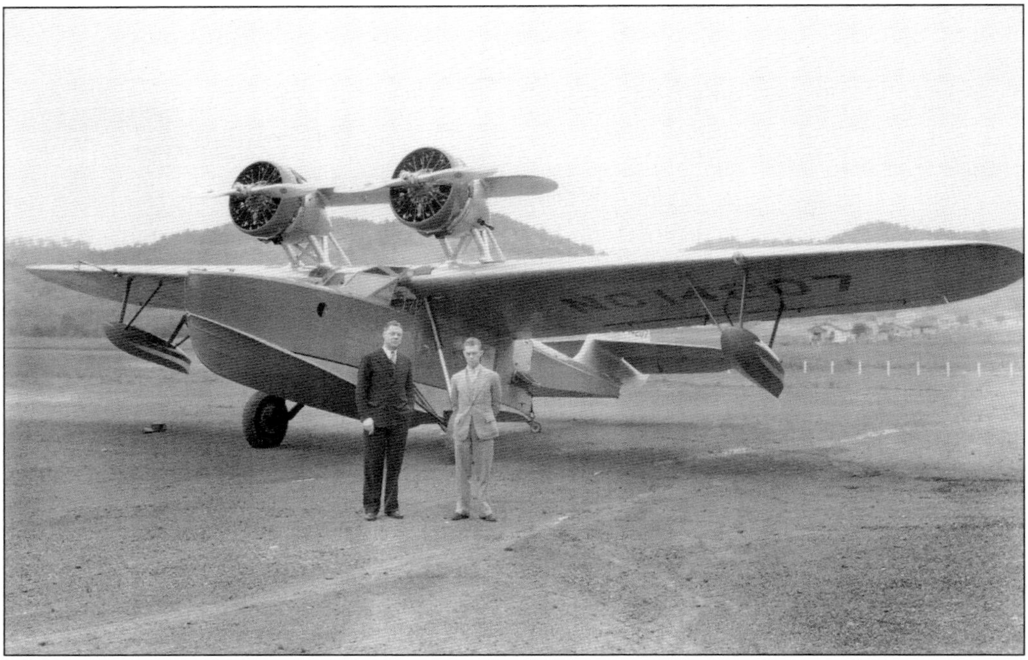

Two unidentified men stand in front of a Douglas 119 Dolphin (registration NC14207) at Wertz Field. The Dolphin was a seaplane introduced in 1931 and used primarily by military operators. This aircraft was registered to A.G. Vanderbilt II of the wealthy Vanderbilt family and was one of two Dolphins used as tenders for their yacht.

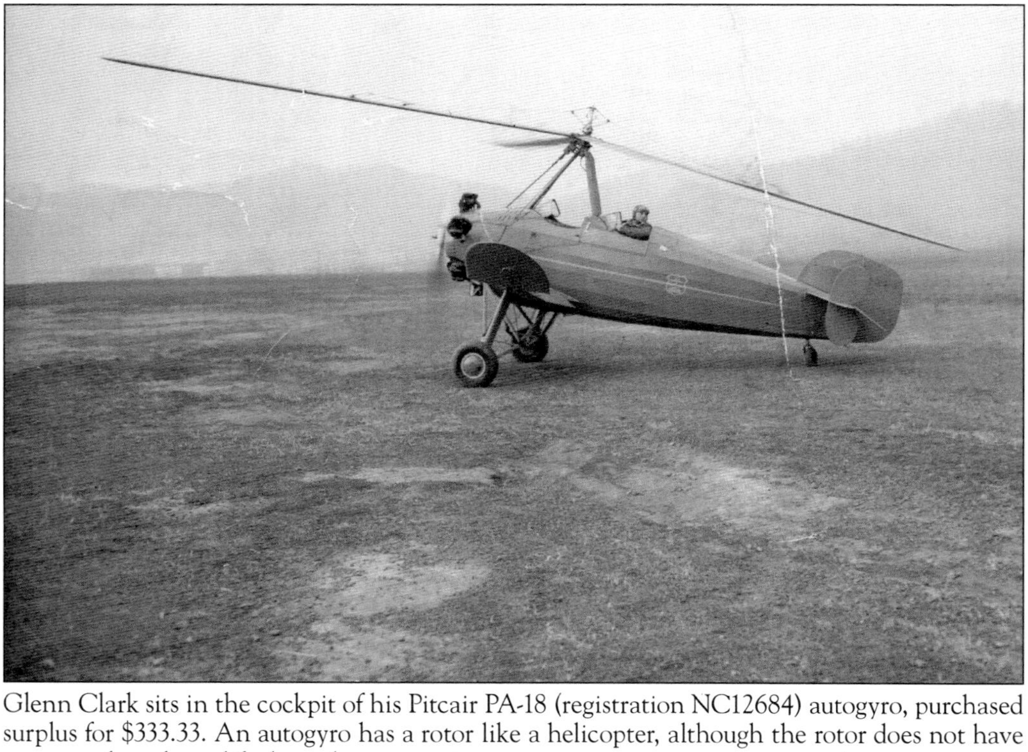

Glenn Clark sits in the cockpit of his Pitcair PA-18 (registration NC12684) autogyro, purchased surplus for $333.33. An autogyro has a rotor like a helicopter, although the rotor does not have power and produces lift through autorotation.

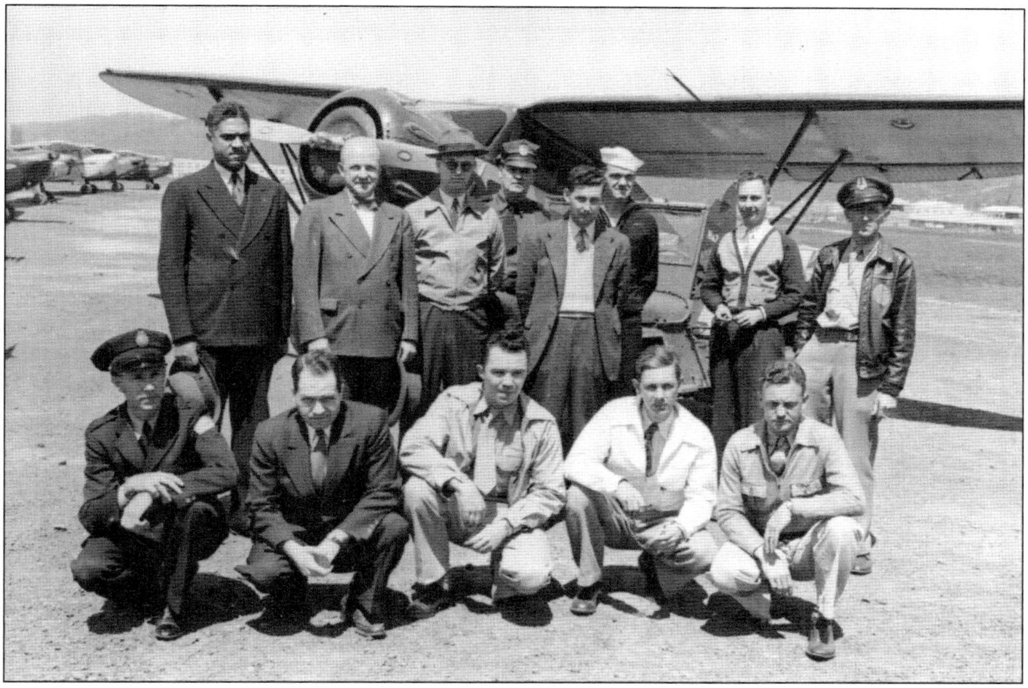

Posing in front of a cabin Waco are from left to right (first row) Jim Jennings, Tom Hill, Harold Young, Cramer Bollinger, and Bob Davis; (second row) Joseph Grider, J.B. Akins, ? Francer, unidentified, Nick Nichols, two unidentified persons, and Omar W. Crim.

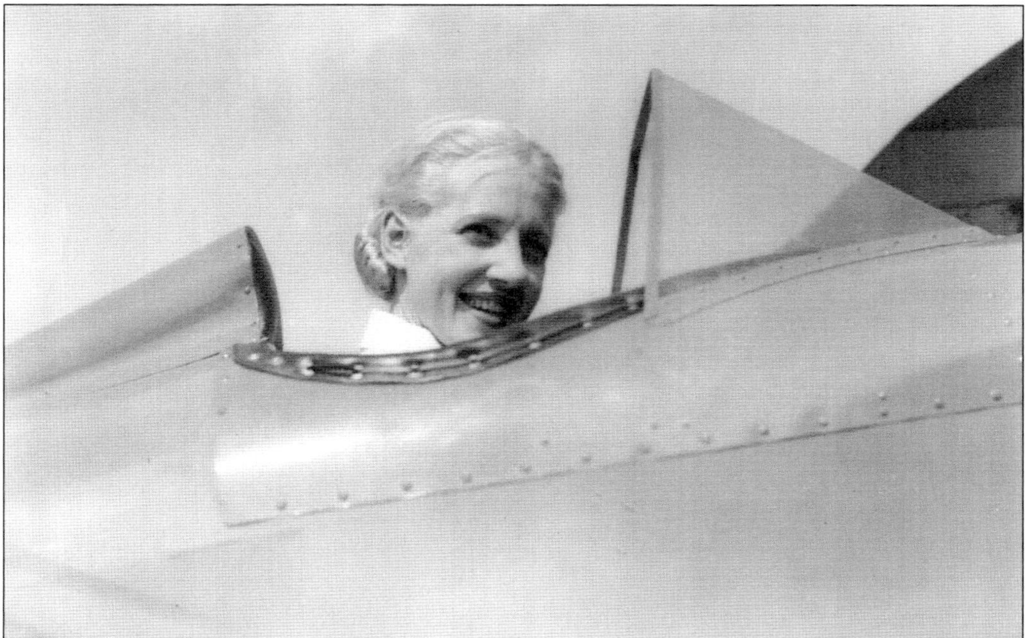

Beulah Stark of Charleston was one of the first females in West Virginia to obtain a pilot's license. Stark earned a private pilot license on December 13, 1933, and a commercial pilot license on May 13, 1934. She helped organize the West Virginia chapter of the Ninety-Nines, an organization of women pilots of which Amelia Earhart was the first president.

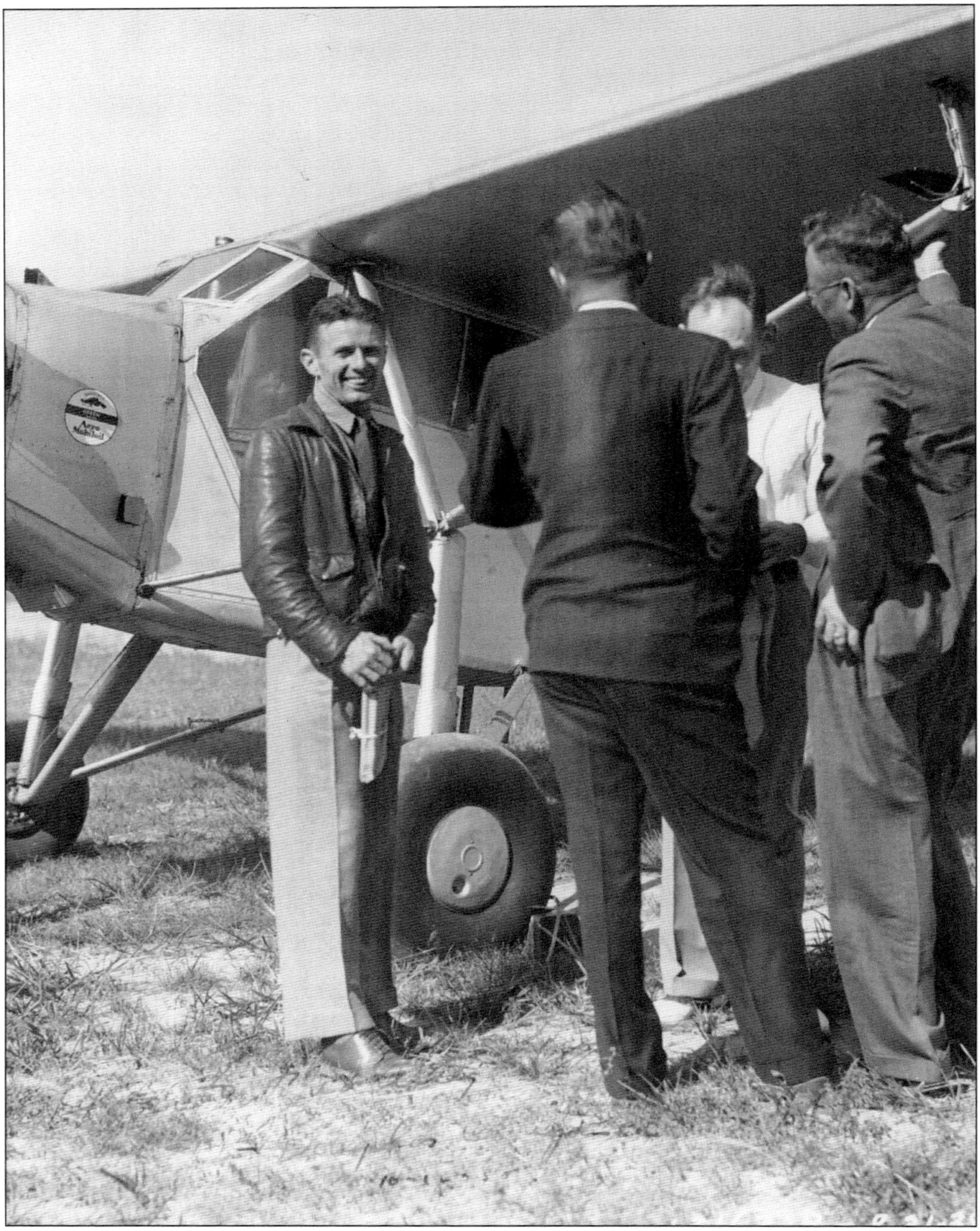

Douglas Corrigan stands in front of an airplane at Wertz Field. In 1938, Corrigan flew nonstop from California to New York. He then filed a flight plan for a transatlantic flight, which was denied by aviation authorities who believed his aircraft would not make the trip. Corrigan filed a new flight plan for a return to California. After he took off, he ended up landing in Ireland 28 hours later, claiming he made a navigation error. Dubbed "Wrong Way Corrigan" by the media, he became a national celebrity and continued to claim until his death in 1995 that he made an error in his transatlantic flight.

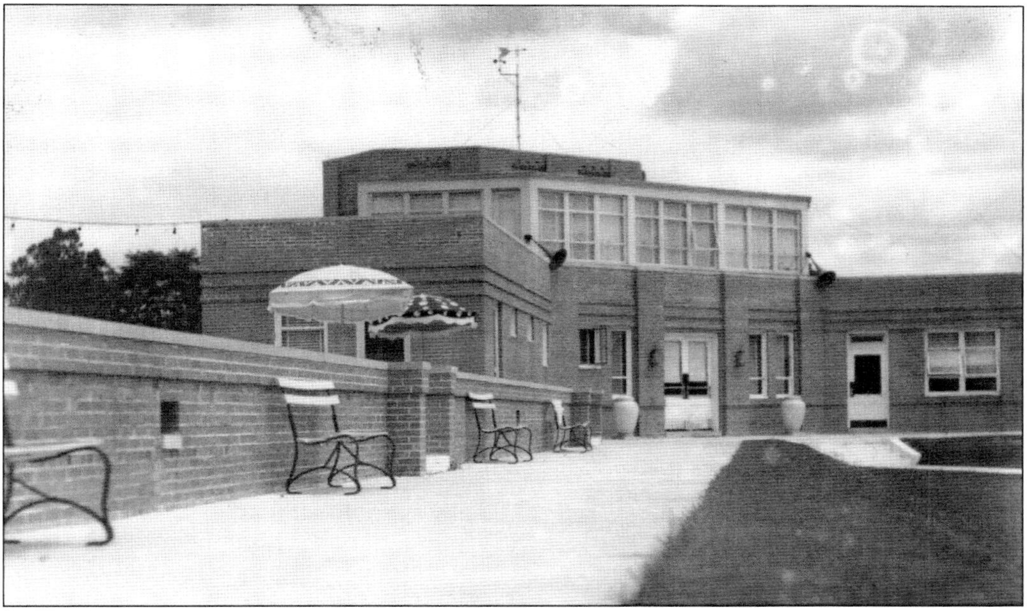

Excavation work on the Wertz Field terminal building began in July 1934. Dedicated on September 22, 1935, the terminal building had two wings with a center lobby and foyer. The lobby was two stories high, offering views of the airfield. The foyer contained a ticket window and the offices of West Virginia Airways Inc. and American Airlines.

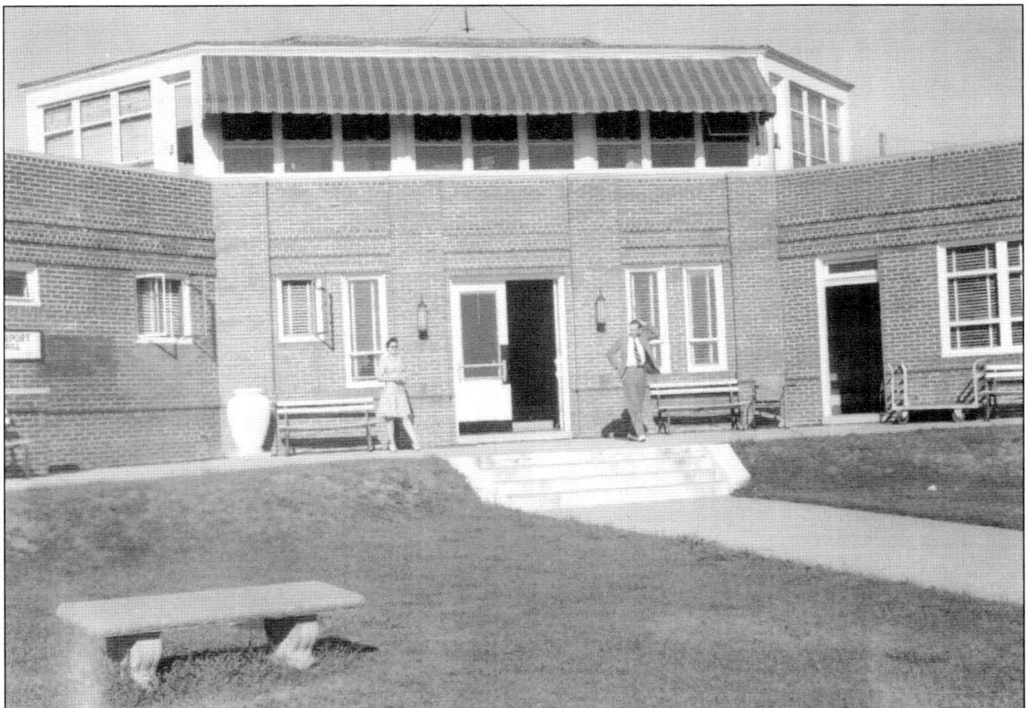

An unidentified man and woman stand in front the terminal building at Wertz Field. The octagonal two-story building contained radio equipment and offices on the second floor and a restaurant with a covered outdoor dining terrace.

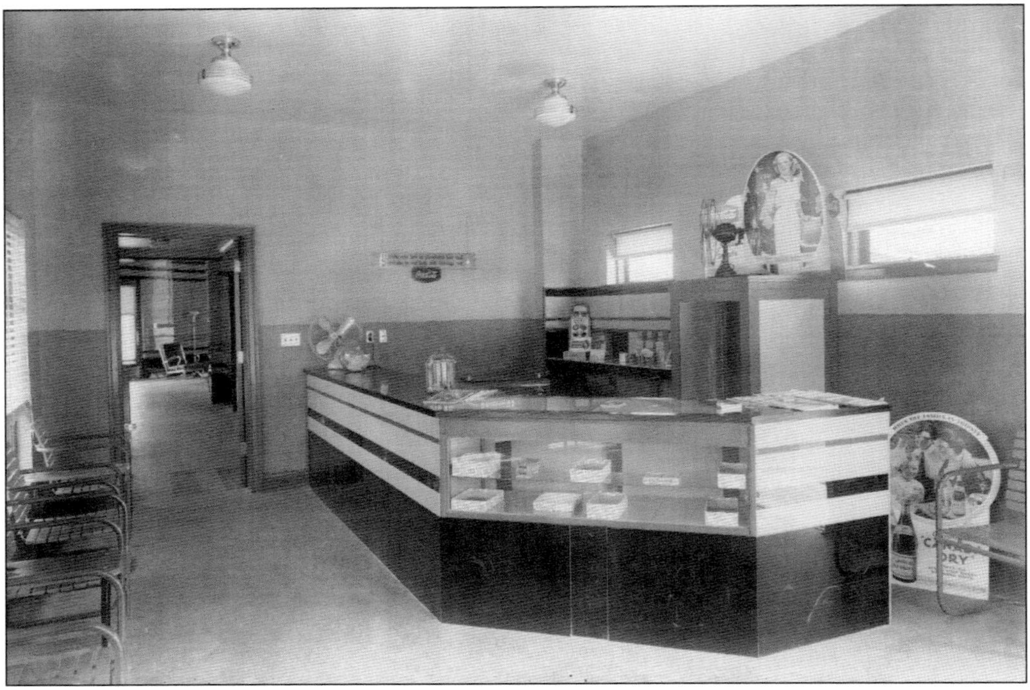

Inside the terminal was a sales counter with advertisements for Coca-Cola and Canada Dry. The basement of the terminal included the kitchen, storage rooms, a pilot and mechanics' club room, and a shower room.

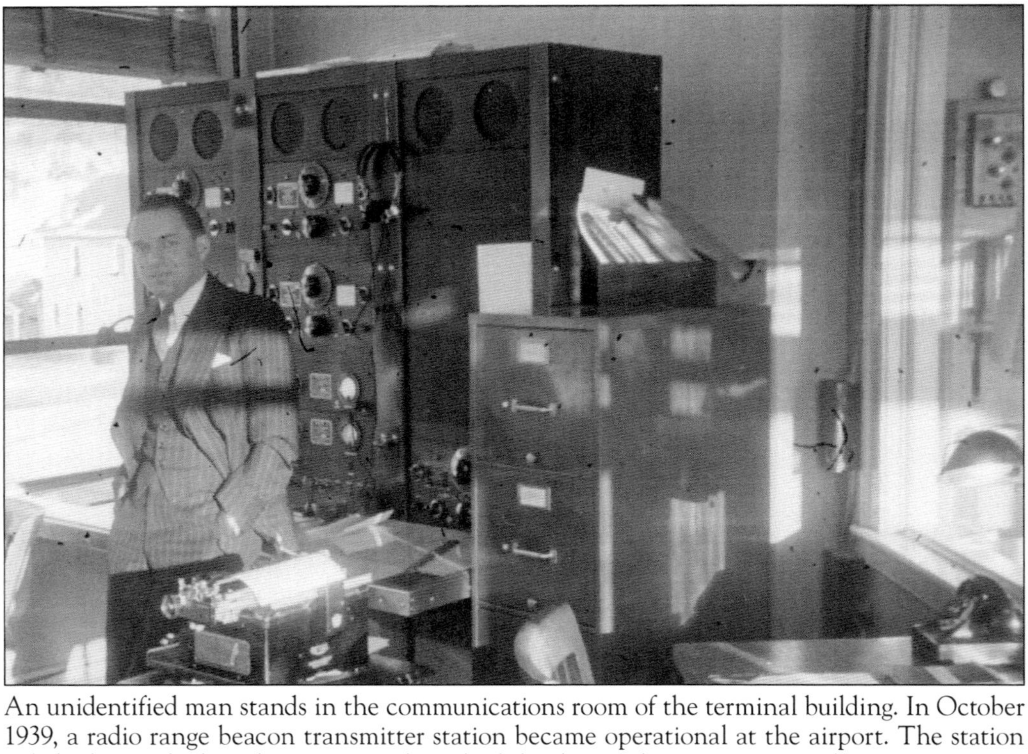

An unidentified man stands in the communications room of the terminal building. In October 1939, a radio range beacon transmitter station became operational at the airport. The station aided pilots in finding the airport and was built by the Civil Aeronautics Authority.

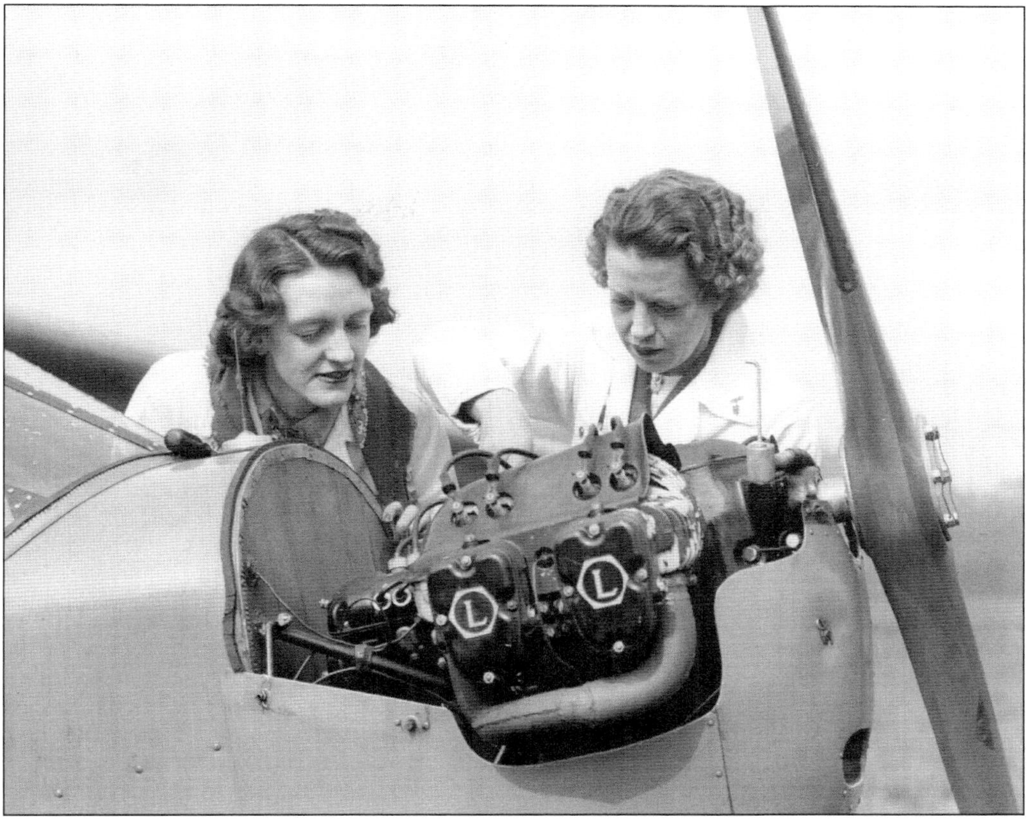

Two unidentified women inspect an aircraft engine at Wertz Field. During the 1930s, many women became pilots in West Virginia.

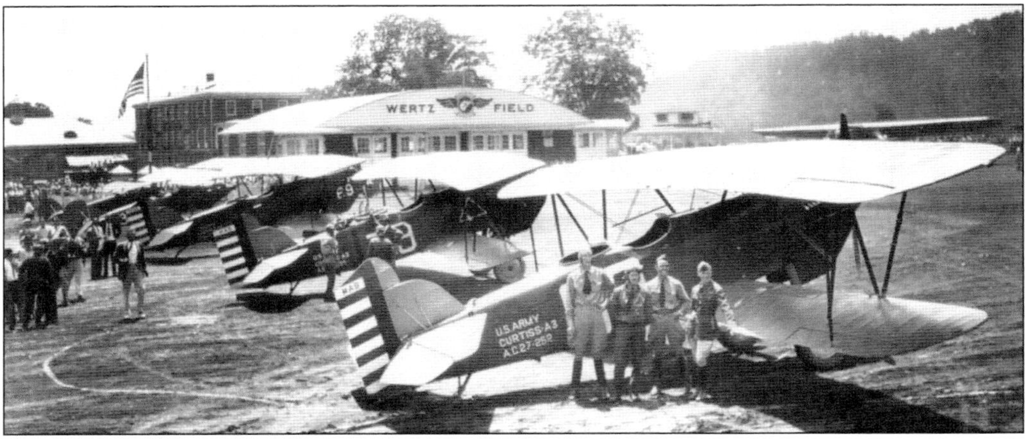

Standing in front of a US Army Air Corps Curtiss A3 attack aircraft at Wertz Field are, from left to right, Lt. M.D. Burnside, Lt. T.S. Power, Lt. J.H. Wallace, and Lt. John Kirby. The A3 could carry two 7.62-millimeter guns and 200 pounds of bombs.

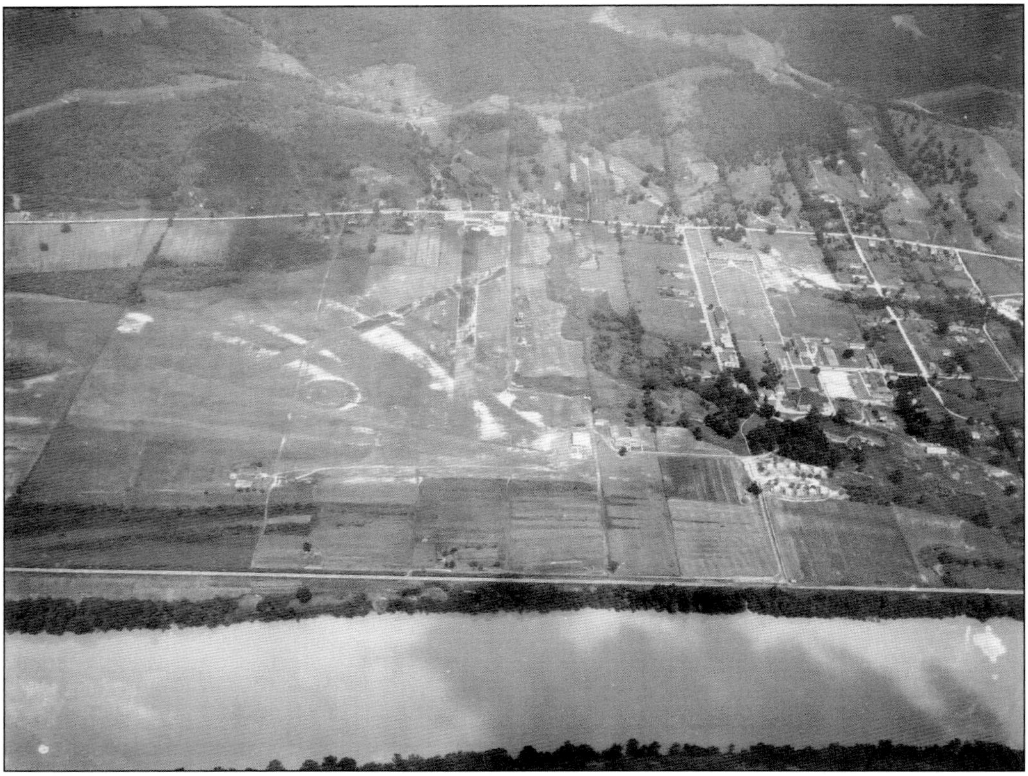

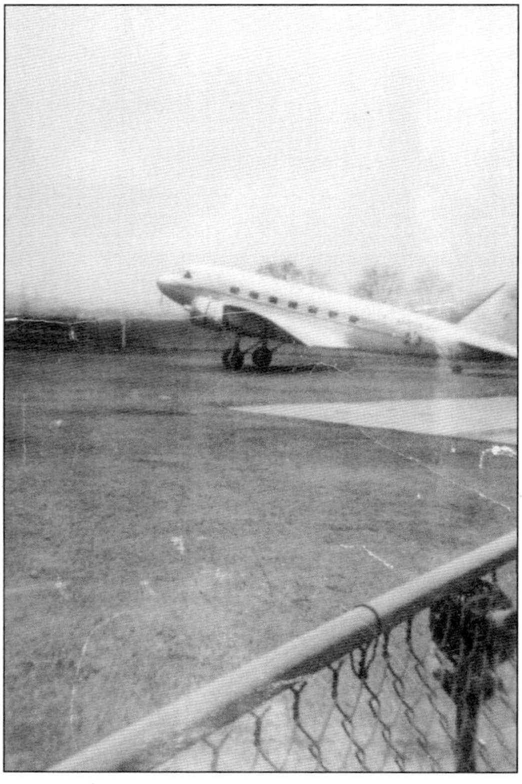

Beginning in late 1932, federal relief funds were used to improve facilities and runways at Wertz Field. In 1935, Wertz Field had three runways. A northwest-facing cinder runway was 2,500 feet long and 100 feet wide. A northeast-southwest blacktop to cinder runway was 2,200 feet long and 100 feet wide. The northwest-southeast turf runway was approximately 4,000 feet long and 100 feet wide, with a power line crossing on the west end, negating the last 1,000 feet for takeoff and landing in that area.

An American Airlines Douglas DC-2 or DC-3 sits near the terminal. As larger aircraft such as the DC-3 were developed, it became evident Wertz Field was inadequate for these planes. In January 1937, American Airlines operated nonstop from Wertz Field to Cincinnati, Ohio, and direct to Washington, DC, with a stop in Elkins, West Virginia, using an eight-passenger Stinson A model.

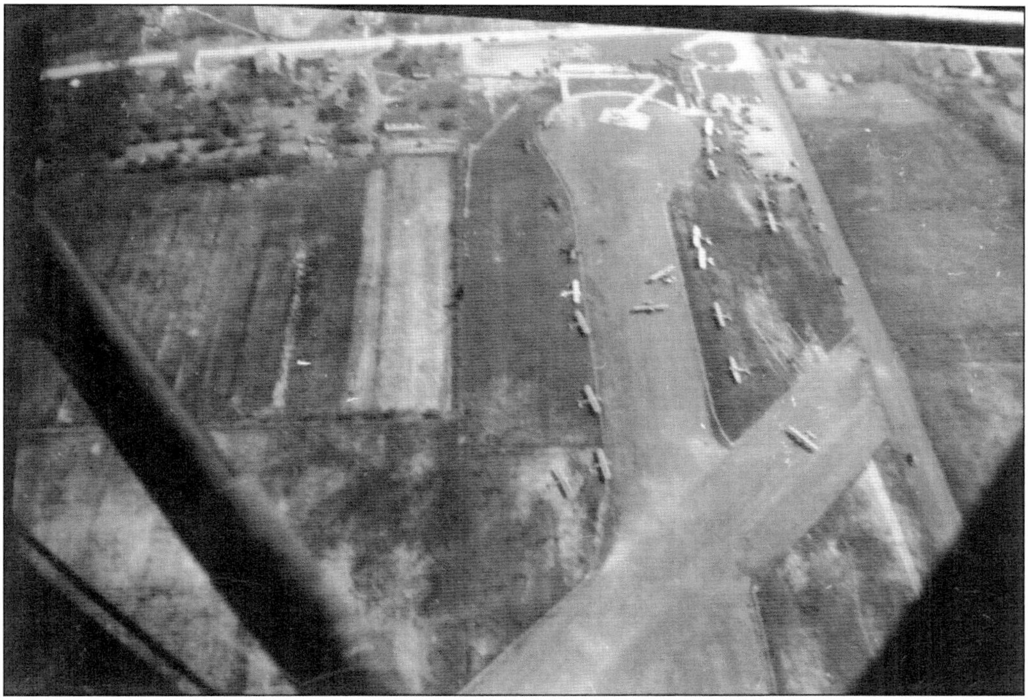

This aerial photograph shows a bustling Wertz Field with 22 aircraft visible and the terminal at the top of the image at the end of a runway.

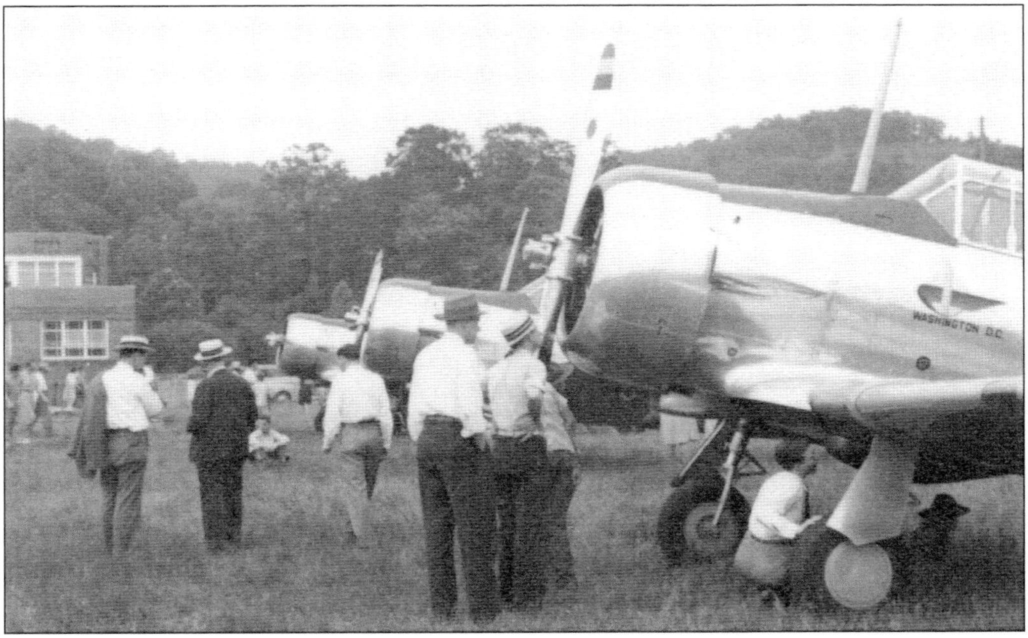

Spectators get an up-close view of military T-6 training aircraft sent to Wertz Field from Washington, DC, sometime after 1934.

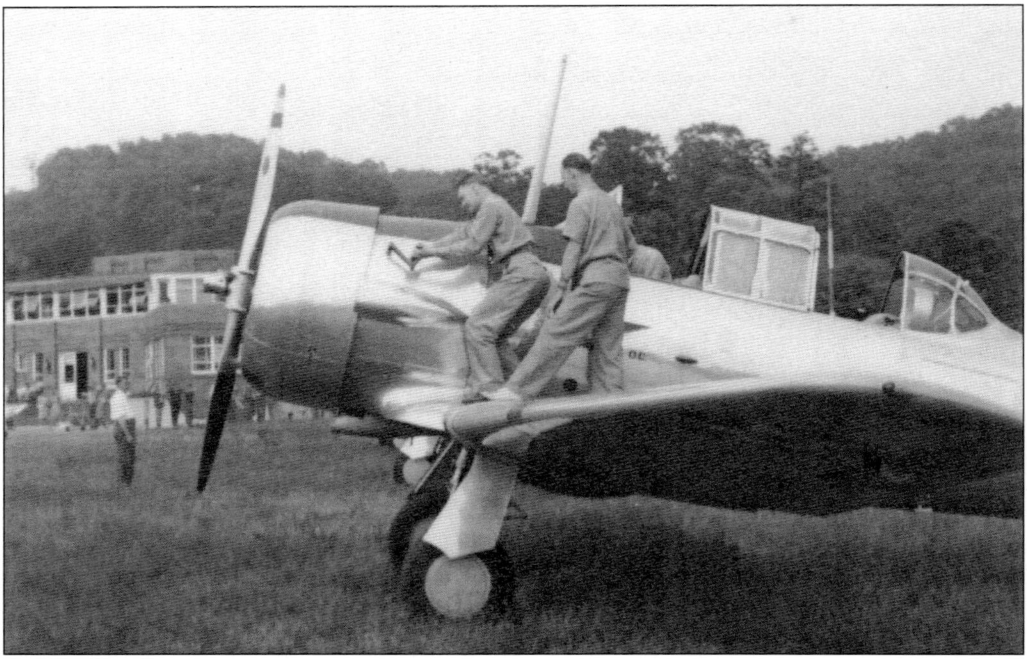

Military personnel operate a crank on a military T-6 training aircraft. Note the large radio antenna sticking up between the military personnel.

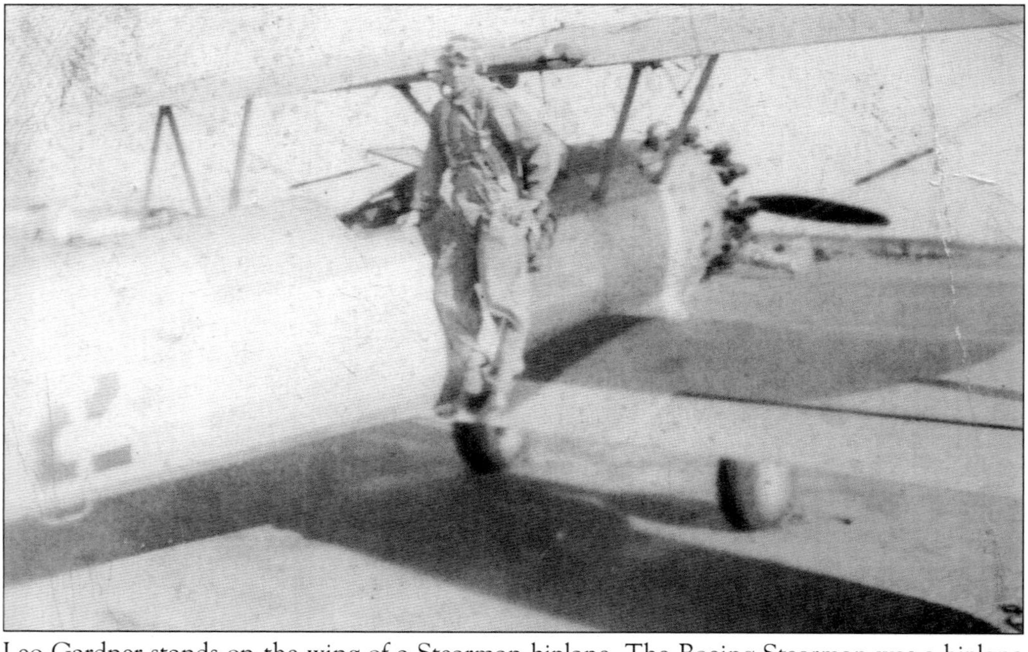

Leo Gardner stands on the wing of a Stearman biplane. The Boeing Stearman was a biplane military trainer introduced in 1934. Over 10,000 were built, and it served as the primary trainer for student pilots in World War II.

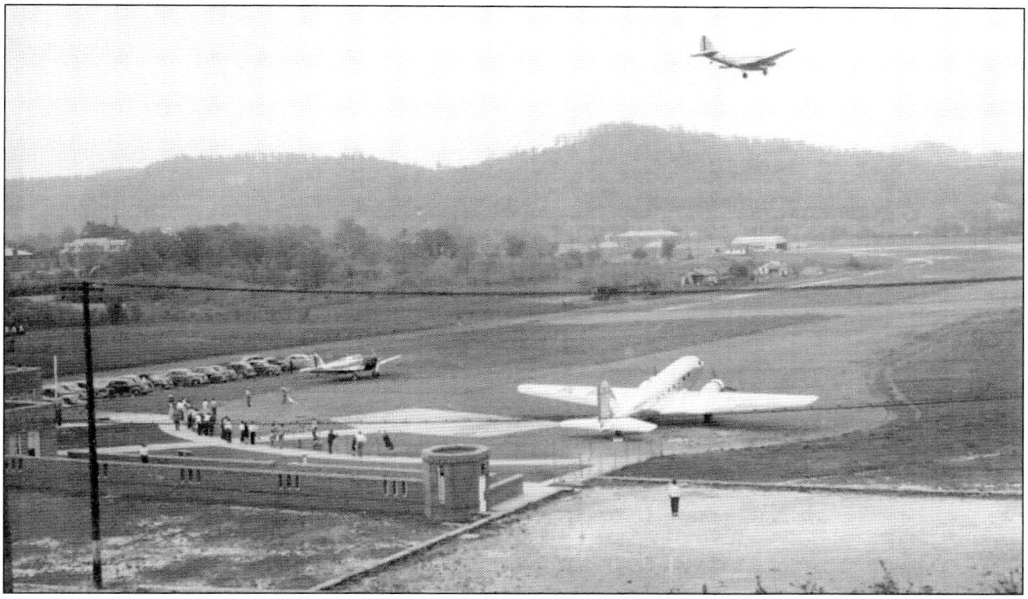

An American Airlines DC-2 or DC-3 sits by the Wertz terminal building as a military airplane flies overhead. After the DC-3 was introduced, American Airlines threatened to cancel service to Wertz Field because the field was not large enough. There is a large group of people along the fence line watching the activities. (Courtesy of the West Virginia State University Archives.)

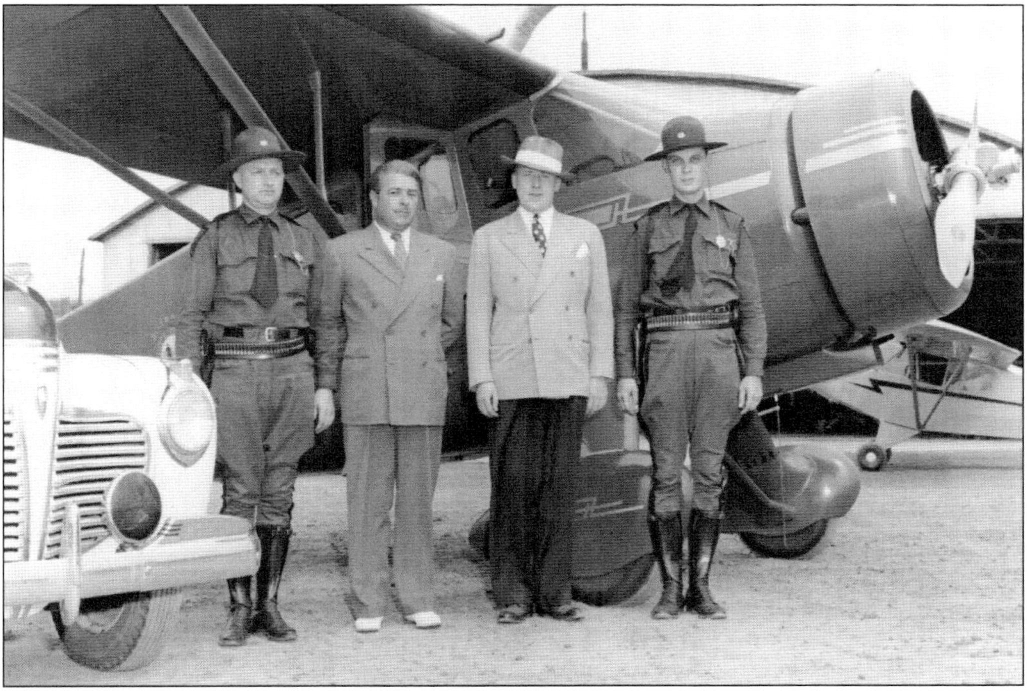

Hubert Stark (second from left) and an unidentified man are flanked by unidentified West Virginia State Troopers, with the state airplane in the background. Stark came to Wertz Field in 1930 as a pilot for West Virginia Airways. He was director of the West Virginia Aeronautics Board from 1937 to 1947 and director of the West Virginia Aeronautics Commission from 1947 to 1963. (Courtesy of the West Virginia State Archives, Beulah Stark Collection.)

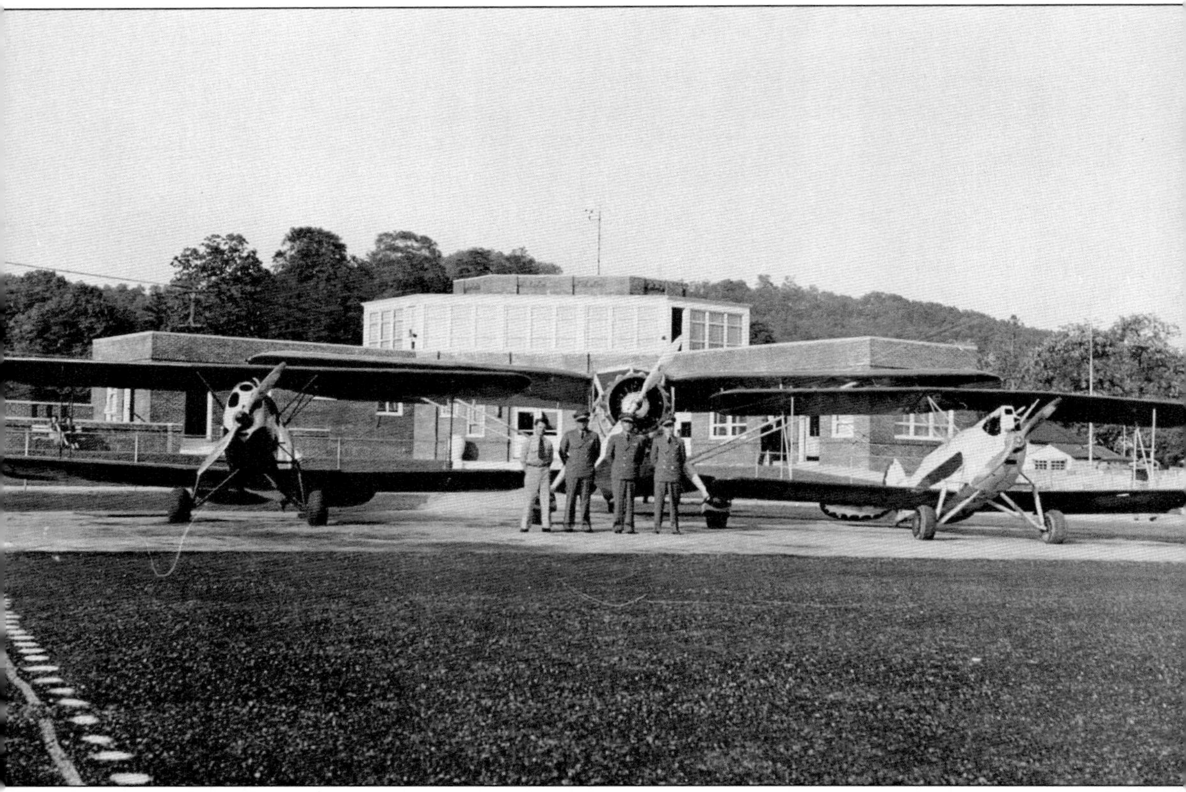

Three aircraft on display in front of the Wertz Field terminal building with unidentified men. The aircraft in the center appears to be a Stinson Reliant. The airport was named after Charleston mayor William W. Wertz, who was instrumental in establishing the field. (Courtesy of the West Virginia State Archives, Beulah Stark Collection.)

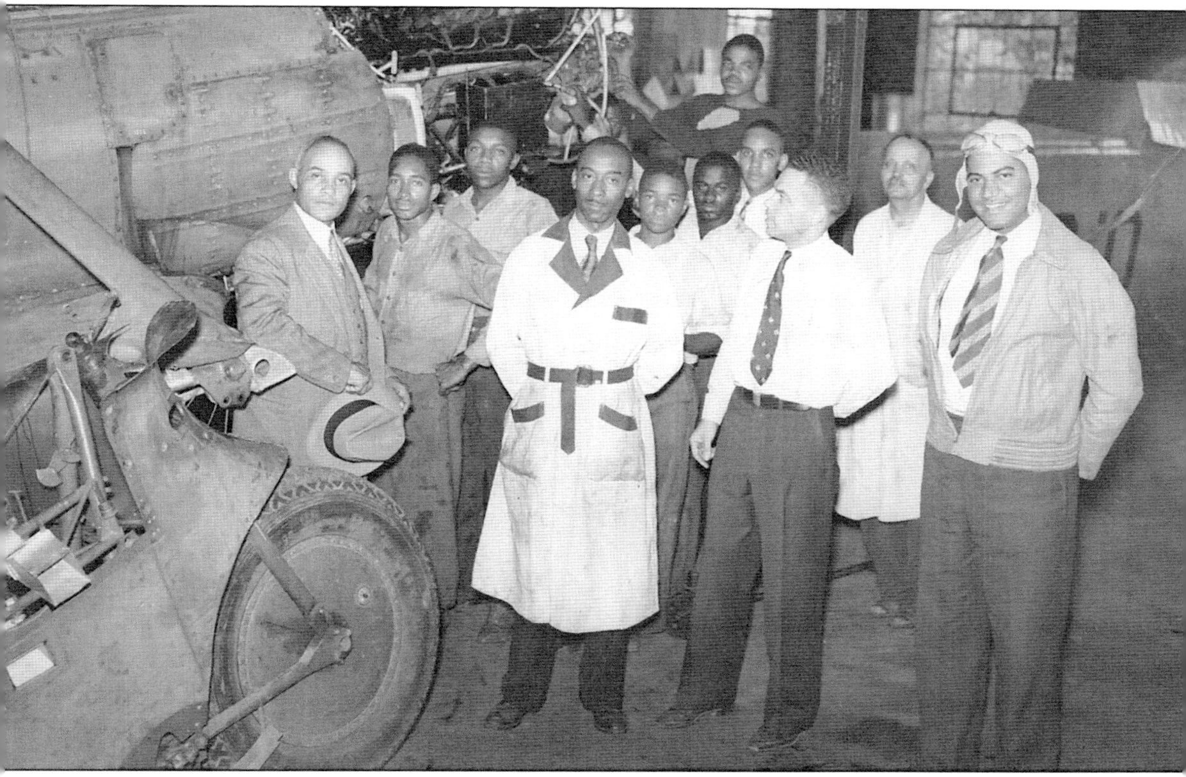

A Curtiss bomber airplane was obtained by the National Youth Administration from the War Department for use at West Virginia State College in the ground training courses. In 1939, Pres. Franklin D. Roosevelt signed the Civilian Pilot Training Act into law. The act created the Civilian Pilot Training Program (CPTP), using educational institutions to provide pilot training so the United States would be better prepared for war. West Virginia State College was the first of six historically black schools to be selected to participate in the program. The school was selected due to the vigorous efforts of Pres. John W. Davis and James C. Evans, administrative assistant to the president and director of mechanical industries and trade and technical education. President Davis sent Evans and Prof. Joseph Grider to Washington, DC, to appeal to the Civil Aeronautics Authority for West Virginia State College's inclusion. It was pointed out that three African Americans had successfully taken flying lessons at Wertz Field and no racial problems would be expected. The three African American men who had taken flying lessons were institute resident Milard Brown, mathematics professor Shefflin Claytor, and Professor Grider. West Virginia State College is thought to be the first institution in West Virginia to racially integrate an educational program, as two white students were admitted into the Civilian Pilot Training Program in 1940. Also unique for the time was the enrollment of African American and white women into the program. Due to the successful racial and gender integration at West Virginia State College in 1940, the Civilian Pilot Training Program became a revolutionary step in the struggle for civil rights that paved the way for future integration. (Courtesy of the West Virginia State University Archives.)

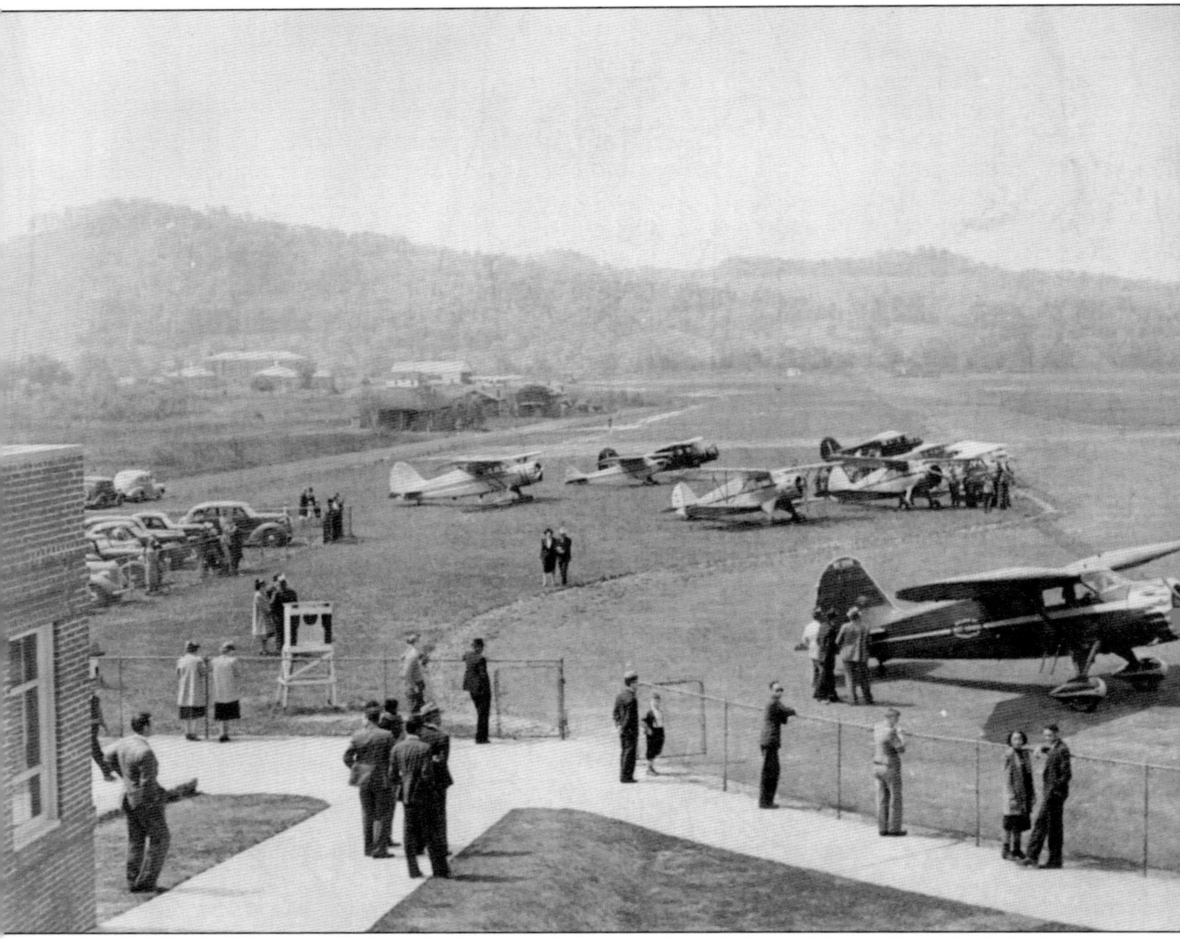

This caption for this photograph in an April 30, 1948, letter by James C. Evans reads, "This picture, dated September 16, 1939, portrays, among other things, the first successful approach of the Negro citizen to participation in federally sponsored training in aeronautics." Evans goes on to identify people: "In this photograph appears in the left foreground, with arms folded across his back and wearing a gray hat, President John W. Davis, who has continued his service to the government

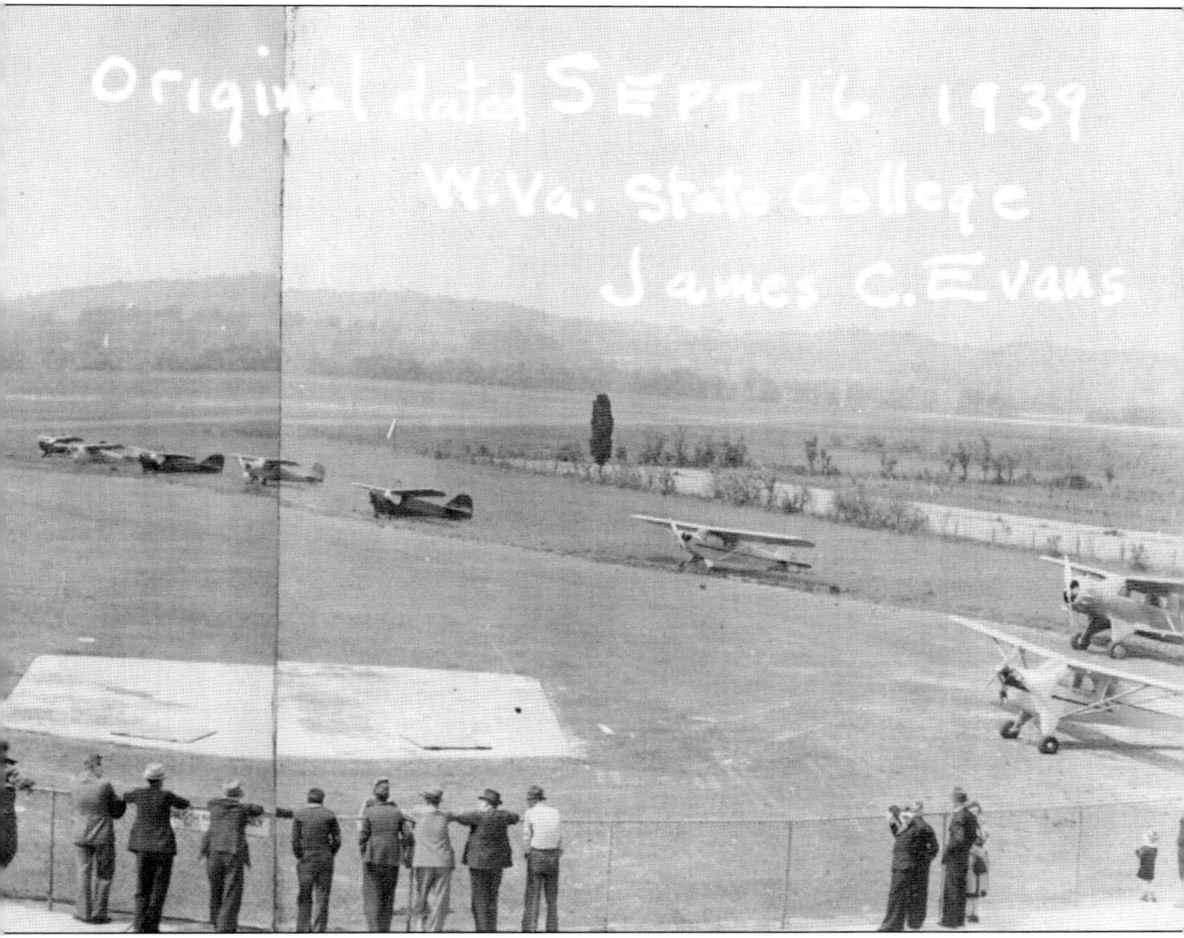

up to participating with you on Monday of this week in the National Defense Conference on Negro Affairs as called by Secretary Forrestal. I appear to his left, slightly behind and looking to my left. At the fence wearing dark glasses is Mr. Hector Strong who became a flight instructor at Tuskegee . . . Pilot trainees and technicians appear further out on the field."

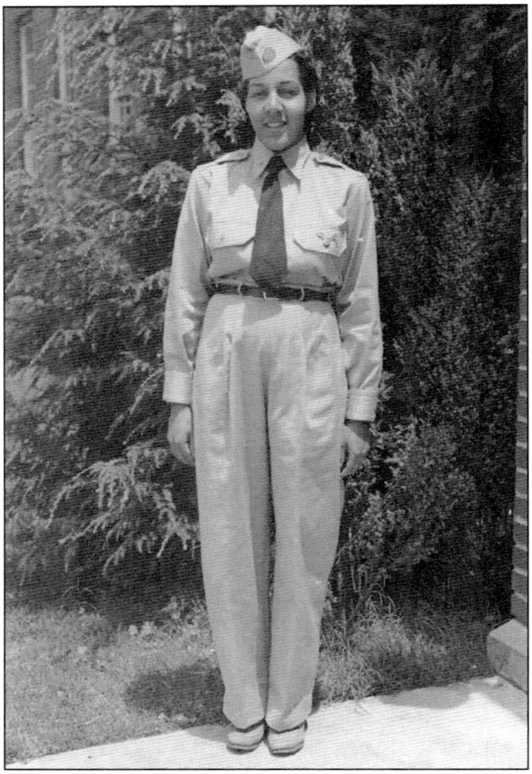

Rose Agnes Rolls successfully completed the Civilian Pilot Training Program at West Virginia State College and was one of the first African American women to receive a private pilot's license in the United States. (Courtesy of the West Virginia State University Archives.)

Rolls stands in front of a West Virginia State Board of Aeronautics aircraft at Wertz Field. Between 1939 and 1941, seventy trainees enrolled in the program at West Virginia State College. (Courtesy of the West Virginia State University Archives.)

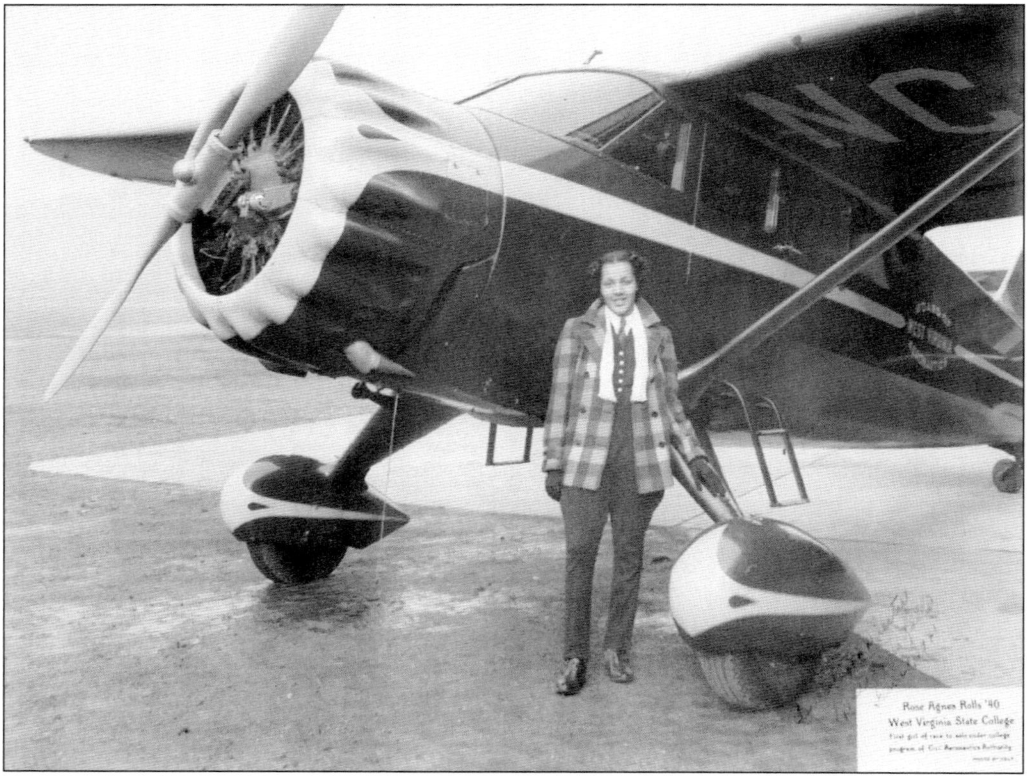

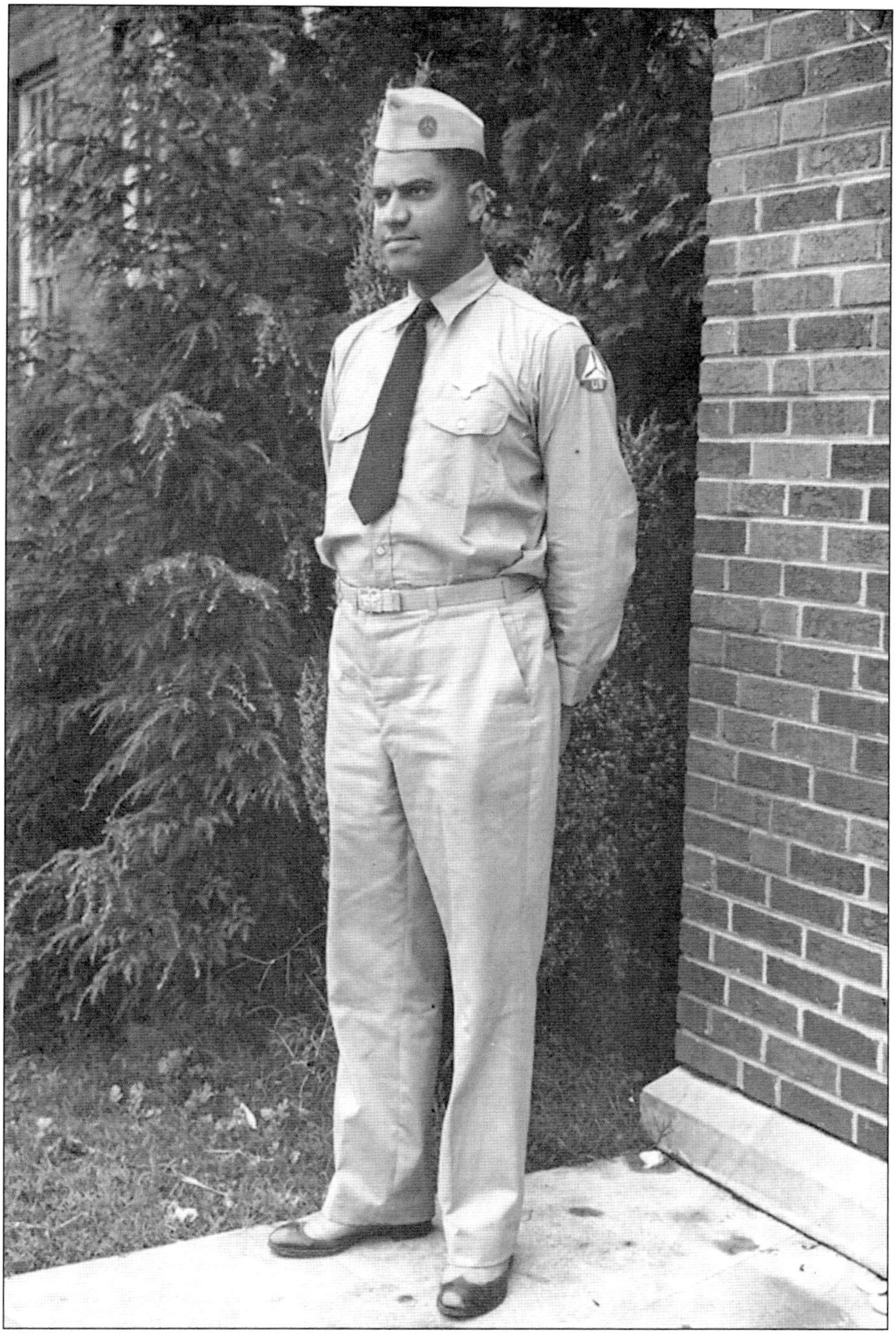

Prof. Joseph Grider stands in his Civilian Pilot Training uniform. The Civilian Pilot Training Program consisted of 72 hours of ground school and 35 hours of flight instruction. The ground courses included physics, calculus, civil air regulations, navigation, aeronautical meteorology, general service of aircraft, aircraft structure and maintenance, practical aerodynamics, airplane power plants, and analytical mechanics. In 1942, the War Department canceled the Civilian Pilot Training Program at all six historically black colleges, consolidating the training at the Tuskegee Army Airfield. (Courtesy of the West Virginia State University Archives.)

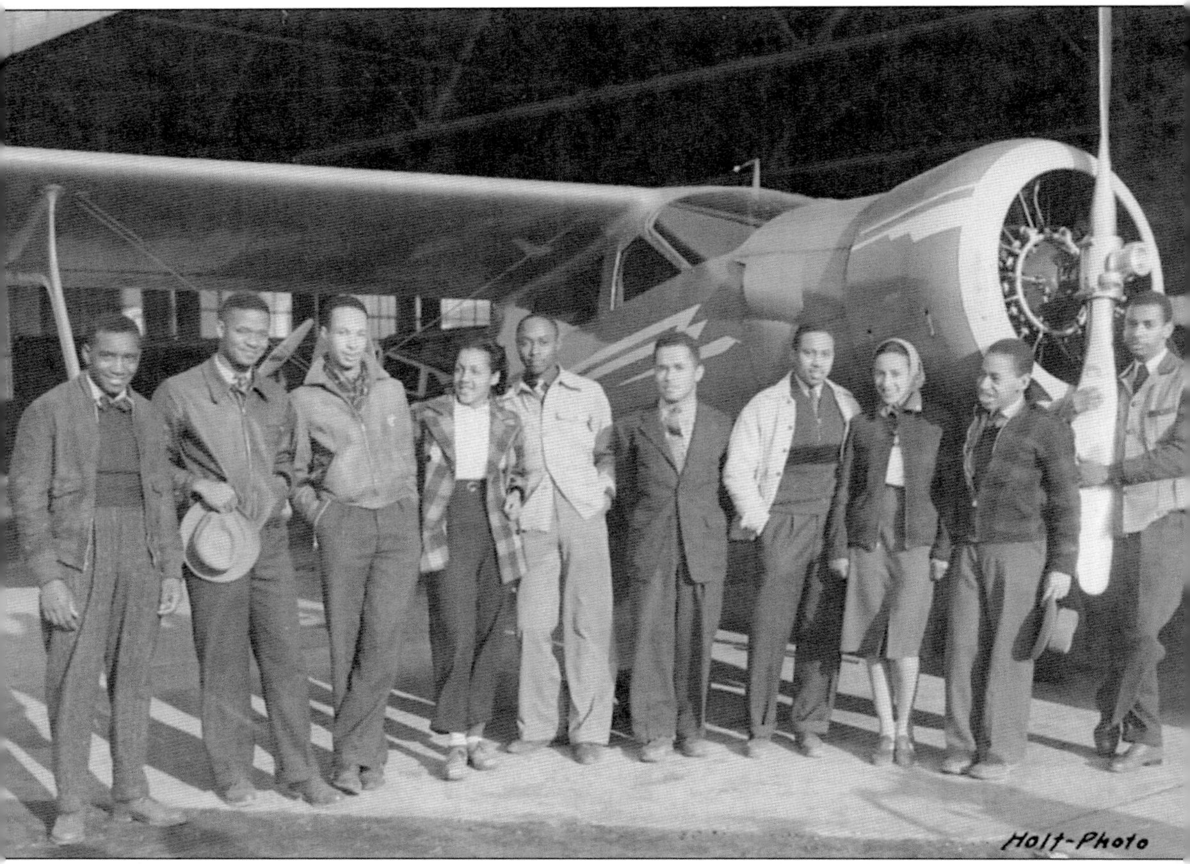

A group of students from the Civilian Pilot Training Program at West Virginia State College poses at Wertz Field. Male African American pilots who graduated the Civilian Pilot Training Program were allowed to apply for military flight training at the Tuskegee Institute in Alabama. The training at Tuskegee led to the first African American military pilots and creation of the first all–African American fighter and bomber groups, known as the Tuskegee Airmen. The Tuskegee Airmen fought racism and segregation to become a respected fighting force in World War II, participating in over 1,500 missions. Approximately 30 African American graduates of West Virginia State College became Tuskegee Airmen during the war. (Courtesy of the West Virginia State University Archives.)

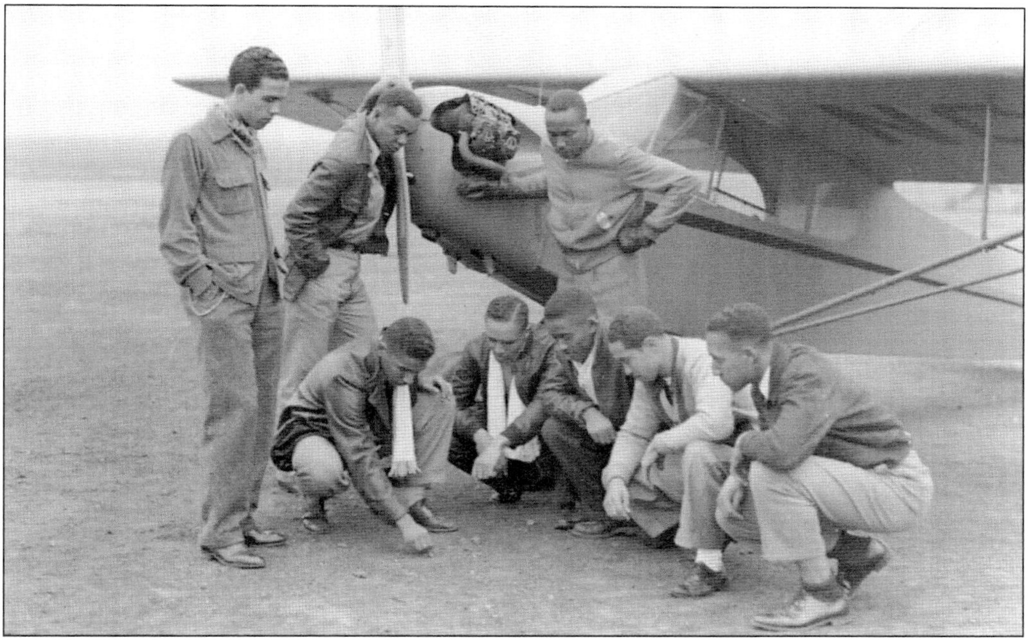

Students in the Civilian Pilot Training Program confer over a navigational problem while at the airfield. (Courtesy of the West Virginia State University Archives.)

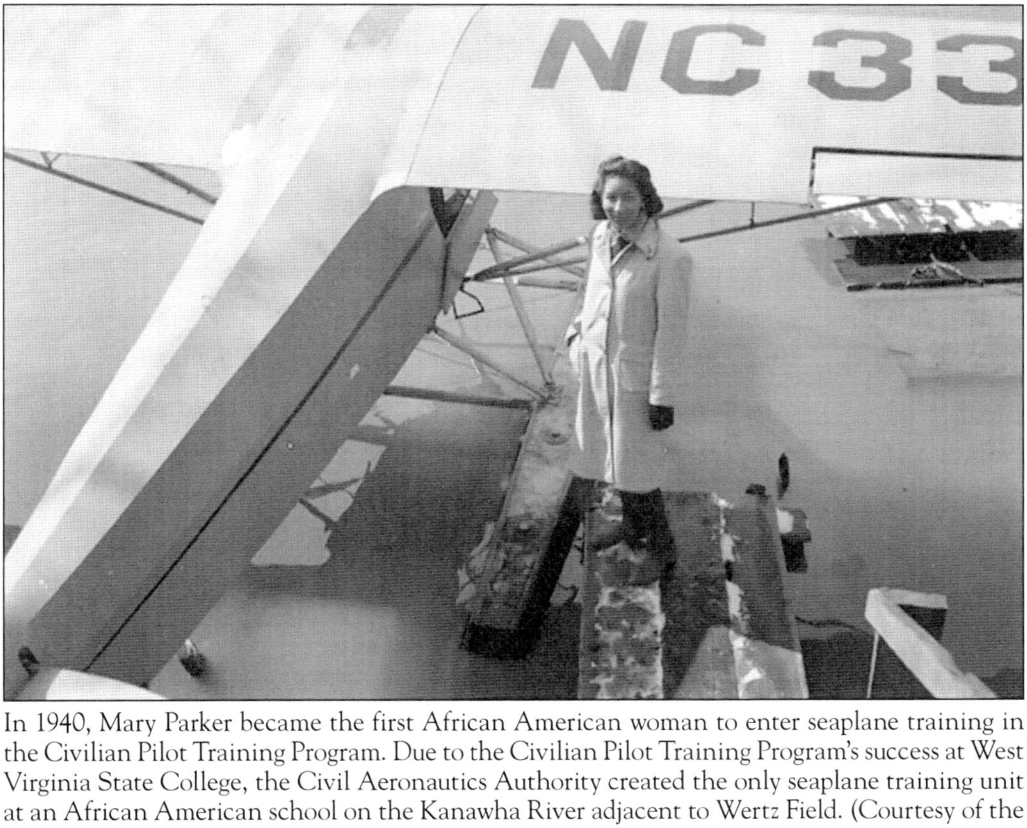

In 1940, Mary Parker became the first African American woman to enter seaplane training in the Civilian Pilot Training Program. Due to the Civilian Pilot Training Program's success at West Virginia State College, the Civil Aeronautics Authority created the only seaplane training unit at an African American school on the Kanawha River adjacent to Wertz Field. (Courtesy of the West Virginia State University Archives.)

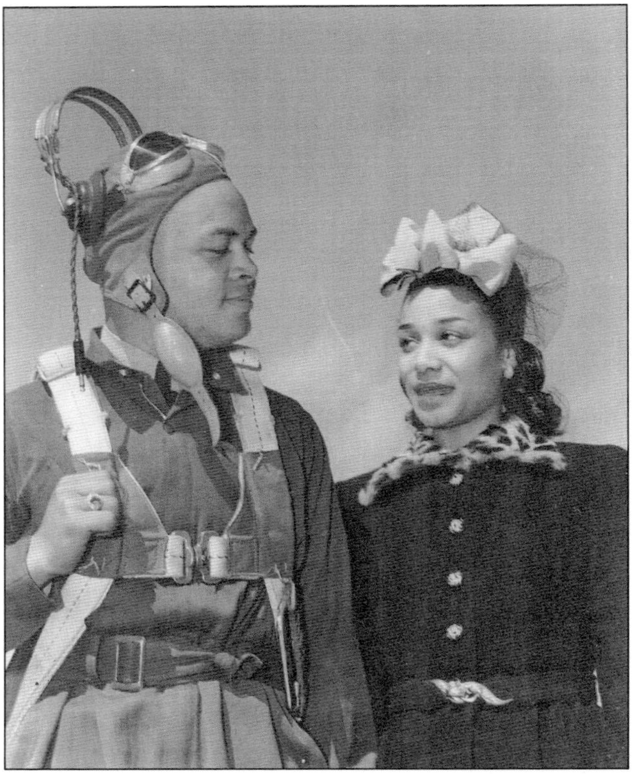

US Army Air Corps second lieutenant George Roberts poses with his wife, Edith. Five of the thirteen cadets in the first training class at Tuskegee graduated and became the first African American Army Air Corps pilots. Among the five were West Virginia State College Civilian Pilot Training Program graduates George Spencer, "Spanky" Roberts, and Mac Ross, who were commissioned second lieutenants in the Army Air Corps on March 7, 1942. Roberts was appointed commander of the 99th Pursuit Squadron, and Ross was appointed commander of the 100th Pursuit Squadron. (Courtesy of the West Virginia State University Archives.)

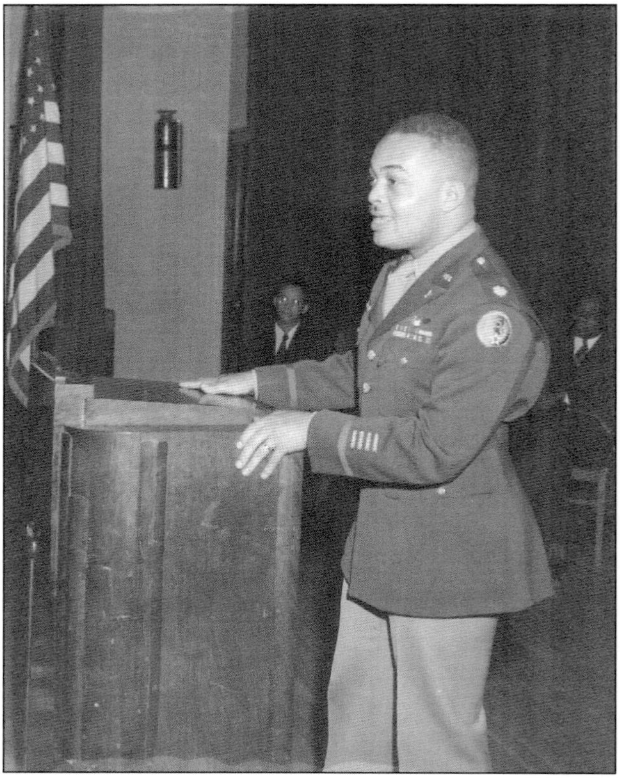

Maj. George Roberts speaks while on the campus of West Virginia State College, in Institute. Roberts was born in London, West Virginia, on September 24, 1918. While attending West Virginia State College, he completed the Civilian Pilot Training Program and entered the first training class to become a Tuskegee Airman. Roberts became the first African American examined and accepted for appointment in the US Army Air Corps. Roberts flew over 100 combat missions in Europe, Africa, and the Middle East. (Courtesy of the West Virginia State University Archives.)

Three

Kanawha Airport from 1947 to 1985

As larger commercial aircraft such as the DC-3 were introduced in the late 1930s, officials were notified by American Airlines that Wertz Field was becoming insufficient and service would be discontinued. A committee was formed in 1937 by the Charleston Chamber of Commerce to search within 25 miles of Charleston for possible sites for a new airport. There being no suitable sites large enough on the valley floor, the decision was made to build an airport on the mountains. In 1940, an area known as Coonskin Ridge was recommended as the site for the new airport. Engineers from the City of Charleston drew up plans for the airport, which were rejected for federal funding by the Work Projects Administration. Since the City of Charleston had no levies to support a bond issue, the Kanawha County Court agreed to take over the project.

In November 1943, a bond issue of $3 million ($41,766,417 in today's dollars) for airport construction was approved by the voters of Kanawha County by a ratio of 22 to 1. The groundbreaking ceremony for Kanawha Airport was held on October 18, 1944. A federal appropriation of $2.75 million ($36,765,514 in today's dollars) was secured in 1945 to aid in construction. The new airport was dedicated on November 3, 1947, and the first airline flights began operating on December 1, 1947. In 1948, the voters of Kanawha County approved $1.1 million ($10,993,290 in today's dollars) in bonds, which the federal government supplemented with $800,000 ($7,995,120 in today's dollars), for the remainder of construction and the new terminal building. Kanawha Airport successfully served the needs of travelers and was expanded several times to keep pace with advances in aviation and the introduction of jet aircraft.

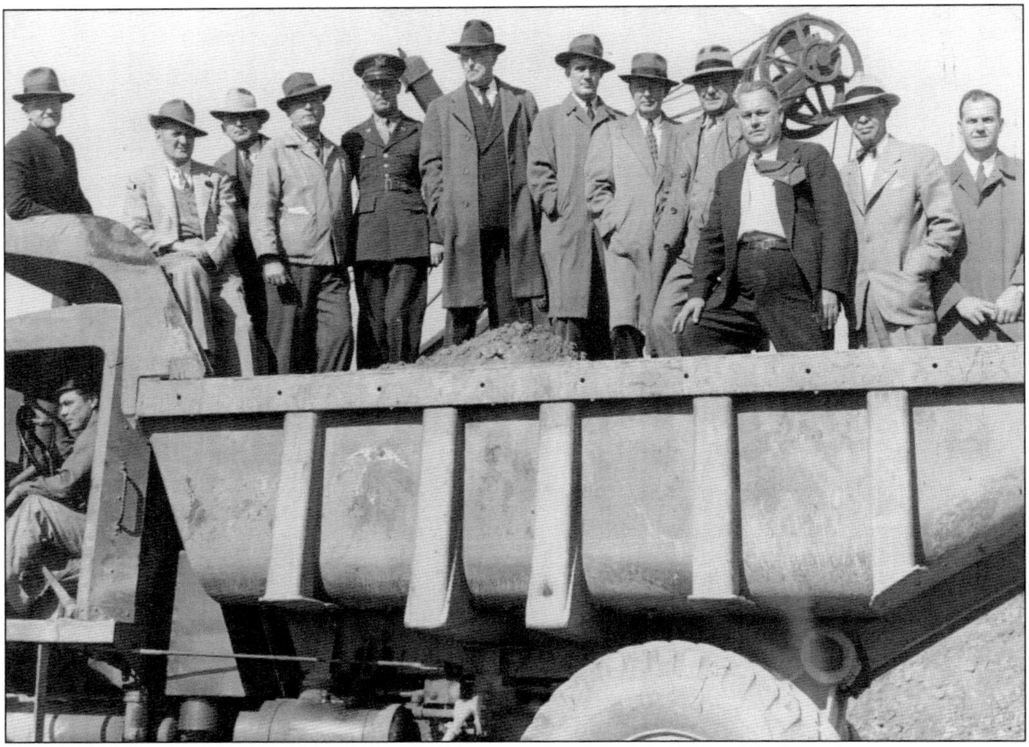

Construction of Kanawha Airport began on October 18, 1944. Posing in the bed of a dump truck after the start of construction are, from left to right, W.F. Picklen, Robert G. Kelly, Mont L. Cavendar, Fred C. Alley, Harry Pockras, James G. Carper, Jack Hilton, Dean P. Reed, Stanley C. Morris, Carl Calvert, Charles E. Hodges, and Pat Bond.

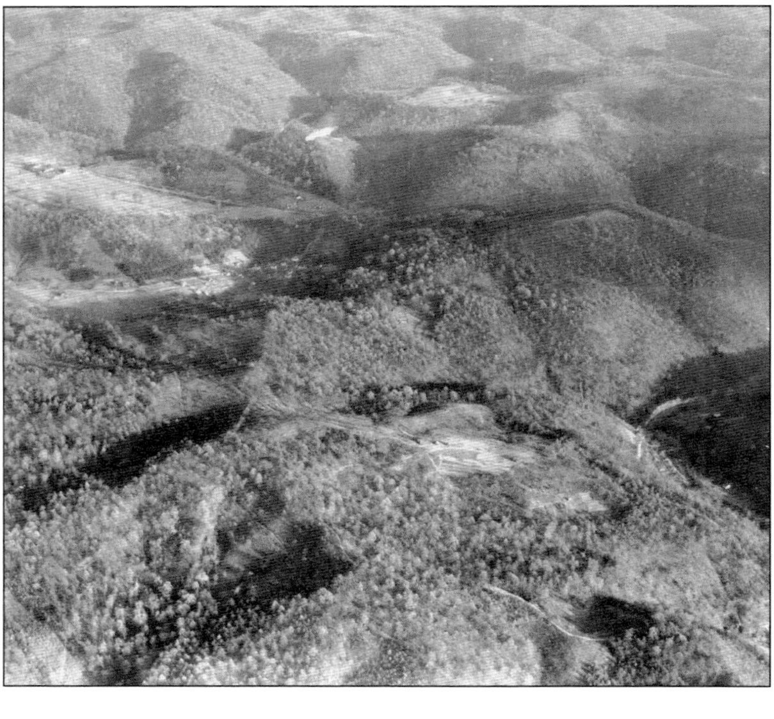

This is a view of the mountains of Coonskin Ridge that would later become Kanawha Airport. When completed, the airport would sit 350 feet above the valley floor and more than nine million cubic yards of rock and dirt would be moved.

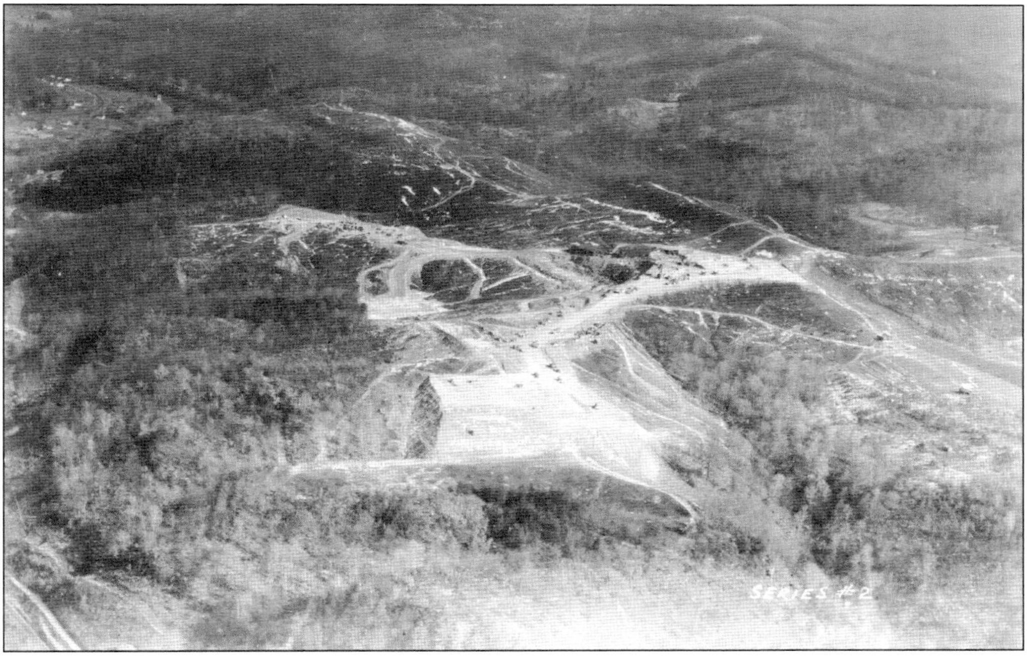

Construction progresses at the Kanawha Airport site. The enormity of the elevation differences that must be leveled out is evident. In 1945, West Virginia senators Harley Kilgore and Chapman Revercomb were able to secure a federal appropriation of $2.75 million ($36,765,514 in today's dollars) to be used in addition to the Kanawha County bonds.

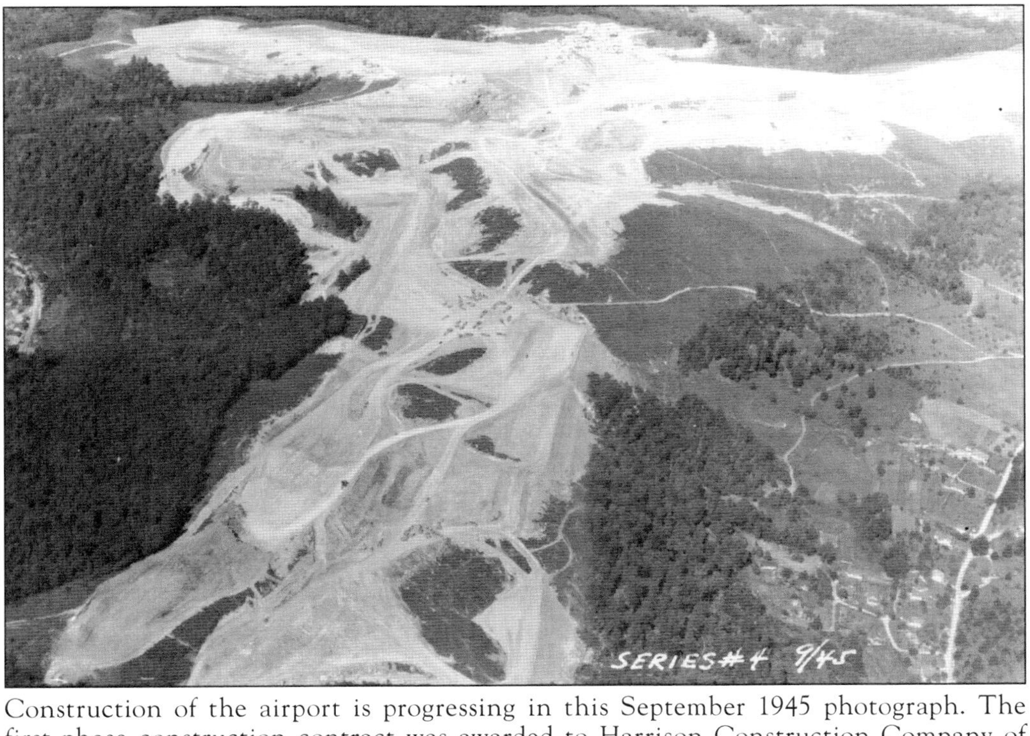

Construction of the airport is progressing in this September 1945 photograph. The first phase construction contract was awarded to Harrison Construction Company of Pittsburgh, Pennsylvania.

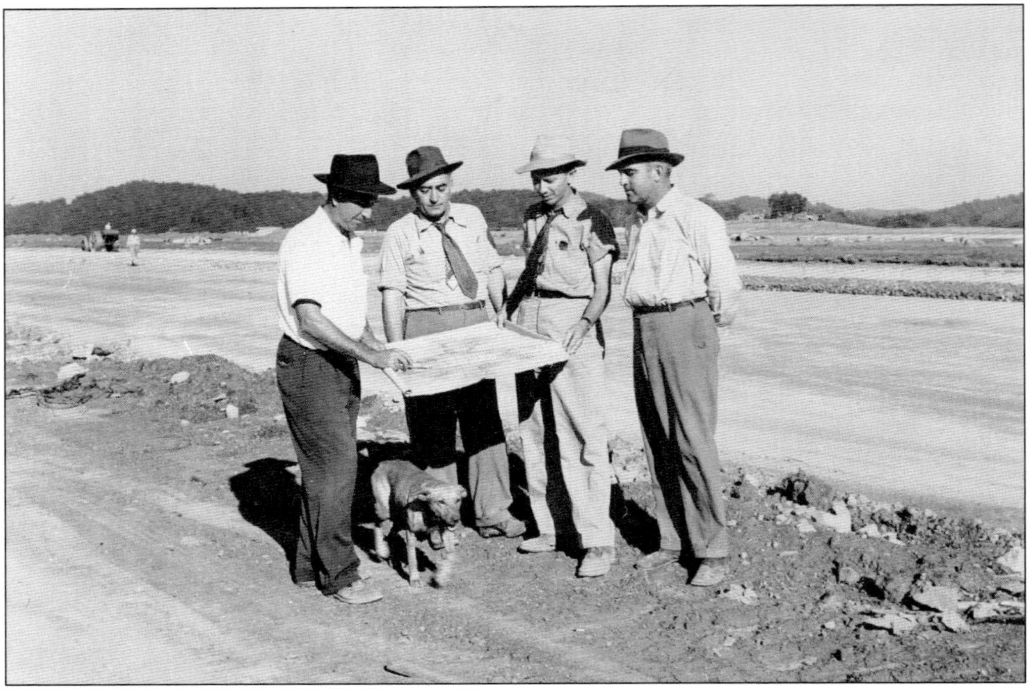

Standing on a future runway are, from left to right, ? Gevell, Tommy the dog, Fred Alley, ? Baker, and ? Reid in September 1946. (Courtesy of the West Virginia State Archives, Judy Escue Collection.)

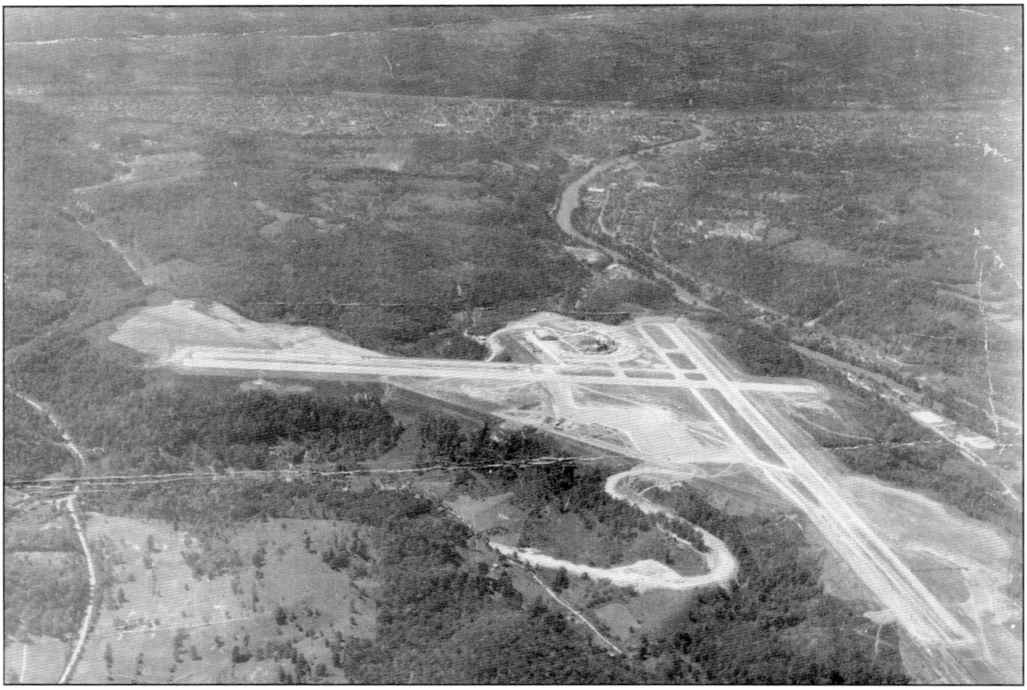

This aerial view shows grading completed after May 1947. The area at the top of the photograph is now the general aviation area. During construction, workers moved approximately 20,000 to 27,000 cubic yards of dirt and rocks each working day.

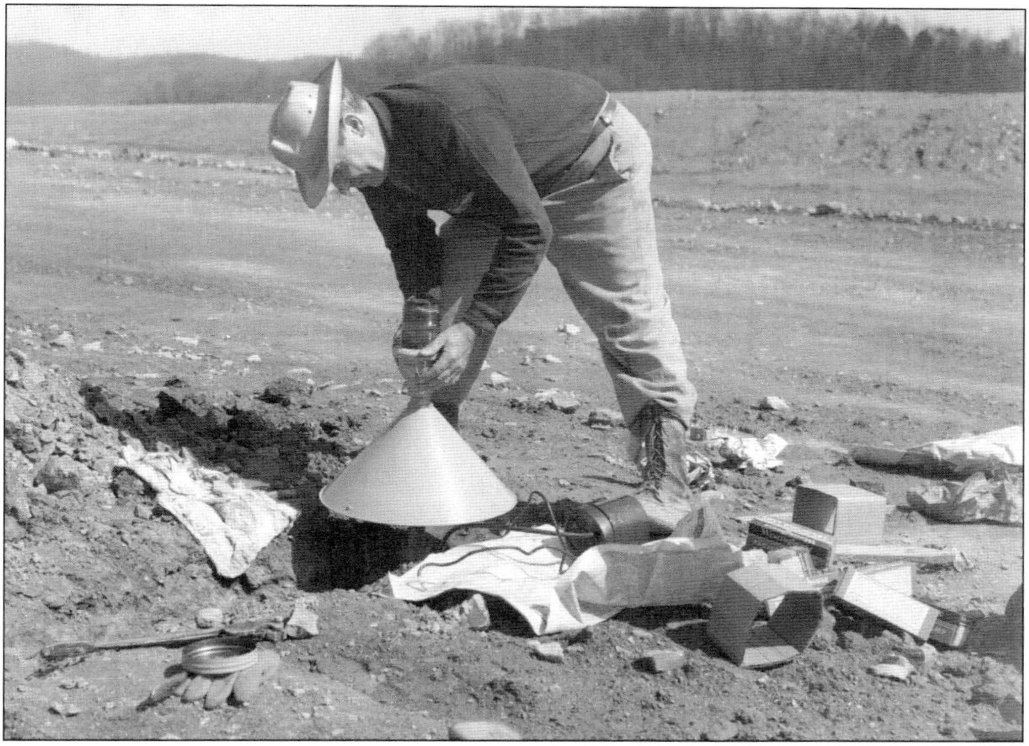

An unidentified worker from the Marigold Electric Company installs a light during construction at Kanawha Airport. The engineering firm for the construction project was Whitman, Requardt and Associates from Baltimore, Maryland.

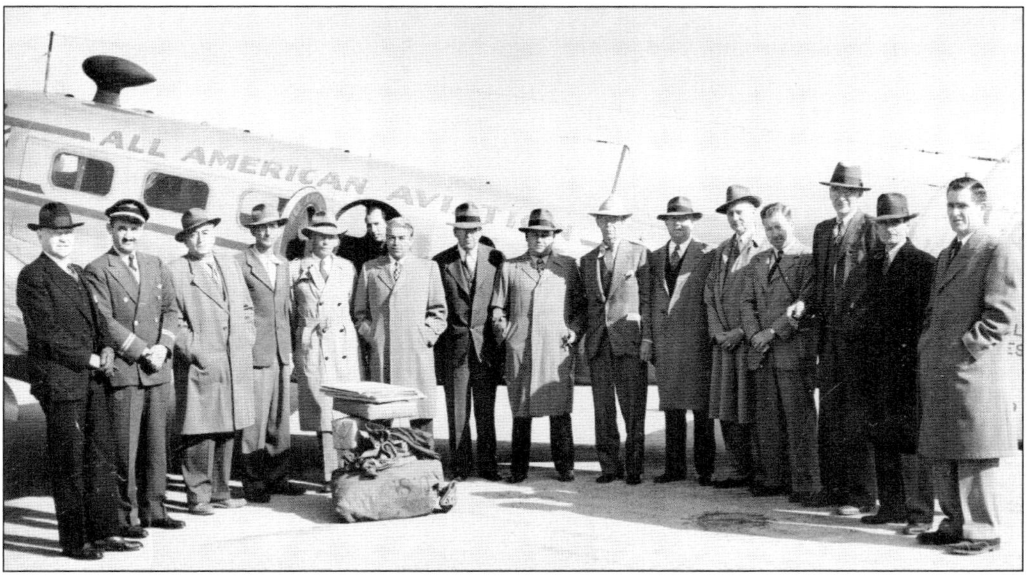

In this October 1, 1947, photograph, an unidentified group of Kanawha County, post office, chamber of commerce, and City of Charleston officials commemorates the first official flight into Kanawha Airport, which carried airmail. All-American Aviation would later become Allegheny Airlines and provide passenger service. (Courtesy of the West Virginia State Archives, Beulah Stark Collection.)

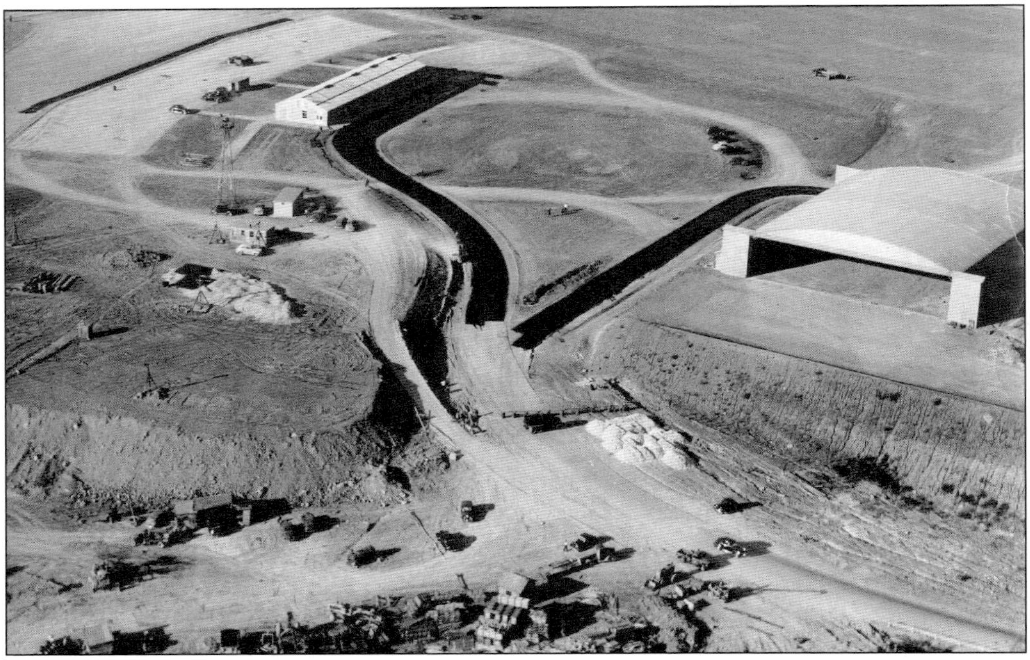

In 1947, work was nearing completion, as evident in this photograph. The runways and taxiways can be clearly seen, and the hangar has been constructed. A temporary administration building has been constructed until the new terminal is built. A tower has been installed, holding a rotating beacon to help pilots locate the airport at night.

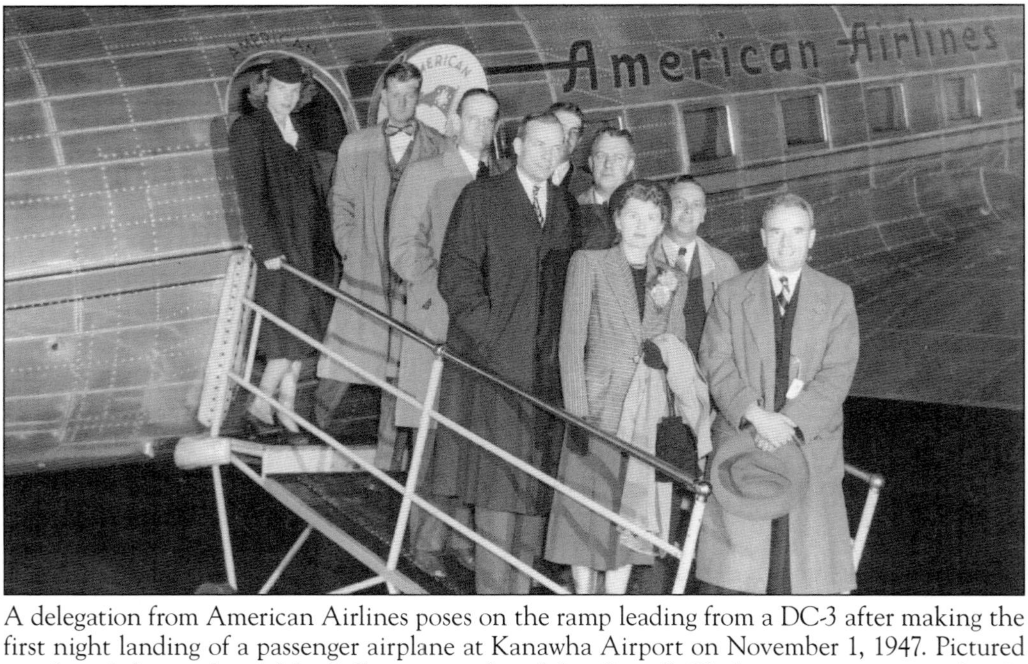

A delegation from American Airlines poses on the ramp leading from a DC-3 after making the first night landing of a passenger airplane at Kanawha Airport on November 1, 1947. Pictured are, from left to right, Adelia Follett, stewardess; John Carroll, Washington operations; Joe C. Lopez, regional manager for airports and buildings; Herbert D. Ford, Washington district sales manager; Charles B. Speers Jr., eastern region vice president; W.H. Miller, assistant vice president of operations; Jack Zevely, general attorney; Mrs. Zevely; and Ralph Damon, president.

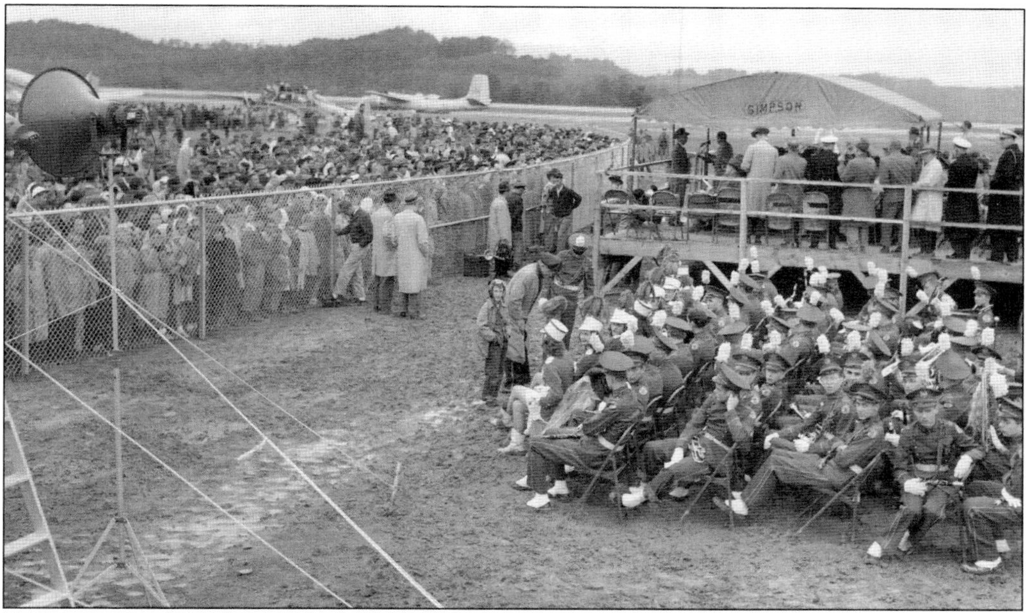

A crowd listens to a speaker at the Kanawha Airport dedication ceremony on November 3, 1947. Marching bands from Charleston High School and Stonewall Jackson High School provided music during the event. (Courtesy of Charleston Newspapers.)

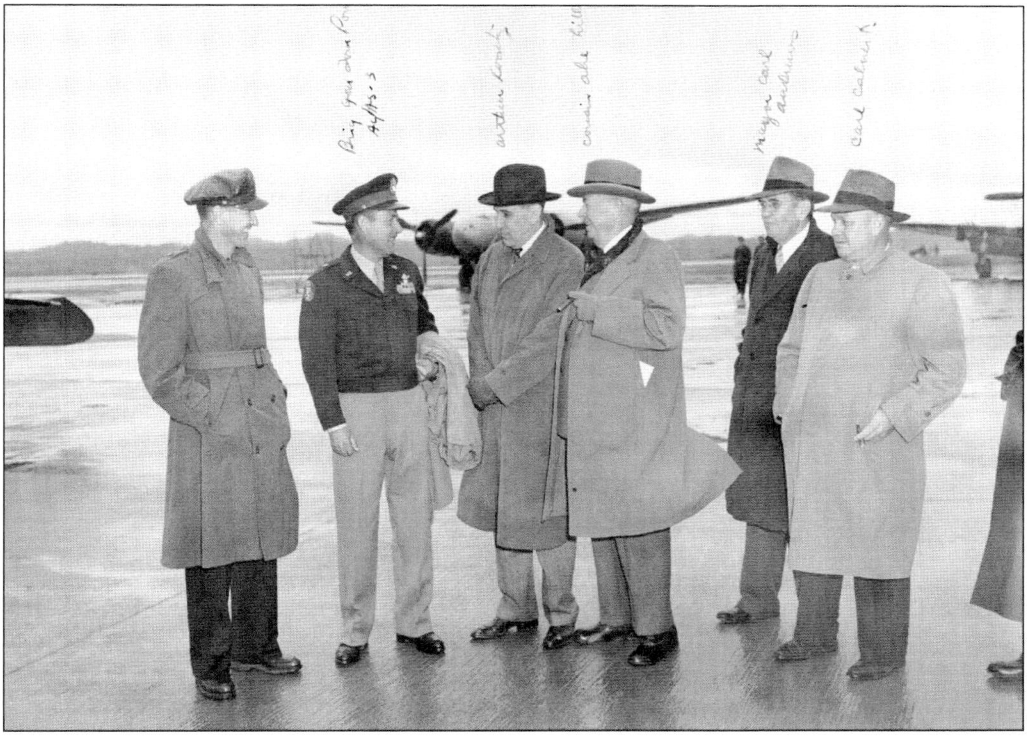

Present at the dedication of Kanawha Airport are, from left to right, Adj. Gen. Charles Fox, Brig. Gen. Tom Power AG/AS-3, Arthur Koontz (state Republican chair), Abe Lilly, Mayor Carl Andrews, and Carl Calvert (Kanawha County Court). (Courtesy of the West Virginia State Archives, General Charles Fox Collection.)

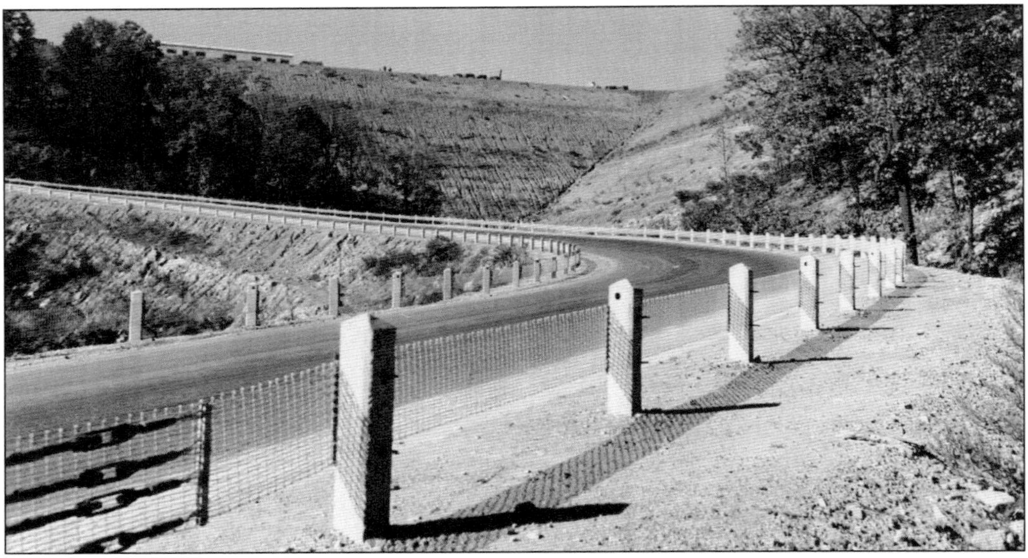

The road to Kanawha Airport is seen in the late 1940s. Built by the West Virginia State Road Commission, the road was initially 22 feet wide and 1.061 miles in length and required moving 300,000 cubic yards of rock and dirt. (Courtesy of the West Virginia State Archives, Judy Escue Collection.)

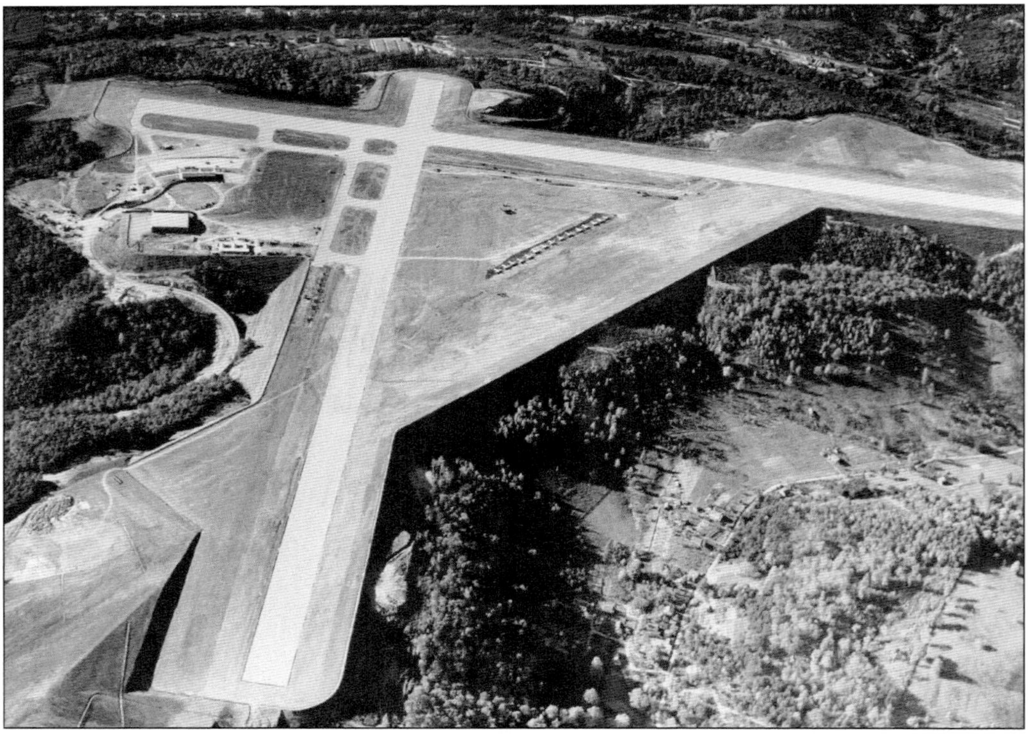

When Kanawha Airport opened in 1947, there was much room for expansion. Fighter aircraft from the West Virginia Air National Guard are lined up in the center of the photograph. The area on the bottom left will become the general aviation area in the 1970s. (Courtesy of the West Virginia State Archives, Judy Escue Collection.)

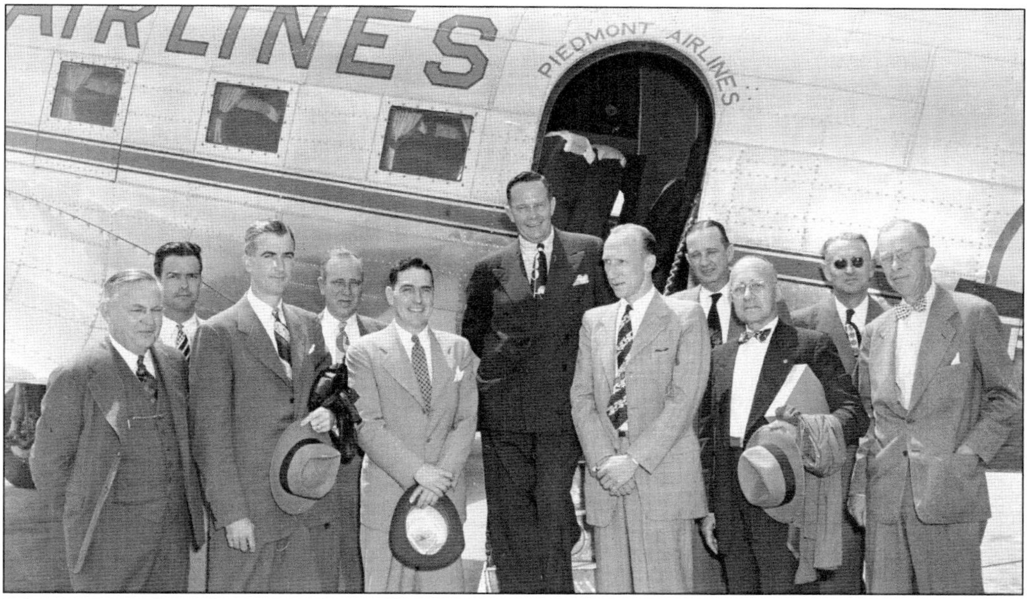

The inaugural Piedmont Airlines flight was on May 13, 1948, using a DC-3 aircraft and the route was Cincinnati, Ohio, to Charleston, West Virginia, to Norfolk, Virginia. Pictured are, from left to right, Wilbur R. Kellogg, R.S. Northington, Edward H. Ould, R.D. Hager, Richard T. Edwards, West Virginia governor Clarence Meadows, T.H. Davis, G. Lyle Kays, B.F. Mooman, Douglas K. Fuller, and Charles E. Hodges. (Courtesy of the West Virginia State Archives, Clarence Meadows Collection.)

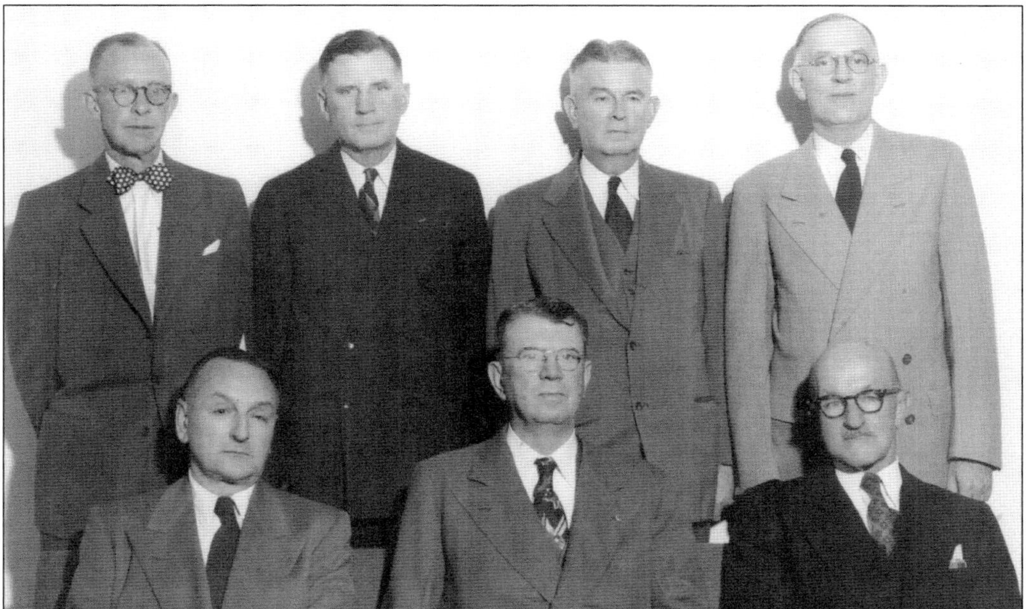

This photograph shows the airport advisory committee members who served from 1944 to 1949. Members of the committee are, from left to right, (first row) Robert G. Kelly, Jesse V. Sullivan, and Fitzhugh Ficklen; (second row) Charles E. Hodges, David M. Giltinan, Dean P. Reed, and Dan N. Mohler.

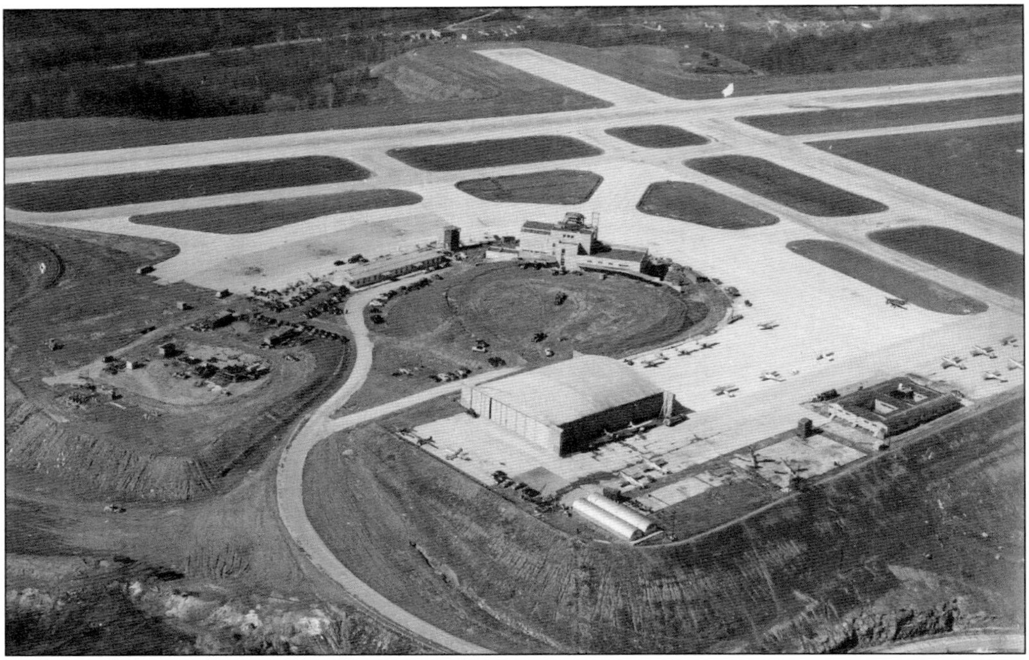

Construction of the new terminal building is progressing and grading is being conducted for the terminal approach and parking lot. Various aircraft occupy the ramp to the right of the terminal, including a mix of T-6 Texans, P-47 Thunderbolts, and P-51 Mustangs. (Courtesy of Charleston Newspapers.)

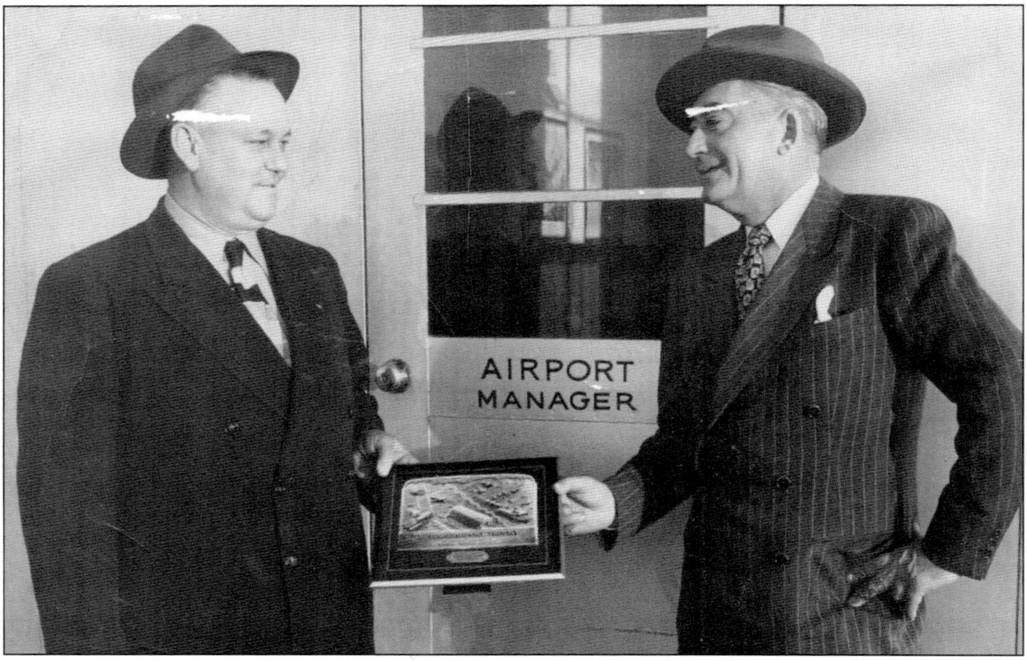

Carl Calvert (left), president of the Kanawha County Court, and Fred Alley, the first manager of Kanawha Airport, hold the Haire Airport Trophy outside of the airport manager's office in 1949. The airport was awarded the trophy as the most outstanding commercial airport for the year 1948. During the first full year of operation, the airport handled a total of 98,733 passengers.

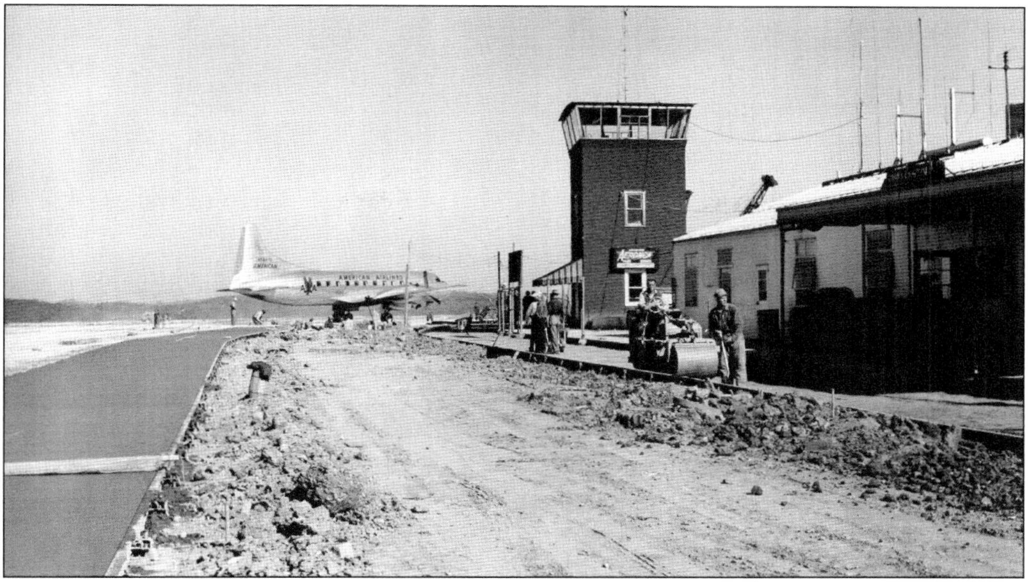

In this 1949 photograph, an American Airlines Convair 240 sits at Kanawha Airport as work continues on the ramp. The temporary administration building is on the right, next to the temporary air traffic control tower. (Courtesy of the West Virginia State Archives, Judy Escue Collection.)

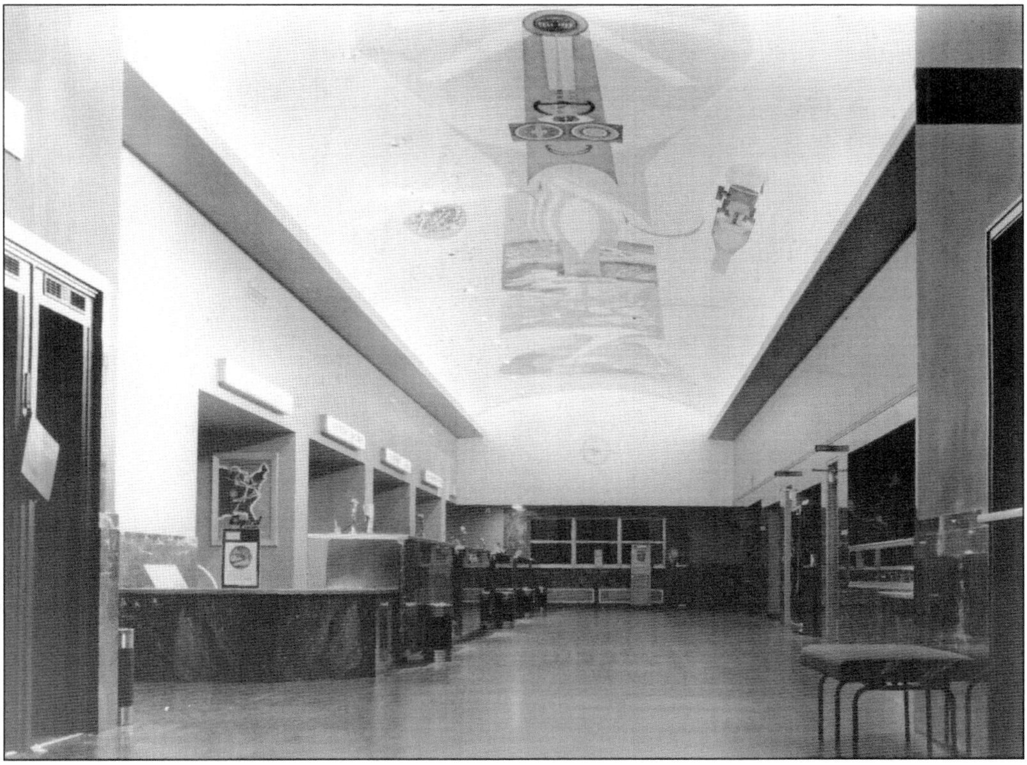

This is a 1950s view of the original ticket lobby including the ceiling mural. Painted by Robert Lepper, the mural featured sections symbolizing Charleston, air travel, aerodynamics, an aircraft wing with airflow around it, and other items representing aviation and travel. The ticket lobby has been expanded several times in the background area of the photograph.

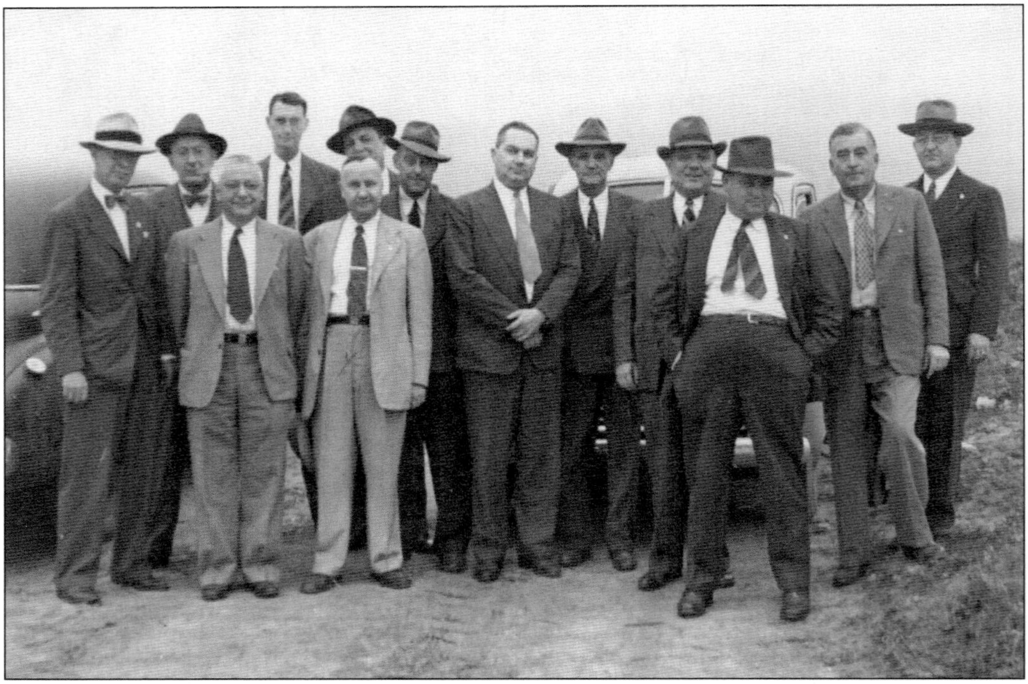

Pictured at Kanawha Airport are, from left to right, Charles Hodges, John Kay, unidentified, Virgil O'Dell, Henry Musser, unidentified, Ruffner Payne, Howard Klostermeyer, unidentified, Roger Creel, Carl Calvert, Fred Alley, and unidentified.

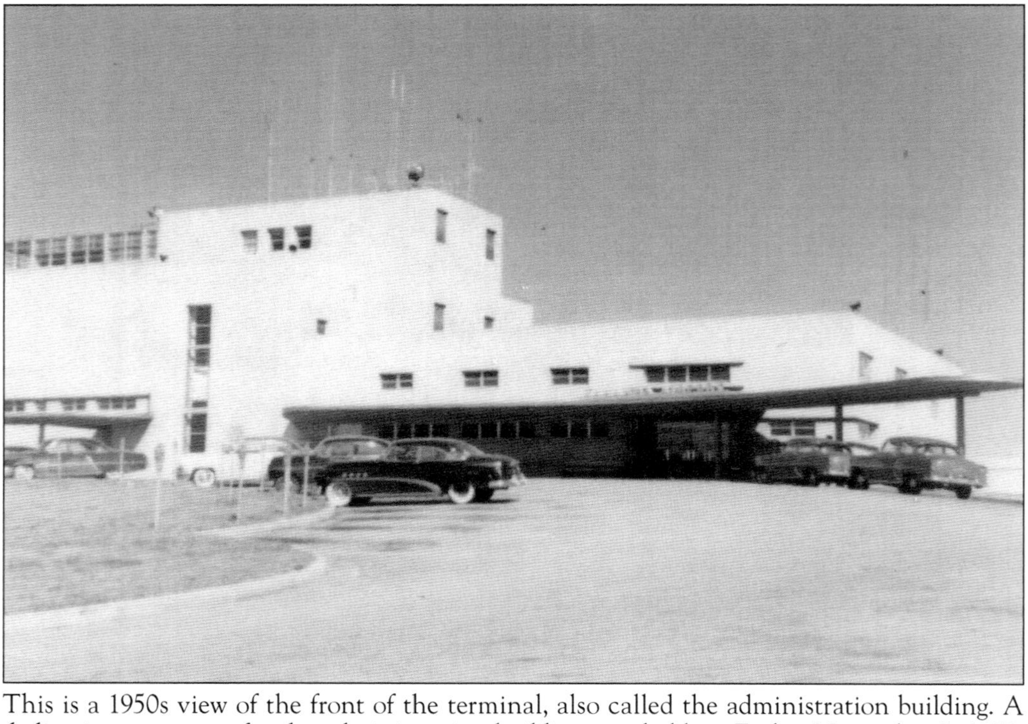

This is a 1950s view of the front of the terminal, also called the administration building. A dedication ceremony for the administration building was held on Friday, November 3, 1950, though the building opened for public use on September 1, 1950.

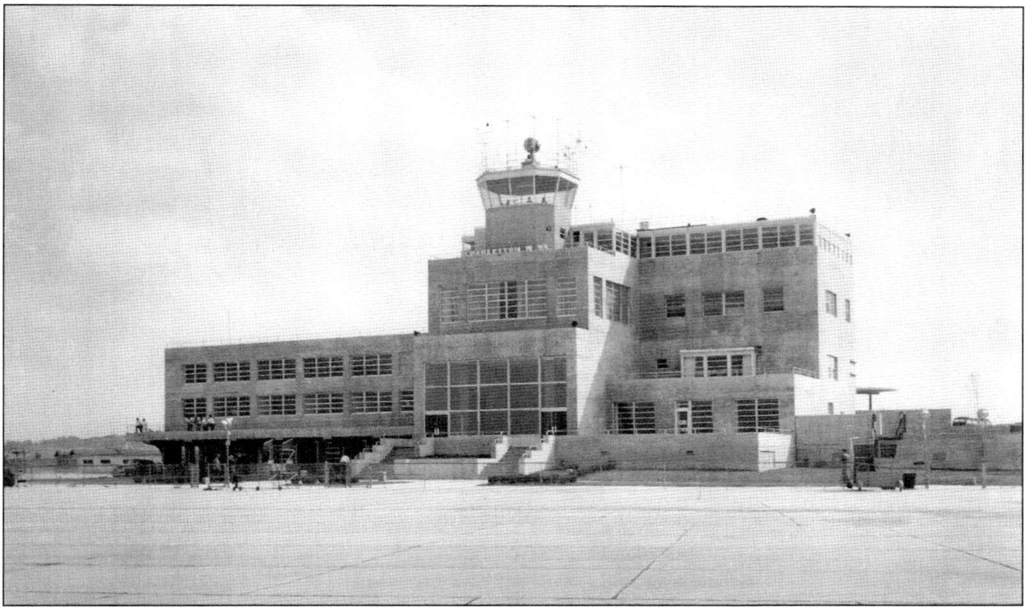

The newly completed terminal building is seen here from the ramp side. A weather station and Civil Aeronautics Administration offices occupied the top floor of the building, and airport offices were located on the mezzanine. The top of one of the ridges leveled for construction once stood in the location of the terminal at an elevation 50 feet higher than the control tower elevation.

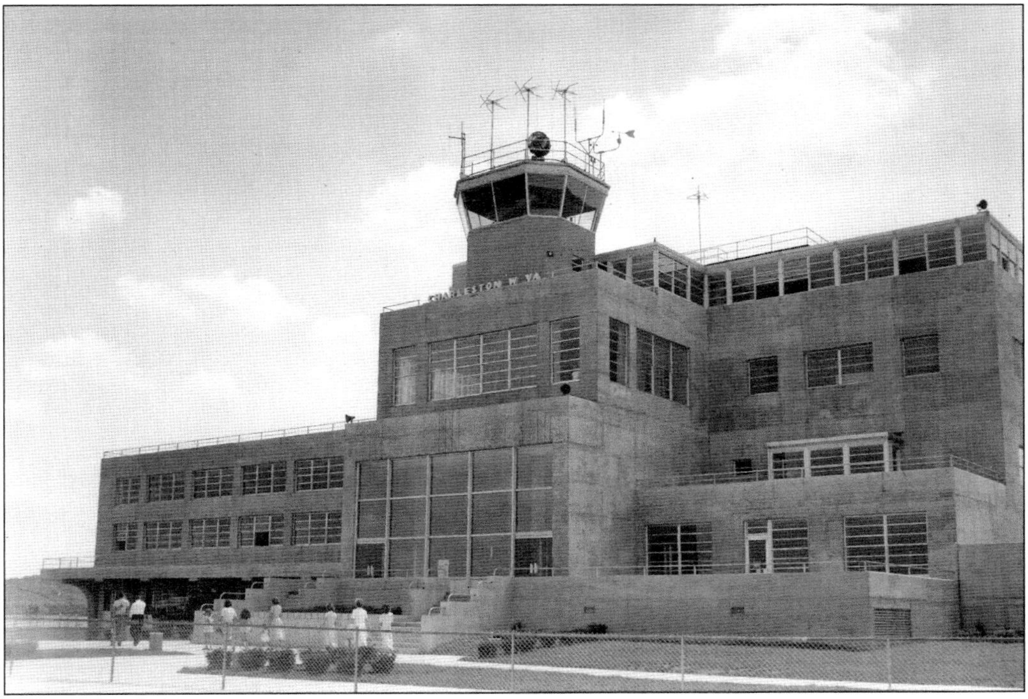

The airport dining facilities were operated by Sky Chefs and included a coffee shop on the ground floor, a club room for private parties on the mezzanine level with an outdoor terrace, and a sky room on the second floor for public dining with an outdoor terrace. A viewing deck extended around the north and east sides of the terminal for the public to view airplanes.

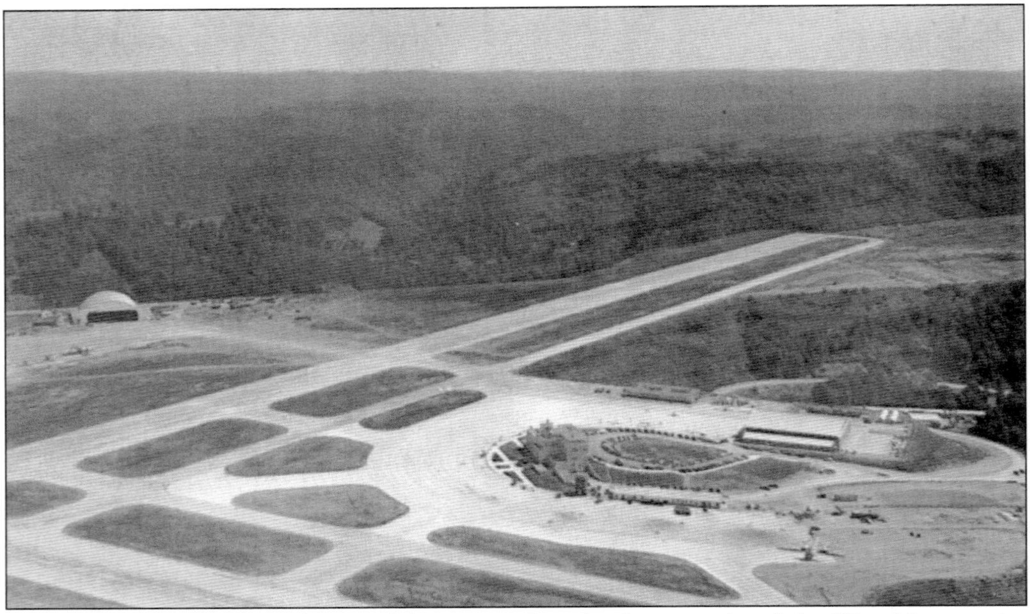

This is an early 1950s aerial view of the terminal in the foreground and the West Virginia Air National Guard on the left. The clear area in the upper right is now the general aviation area.

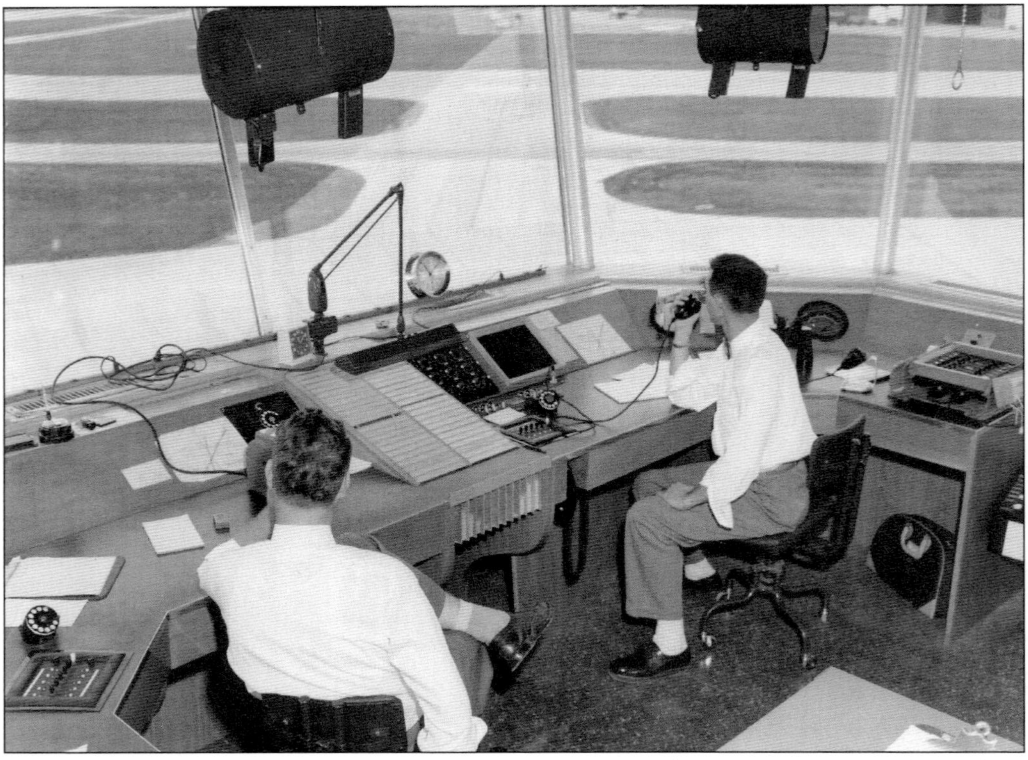

Two air traffic controllers sit in the Kanawha Airport control tower cab. The two large black objects hanging from the ceiling are known as light guns, used to control aircraft or ground vehicles with a radio failure. Air traffic controllers can use them to send different instructions based on light color and flashes. (Courtesy of Charleston Newspapers.)

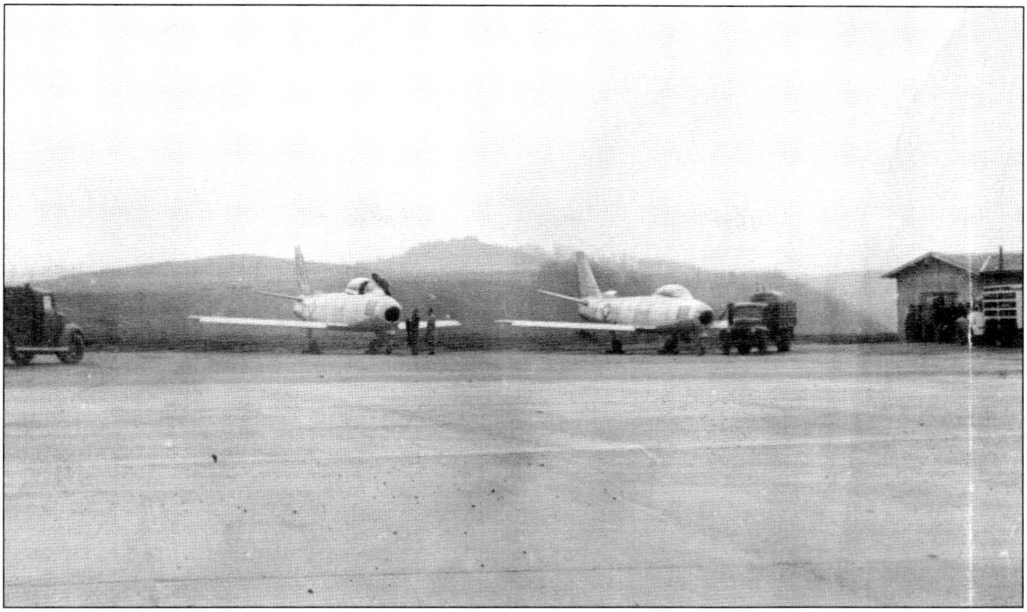

Two US Air Force F-86 Sabre fighter jets were forced to make an emergency landing at Kanawha Airport on March 21, 1950, due to low fuel. There being no jet fuel available in Charleston, a shipment of 800 gallons had to be trucked in from Dayton, Ohio. The two aircraft are seen here on March 22, 1950, as they prepare for takeoff. Only three minutes after takeoff, both aircraft would crash near Emmons, West Virginia, killing the pilots.

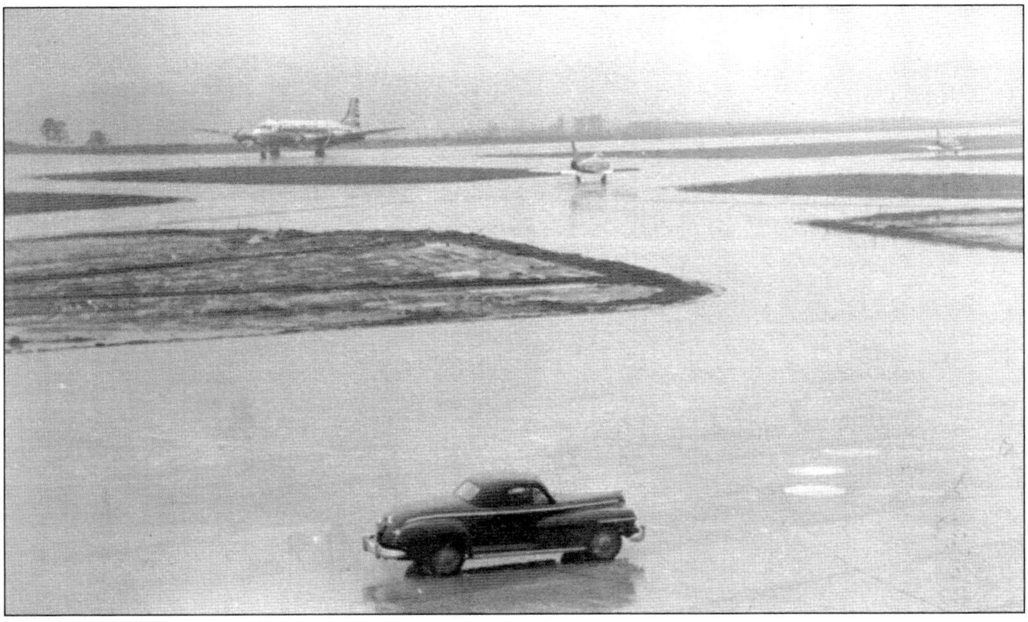

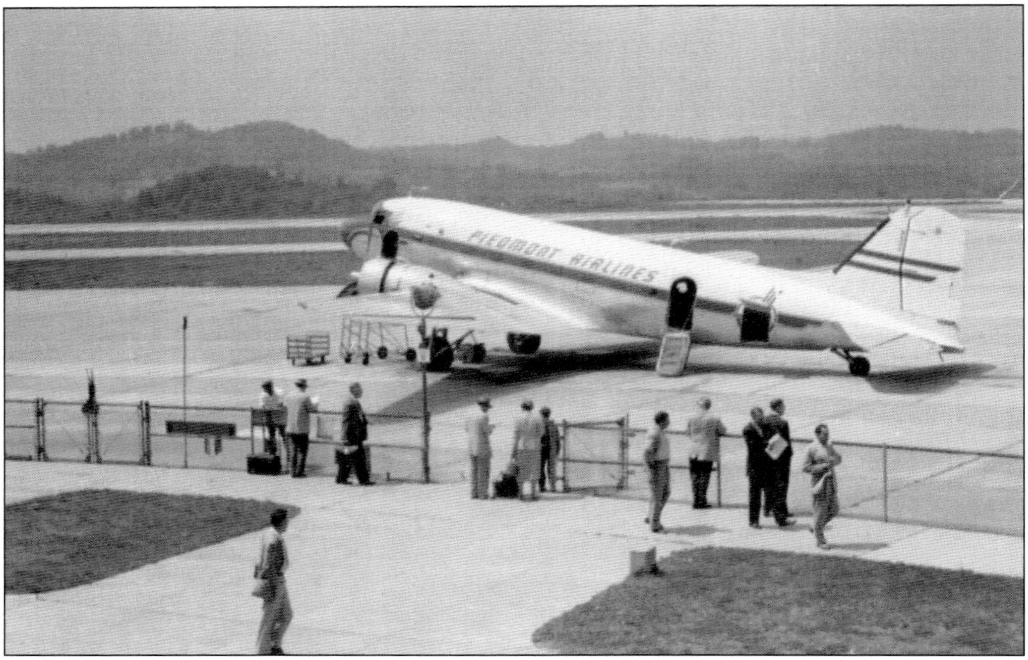

A Piedmont Airlines DC-3 (registration N53V), the *Hampton Roads Pacemaker*, is seen on the ramp at Kanawha Airport. The DC-3, a common visitor to Kanawha Airport into the 1960s, was operated by Piedmont Airlines from 1948 to 1963.

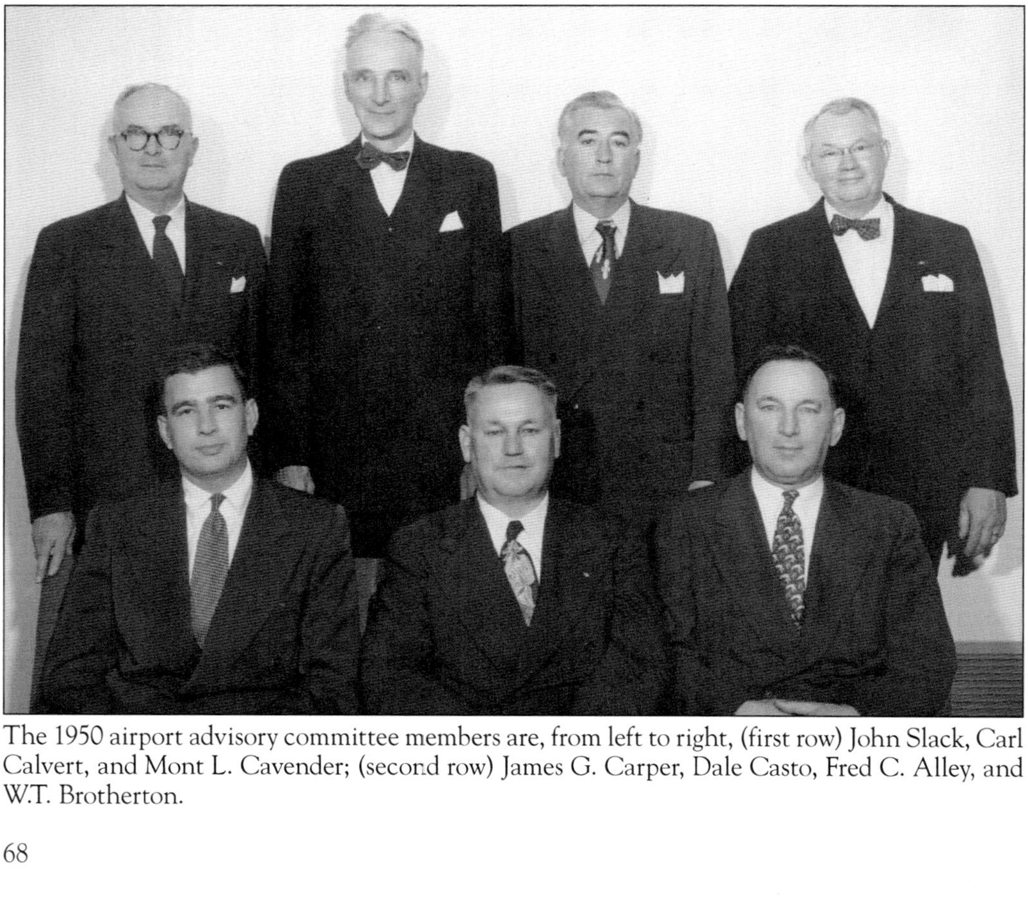

The 1950 airport advisory committee members are, from left to right, (first row) John Slack, Carl Calvert, and Mont L. Cavender; (second row) James G. Carper, Dale Casto, Fred C. Alley, and W.T. Brotherton.

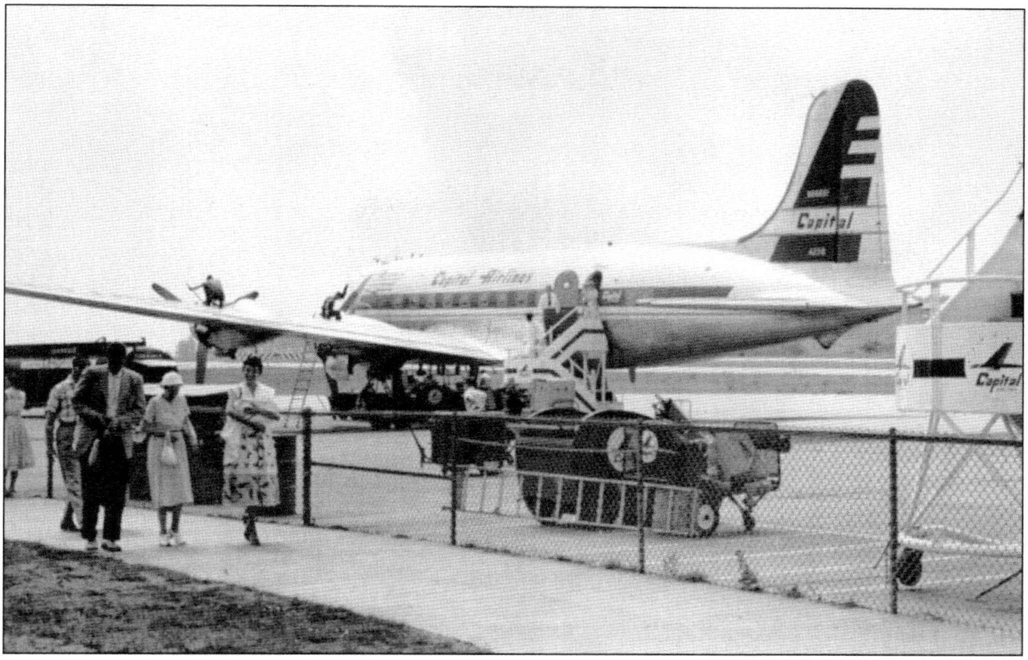

A Capital Airlines DC-4 sits on the ramp of Kanawha Airport. Capital Airlines served the following destinations from Charleston in 1955: Pittsburgh, Pennsylvania, with stops in Clarksburg, West Virginia, and Morgantown, West Virginia, or Wheeling, West Virginia; New York, New York; and Atlanta, Georgia, with some flights stopping at Tri-Cities Airport in Tennessee.

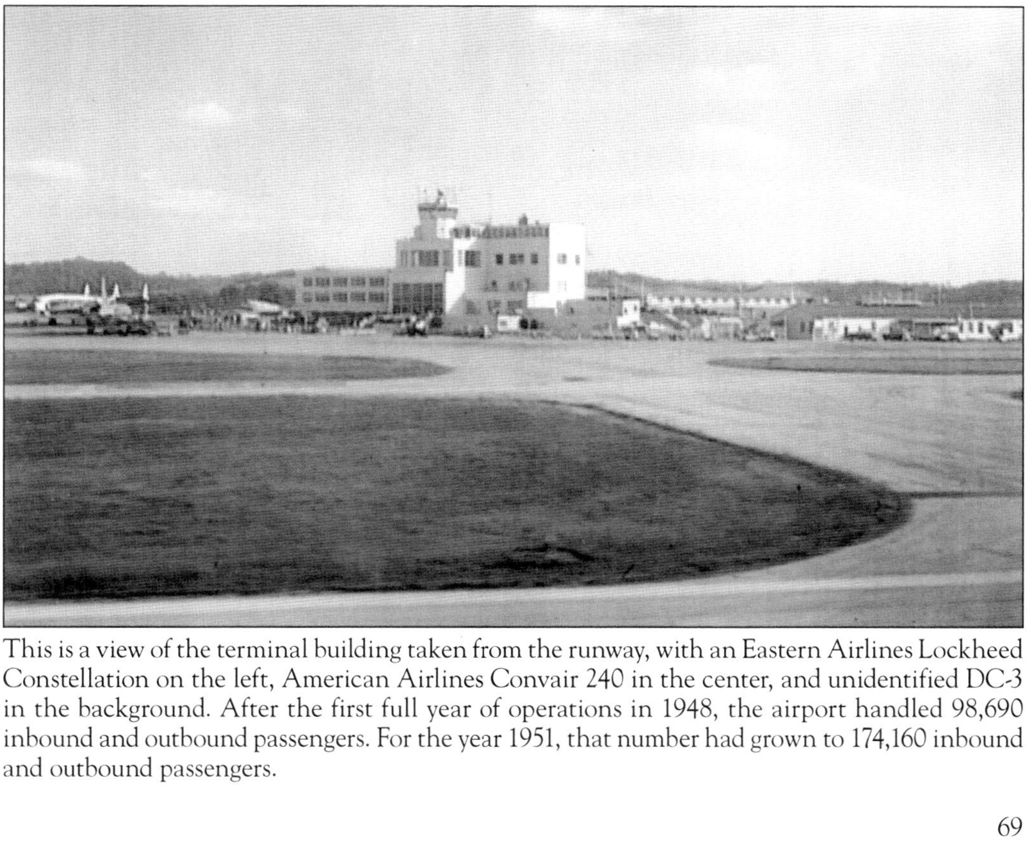

This is a view of the terminal building taken from the runway, with an Eastern Airlines Lockheed Constellation on the left, American Airlines Convair 240 in the center, and unidentified DC-3 in the background. After the first full year of operations in 1948, the airport handled 98,690 inbound and outbound passengers. For the year 1951, that number had grown to 174,160 inbound and outbound passengers.

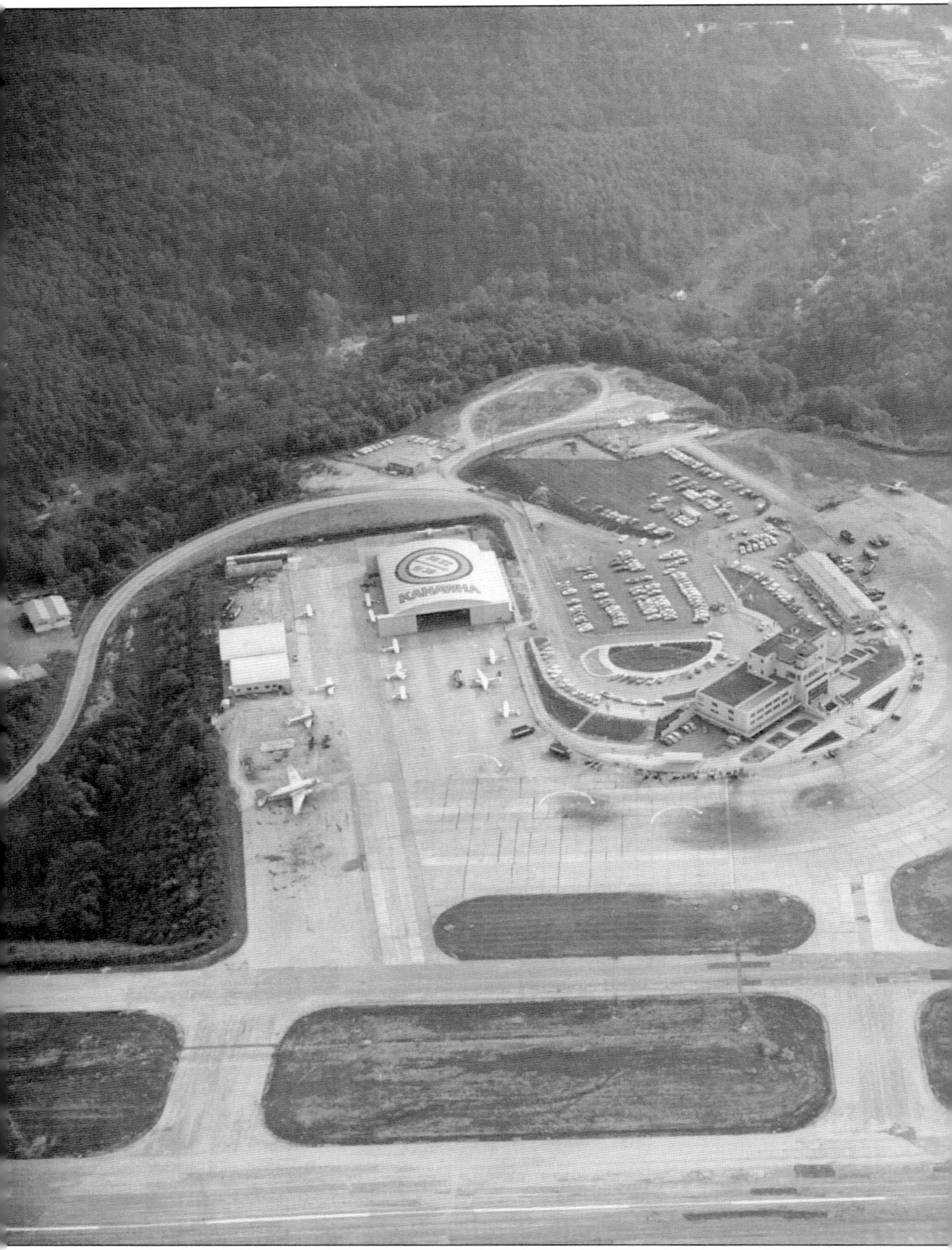
KANAWHA

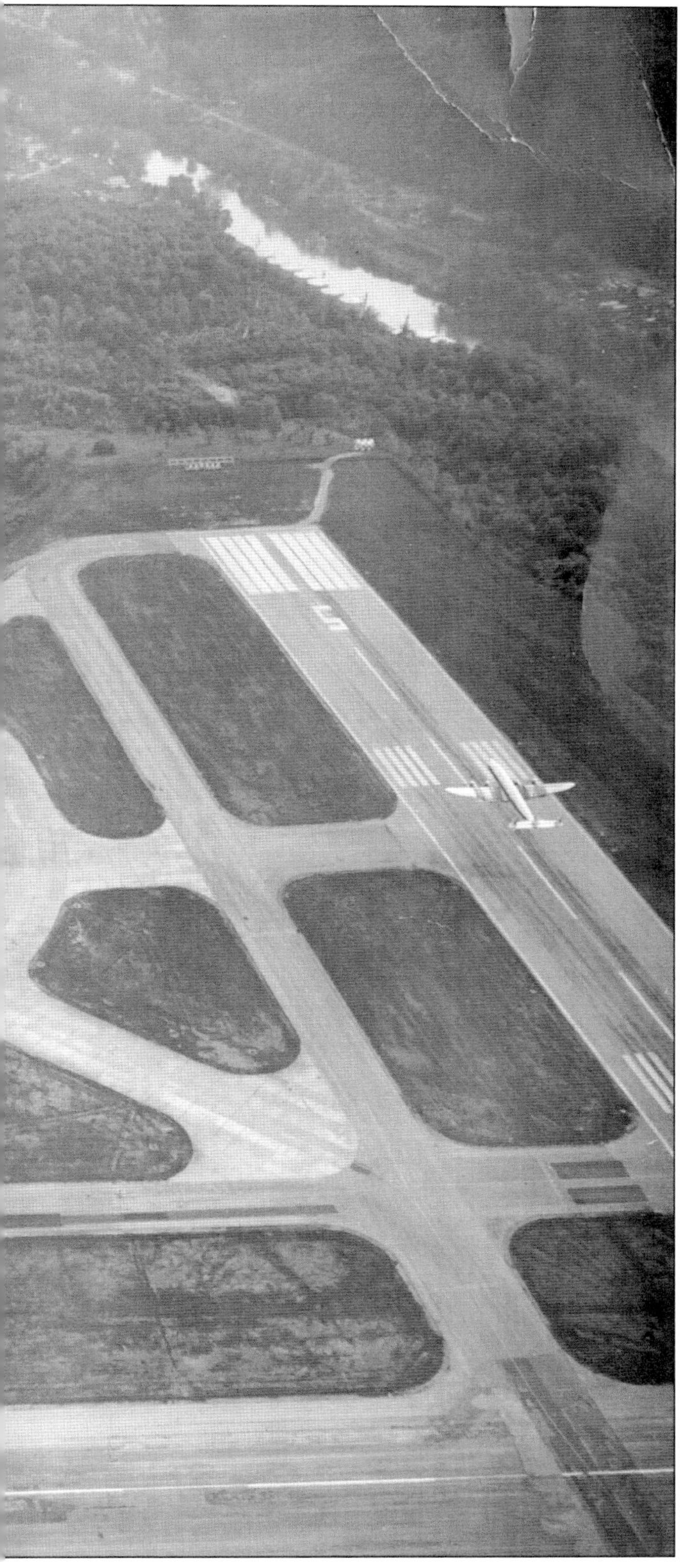

An Eastern Airlines Lockheed L-1049 Super Constellation takes off from Runway 23 as a Capital Airlines DC-3 sits on the commercial ramp in front of the terminal. The Super Constellation had four propeller engines with a cruising speed of 340 miles per hour and more-than-5,000-mile range. In 1960, Eastern Airlines provided nonstop service from Charleston to Roanoke, Virginia, and Akron/Canton, Ohio. The general aviation area is seen to the left of the terminal, where long-term parking garages are presently located.

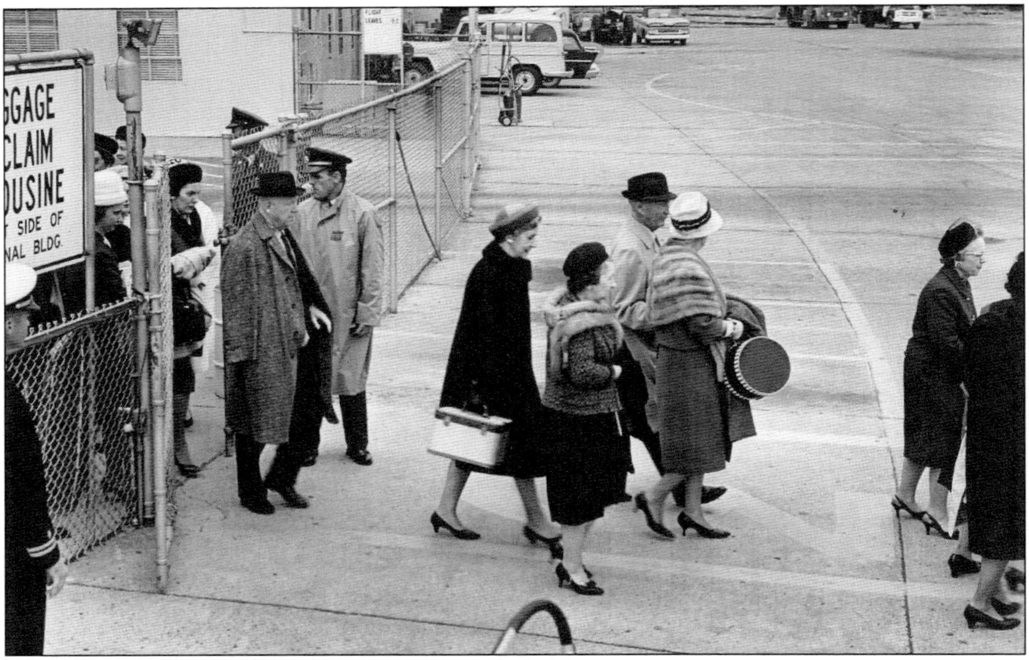

Passengers board a United Airlines plane using the aircraft stairs in the 1960s. Before airport security become a concern, the public and passengers were allowed outside next to the ramp up to a low chain-link fence. All passengers were forced to go outside to board aircraft. Today, jet bridges are commonly used for many aircraft. (Courtesy of Charleston Newspapers.)

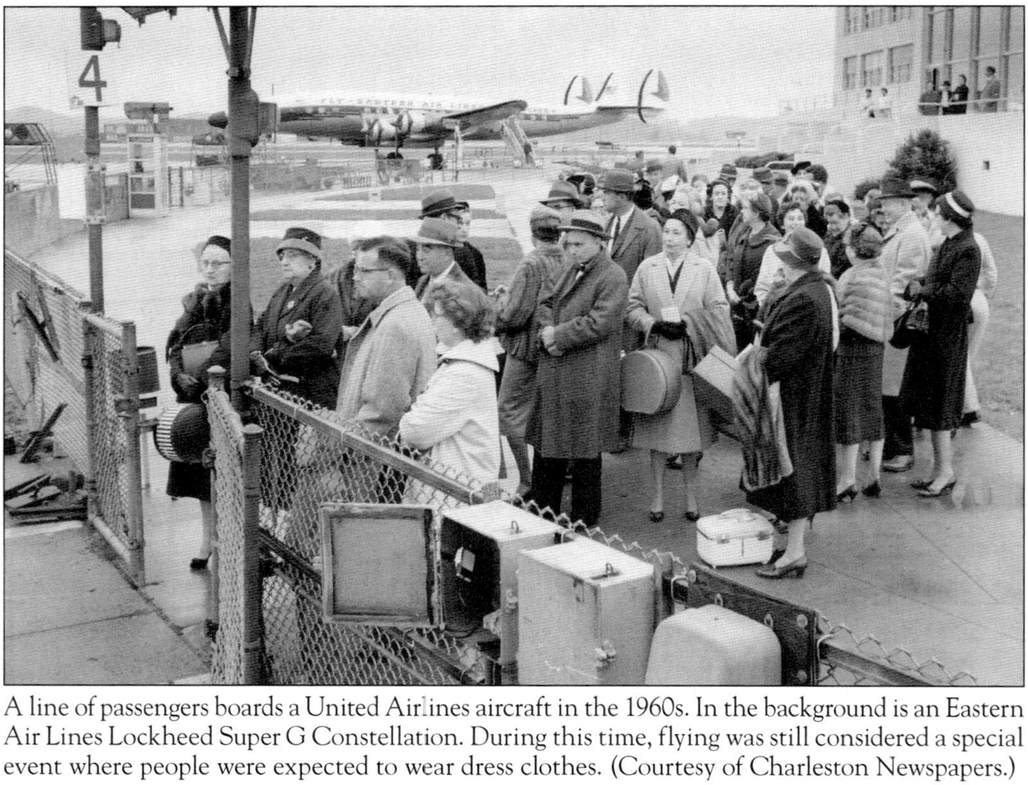

A line of passengers boards a United Airlines aircraft in the 1960s. In the background is an Eastern Air Lines Lockheed Super G Constellation. During this time, flying was still considered a special event where people were expected to wear dress clothes. (Courtesy of Charleston Newspapers.)

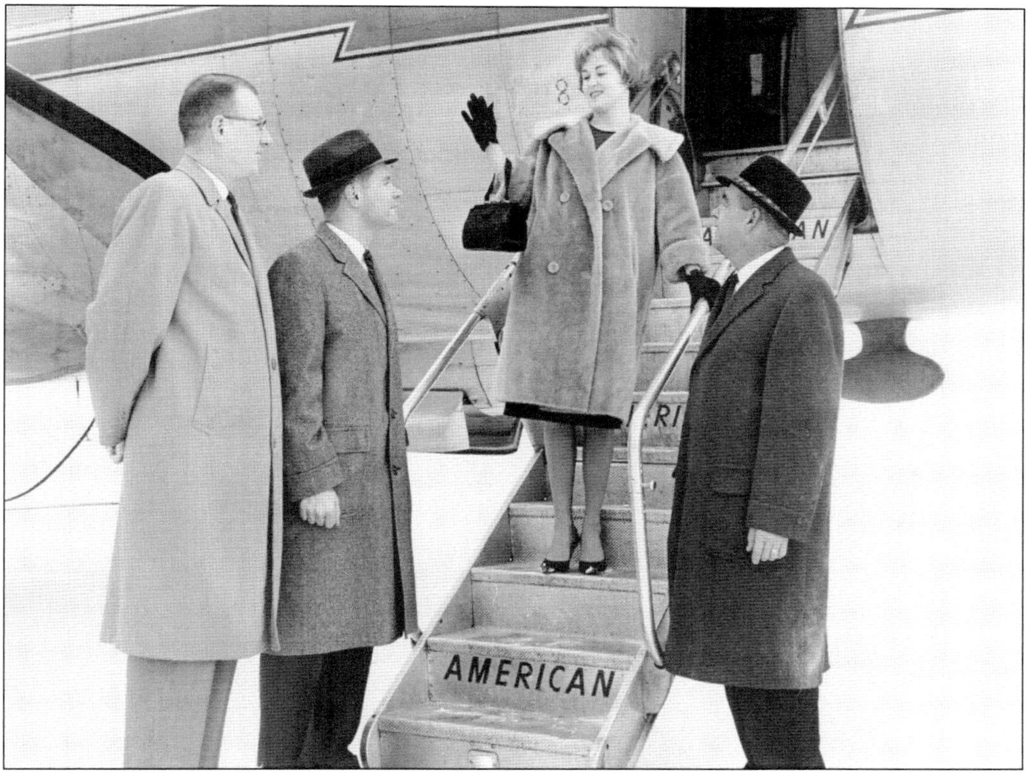

From left to right are Robert M. Burrows, American Airlines Charleston manager; Thomas W. Lewis, district sales manager; Patti Harrison, Charleston's representative 100 millionth passenger on American Airlines; and Calvin Wilson, Kanawha Airport manager. They pose as Harrison boards flight 578 on December 28, 1961. (Courtesy of the West Virginia State Archives, Emil Varney Collection.)

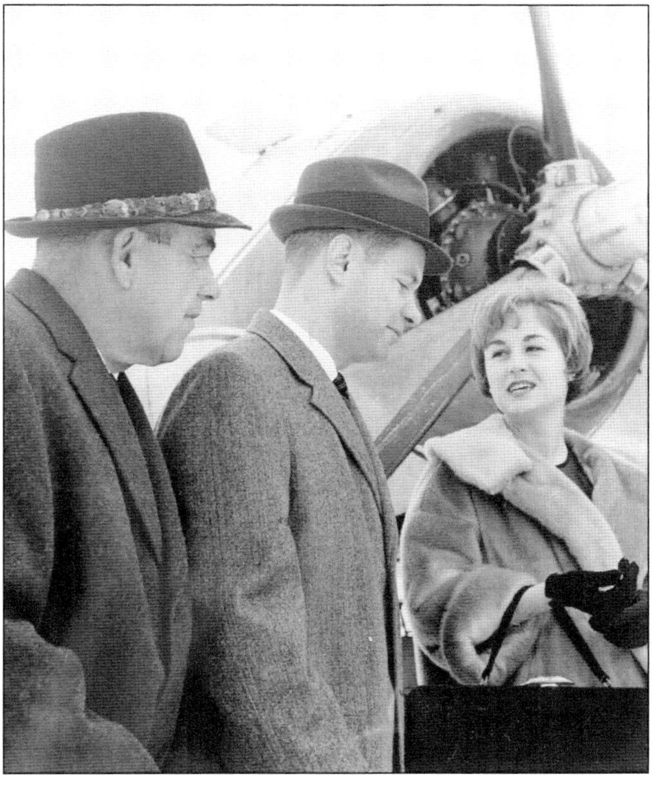

Seen from left to right are Calvin Wilson, Kanawha Airport manager; Thomas W. Lewis, American Airlines district sales manager, and Patti Harrison, passenger. Before taking flight 578 to Washington DC, on December 28, 1961, Harrison was presented with a gold key ring. (Courtesy of the West Virginia State Archives, Emil Varney Collection.)

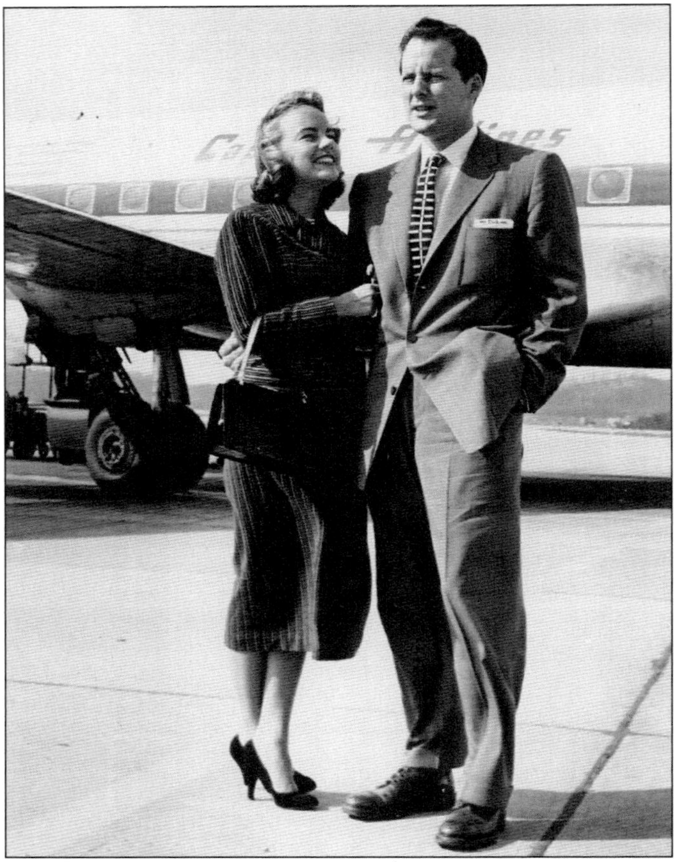

Actress Terry Moore and her husband are seen at Kanawha Airport in this undated photograph. (Courtesy of the West Virginia State Archives, Frank Wilkin Collection.)

This is a view of the front of the terminal building in the 1960s. Since this photograph was taken, the terminal and parking areas have been expanded several times. The area directly in front of the terminal once had parking meters and is now a free 20-minute parking lot.

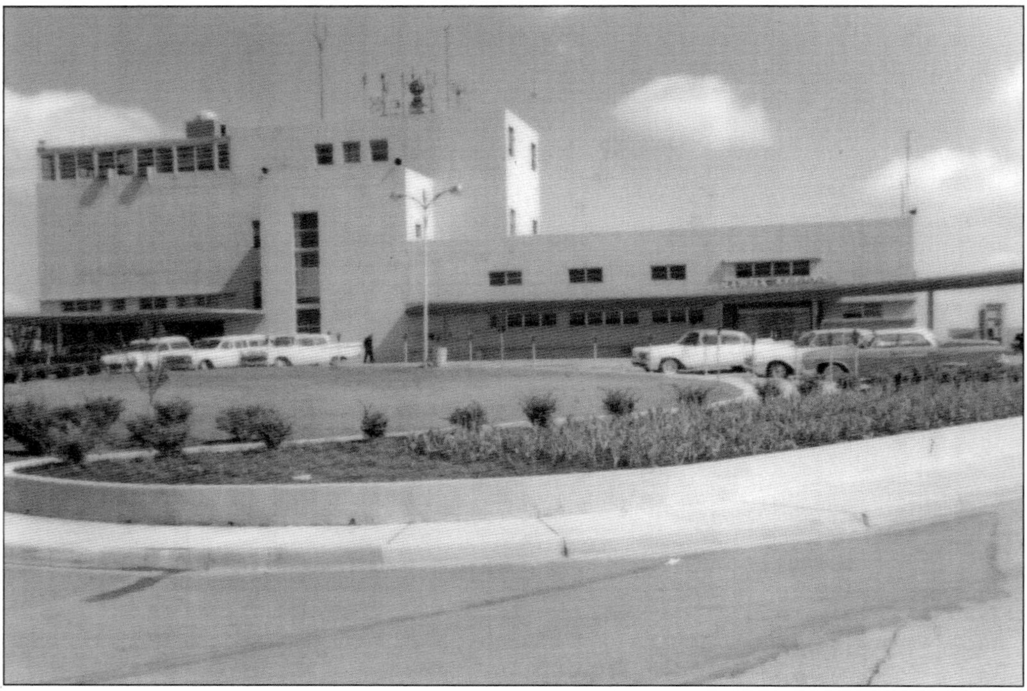

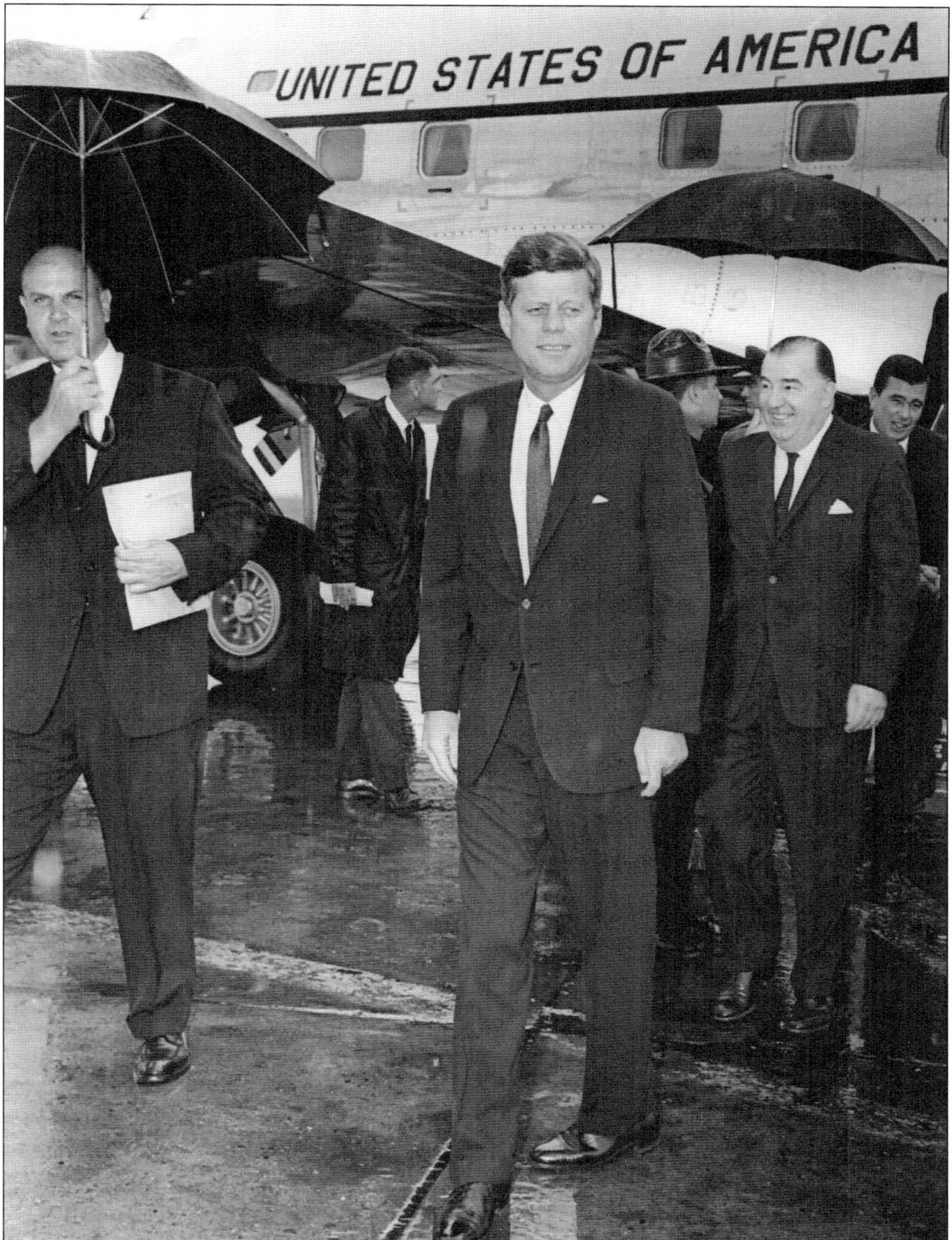

Pres. John F. Kennedy arrives at Kanawha Airport on June 20, 1963. President Kennedy spoke to a crowd at the state capitol commemorating the centennial of the State of West Virginia. Sen. Jennings Randolph is seen smiling on the right. (Courtesy of Charleston Newspapers.)

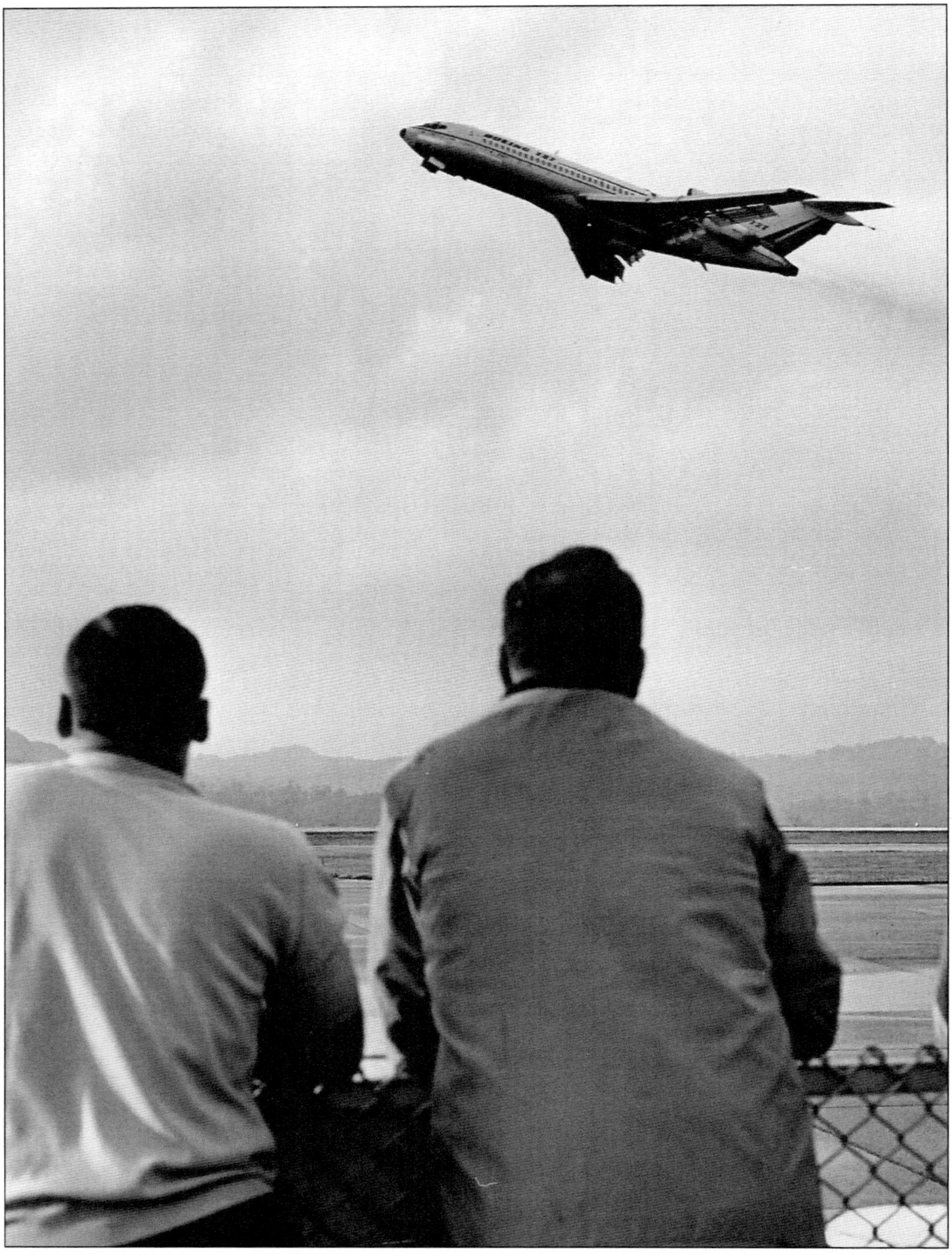

Two men watch a Boeing 727 takeoff on October 7, 1965. The aircraft was flown into Kanawha Airport for evaluation tests by Piedmont Airlines and used 3,800 feet of runway with a light load.

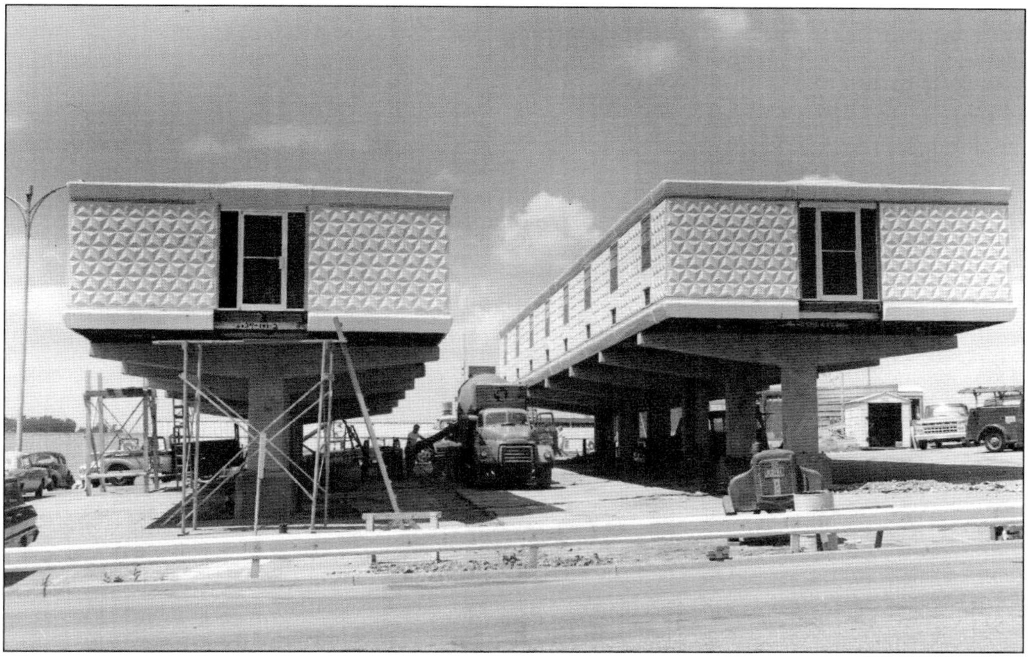

The Airport Motel is under construction in this 1965 photograph. According to the *Charleston Gazette*, the $100,000 Holiday Inn had 32 rooms, fiberglass-covered outer walls, and building sections of eight rooms that were each trucked to Charleston with their beds, bathrooms, and television sets in place. The unique design allowed for vehicle parking under the motel. In 1969, Airporters Inc. of Cleveland, Ohio, offered the motel to the airport authority, which agreed to the takeover. In 1974, double rooms at the motel were advertised for $12 nightly, $54 weekly, and $169 monthly. (Courtesy of Charleston Newspapers.)

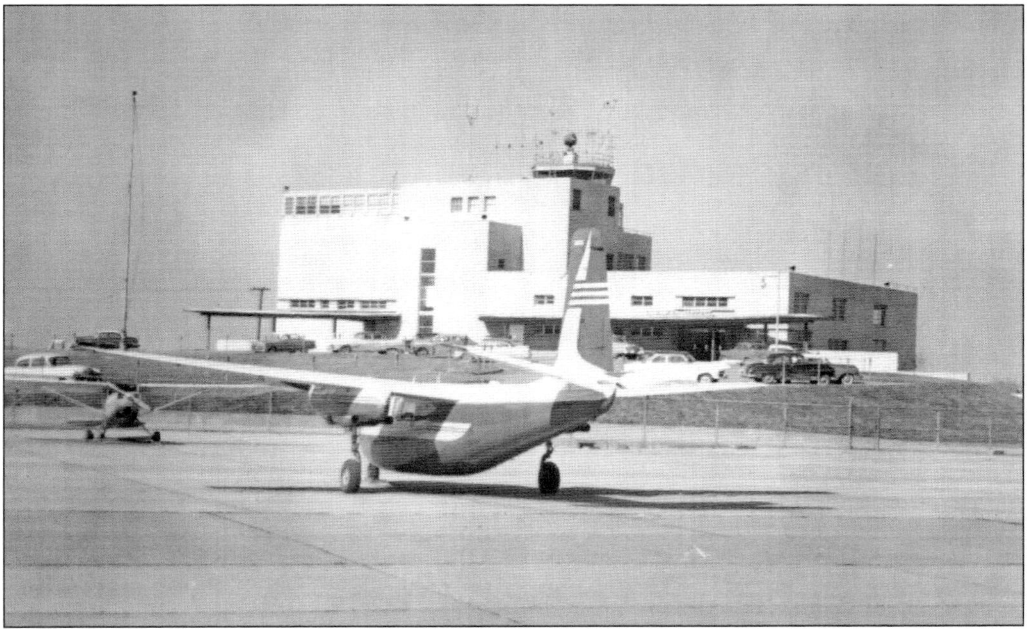

Aircraft sit in the original general aviation area next to the terminal. This area is now occupied by the long-term parking garages.

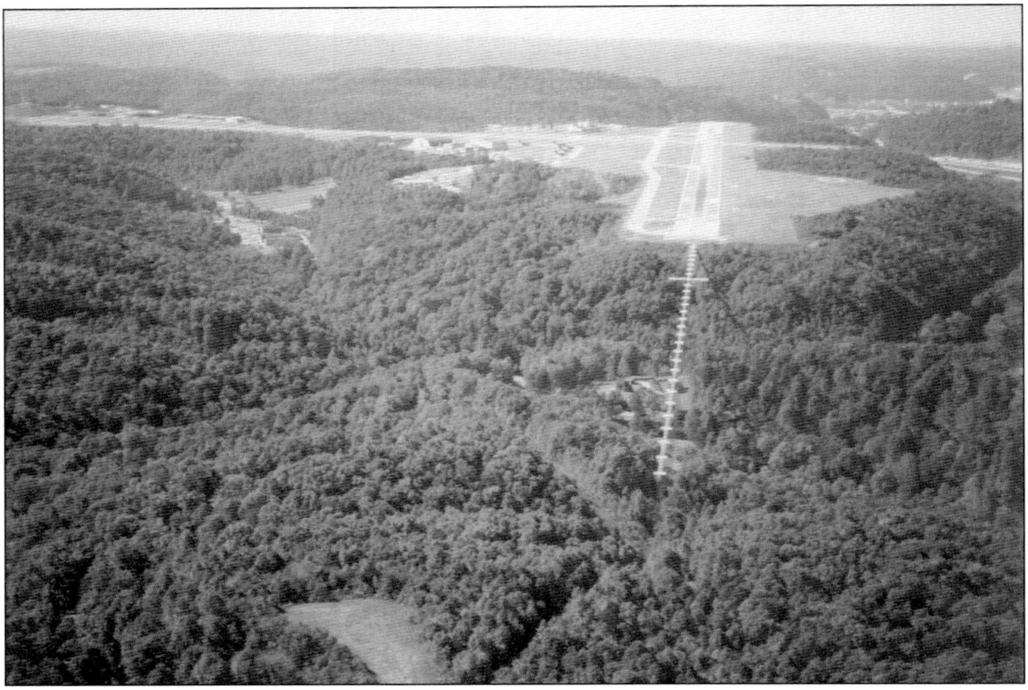

While approaching Runway 23 for landing, pilots would see the approach lighting system constructed in August 1961 to enhance visibility during night and poor weather. To the left of the runway is Taxiway A; notice the dogleg causing pilots to turn as they taxi to the end of the runway.

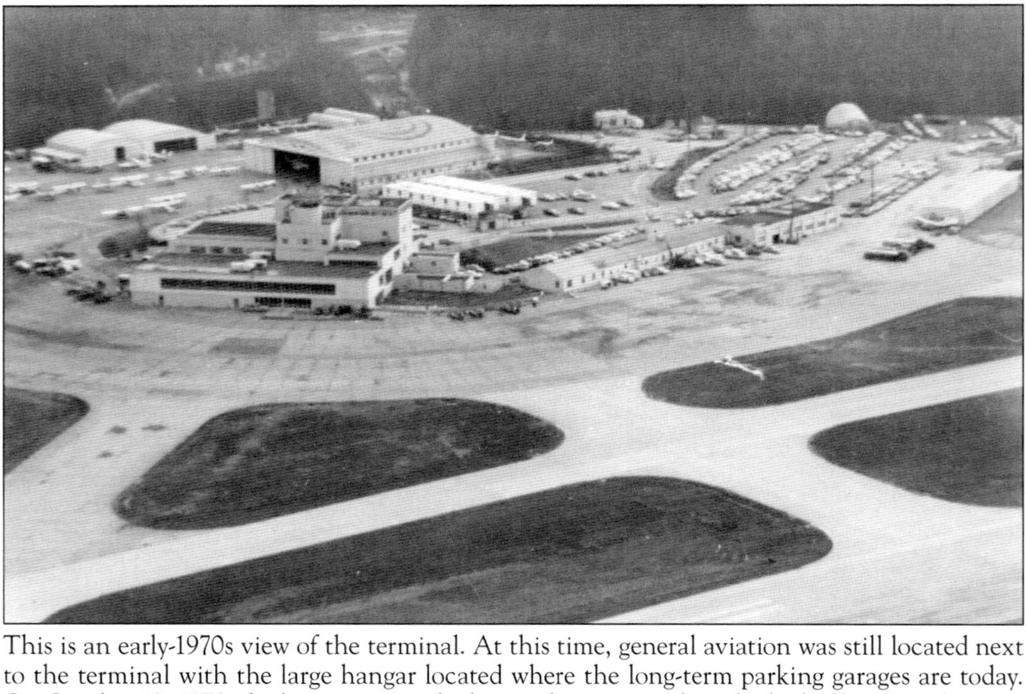

This is an early-1970s view of the terminal. At this time, general aviation was still located next to the terminal with the large hangar located where the long-term parking garages are today. On October 18, 1973, the hangar was jacked up and transported on the bed of large trucks to its present-day location at general aviation. The two long white buildings are a motel that briefly operated where short-term parking now resides.

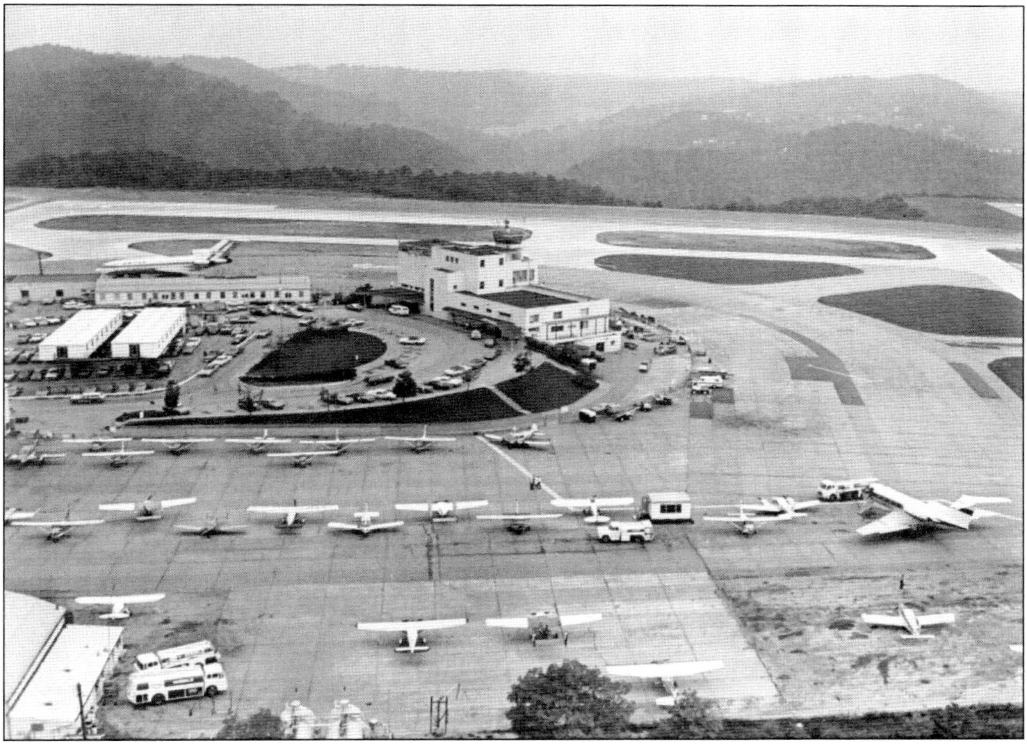

Taken sometime between 1969 and 1973, this view shows a busy general aviation ramp with a United Airlines Boeing 727 next to the terminal. Note how few parking spots existed between the motel and terminal building. (Courtesy of Charleston Newspapers.)

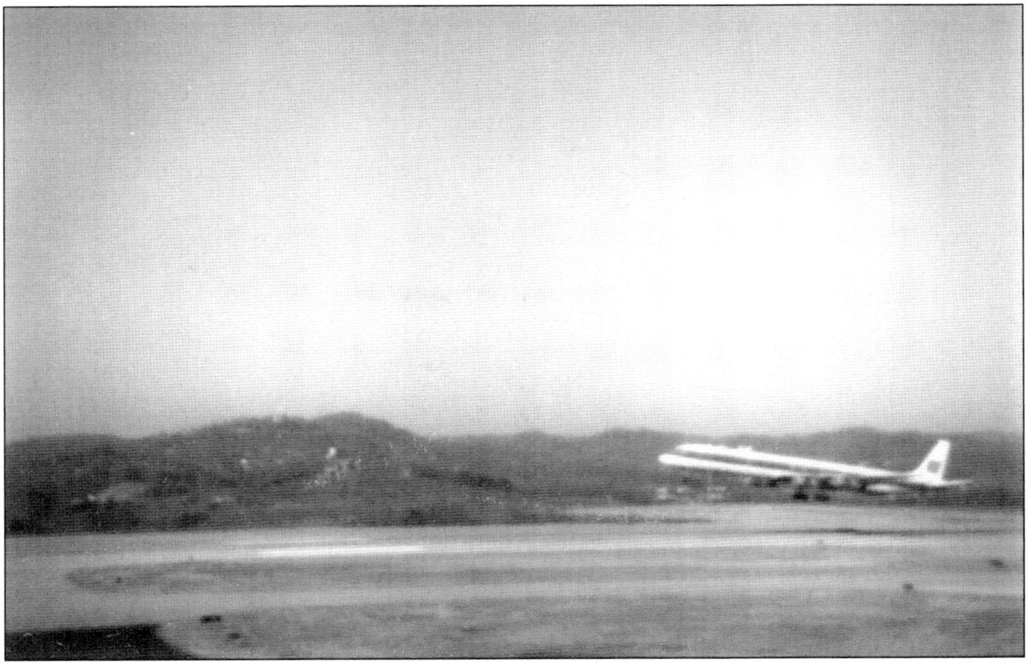

A United Airlines Douglas DC-8 takes off from Runway 23. This aircraft was probably a charter flight and is one of the largest commercial aircraft to ever use Kanawha Airport.

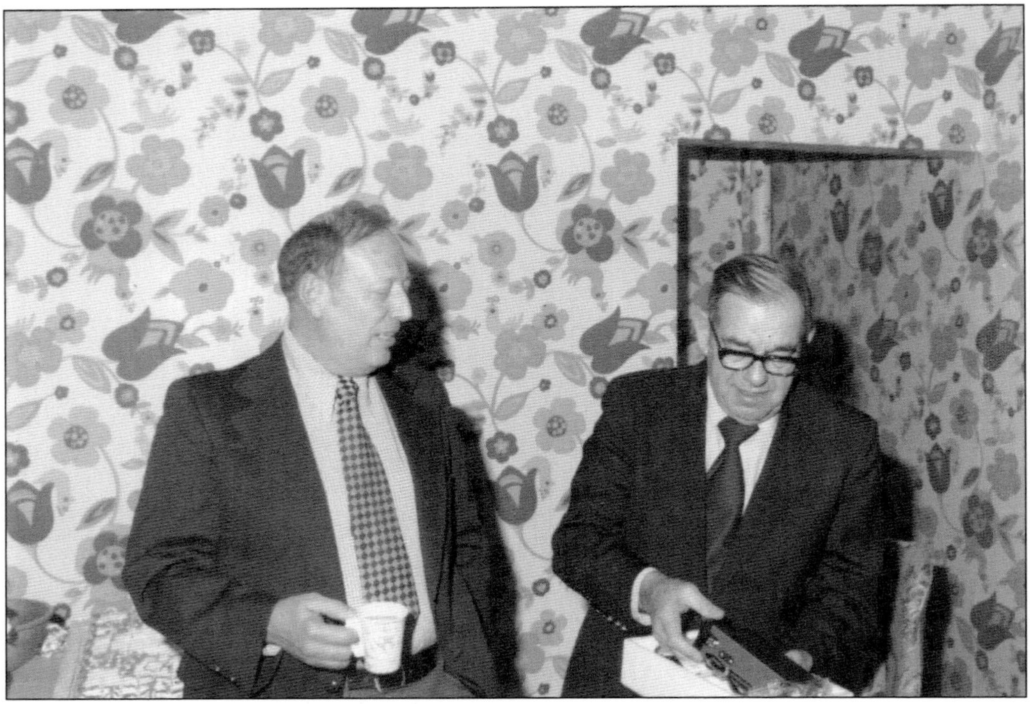

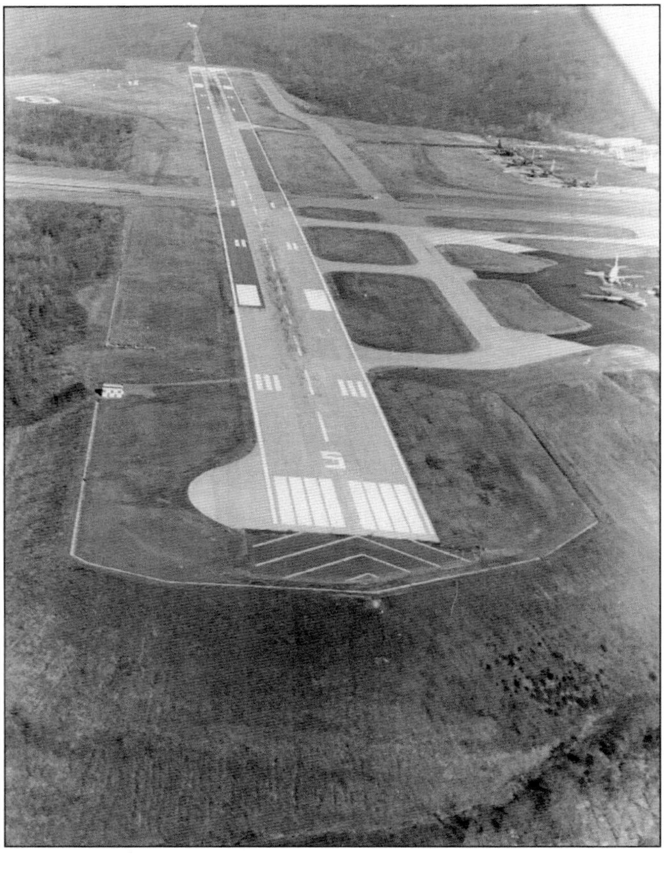

Ralph Cowgill (left) watches as Calvin Wilson removes a gift from a box during a Christmas party at the airport. Wilson served as manager of the airport from 1959 to 1976. Cowgill served as manager of the airport from 1976 to 1981.

This is a view of the approach end of Runway 5. Runways are numbered between 1 and 36 based on magnetic compass bearing with the last number of the bearing removed. Therefore, Runway 5 means it is on a bearing of 50 degrees. Facing the opposite direction, Runway 23 is on a bearing of 230 degrees.

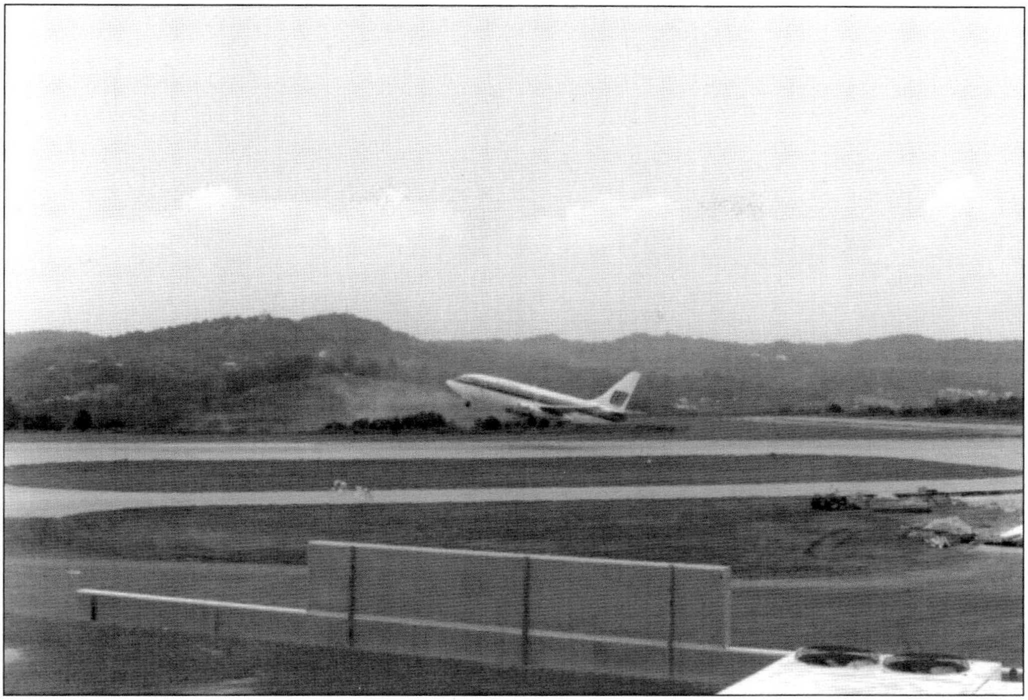

A United Airlines Boeing 737 takes off from Runway 23. In November 1968, United began operating the first scheduled jet service to Charleston using the Boeing 737.

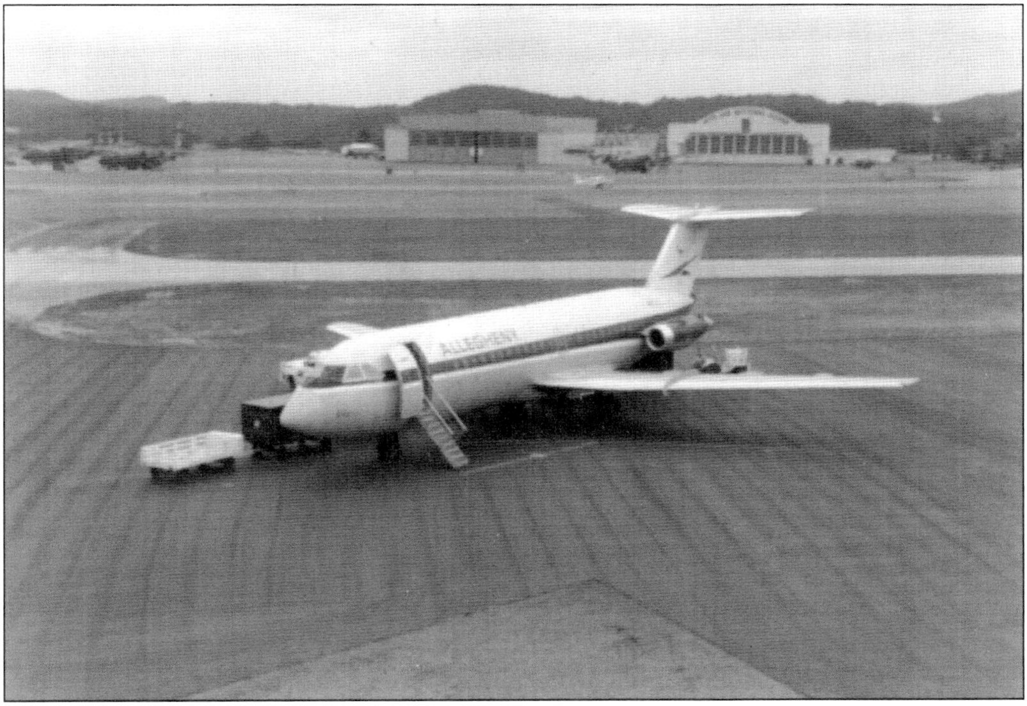

An Allegheny Airlines British Aerospace Corporation One Eleven (BAC-111) sits on the commercial ramp. The BAC-111 was operated by Allegheny from 1972 until its name change to USAir in 1979.

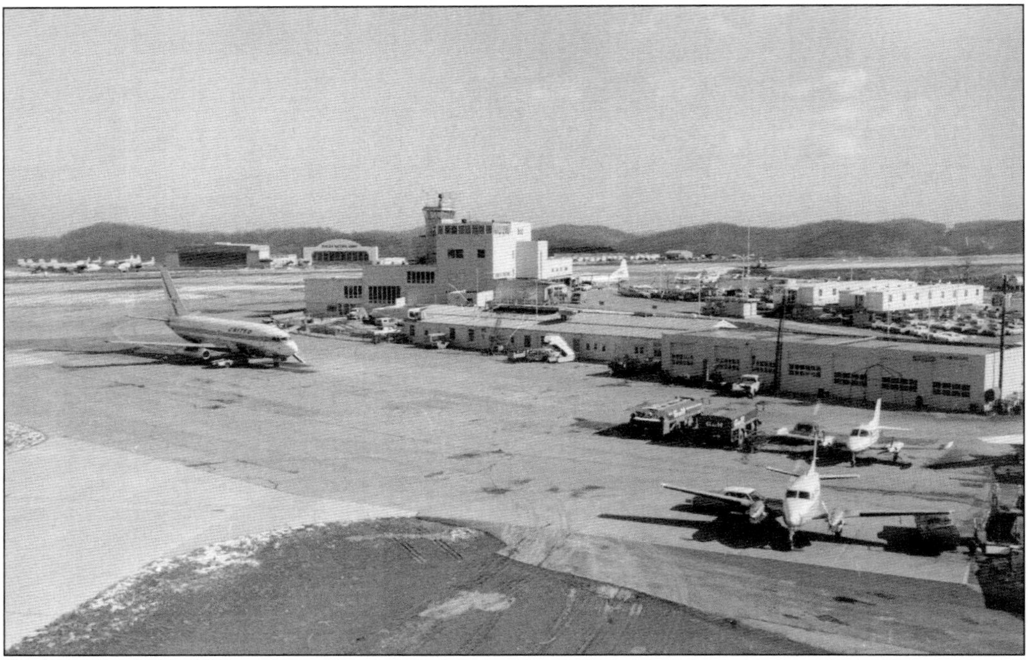

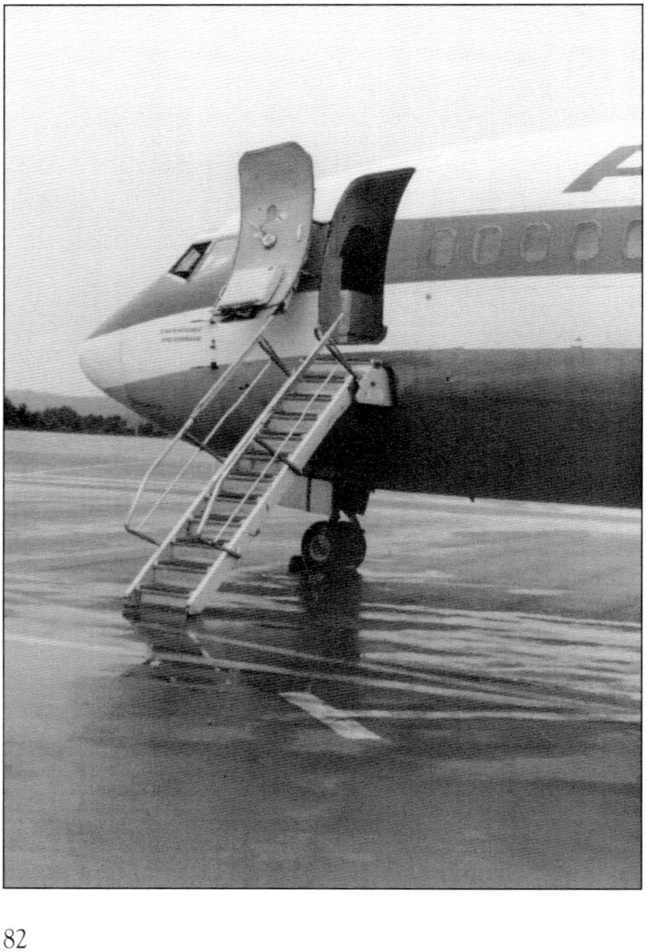

The view in this c. 1970 image looks at the terminal from Runway 5, with a United 737 parked next to the expanded terminal building. Two twin-engine propeller aircraft sit on the right in front of the airport maintenance building. The building in between maintenance and the terminal served as the temporary terminal building between 1947 and 1950. (Courtesy of Charleston Newspapers.)

Before jet bridges became standard, many aircraft used their own stairs, like this Piedmont Airlines Boeing 737-200, the *Chesapeake Pacemaker*. Piedmont Airlines operated the 737-200, with a total of 118 seats in an all-coach configuration.

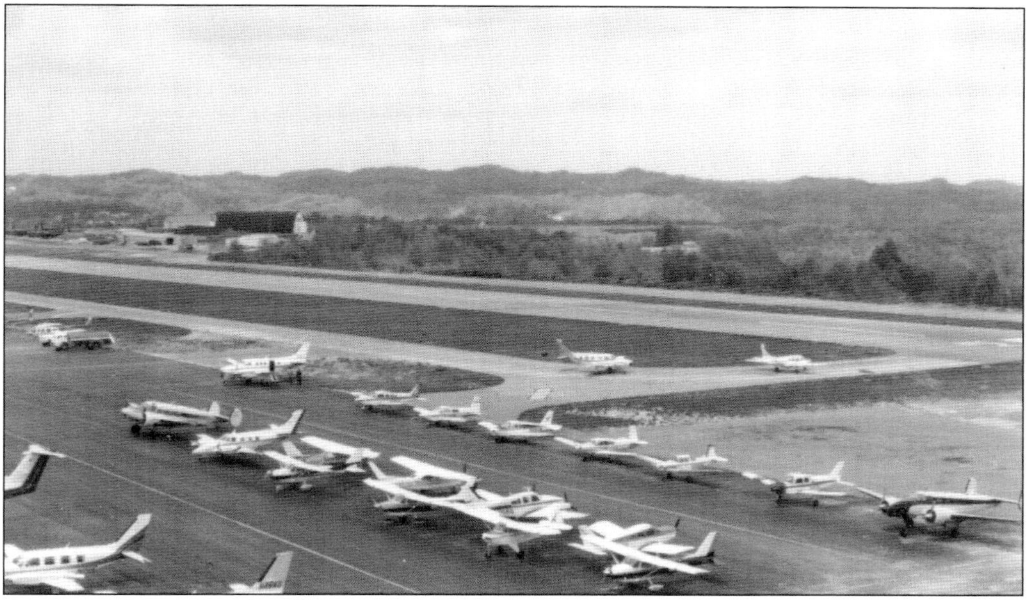

Two aircraft taxi to takeoff on Runway 33. Known as the crosswind runway, 15/33 was 4,750 feet long and 150 feet wide. It was primarily used for general aviation traffic and was originally designated Runway 14/32.

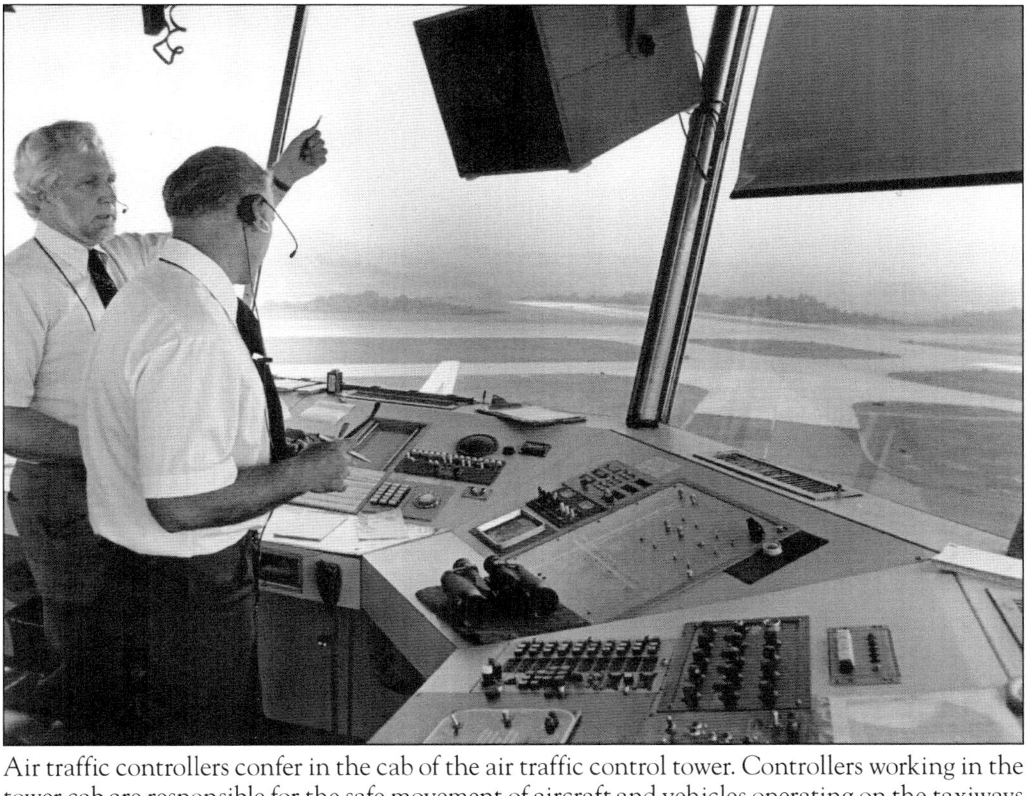

Air traffic controllers confer in the cab of the air traffic control tower. Controllers working in the tower cab are responsible for the safe movement of aircraft and vehicles operating on the taxiways and runway of the airport and for aircraft flying near the airport. The tail of a Piedmont Airlines Boeing 737 is barely visible. (Courtesy of Charleston Newspapers.)

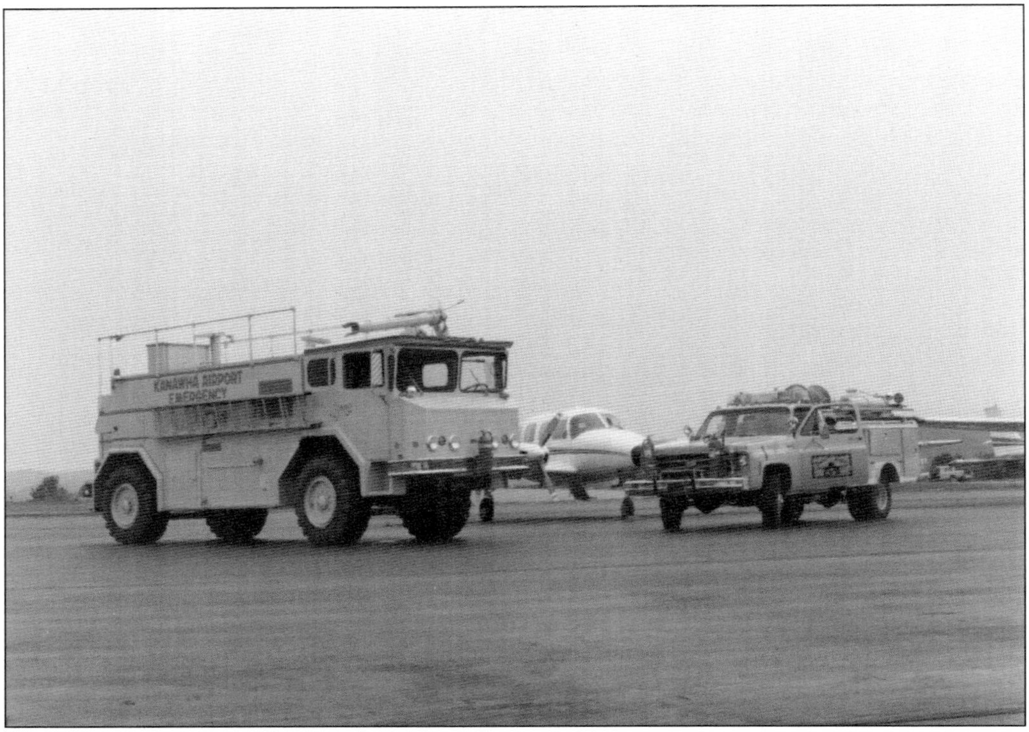

Two fire trucks from the Kanawha Airport Fire Department are on display. For years, the Central West Virginia Regional Airport Authority and the West Virginia Air National Guard each operated separate fire departments. Today, the West Virginia Air National Guard operates the only fire department and provides primary fire service for all airport users in exchange for a $1-per-year lease of land for its base.

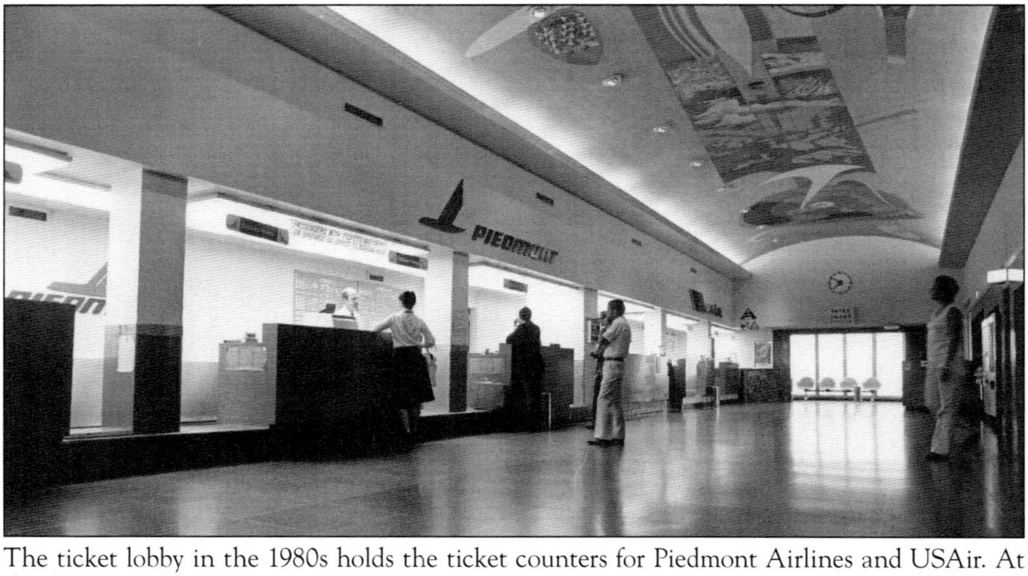

The ticket lobby in the 1980s holds the ticket counters for Piedmont Airlines and USAir. At the far end of the lobby, passengers could access Gates 5–9. The ticket lobby has been extended several times since this photograph was taken. (Courtesy of Charleston Newspapers.)

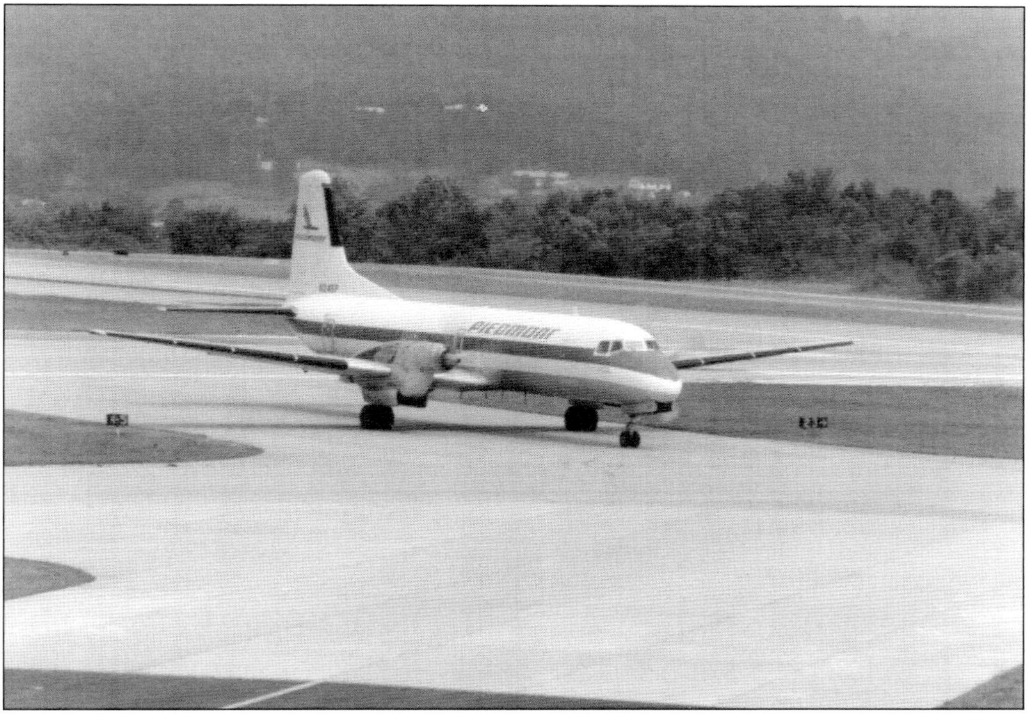

A Piedmont Airlines YS-11 at Kanawha Airport is seen in this early-1980s photograph. Piedmont operated 21 of these Japanese built 58-passenger aircraft between 1968 and 1982.

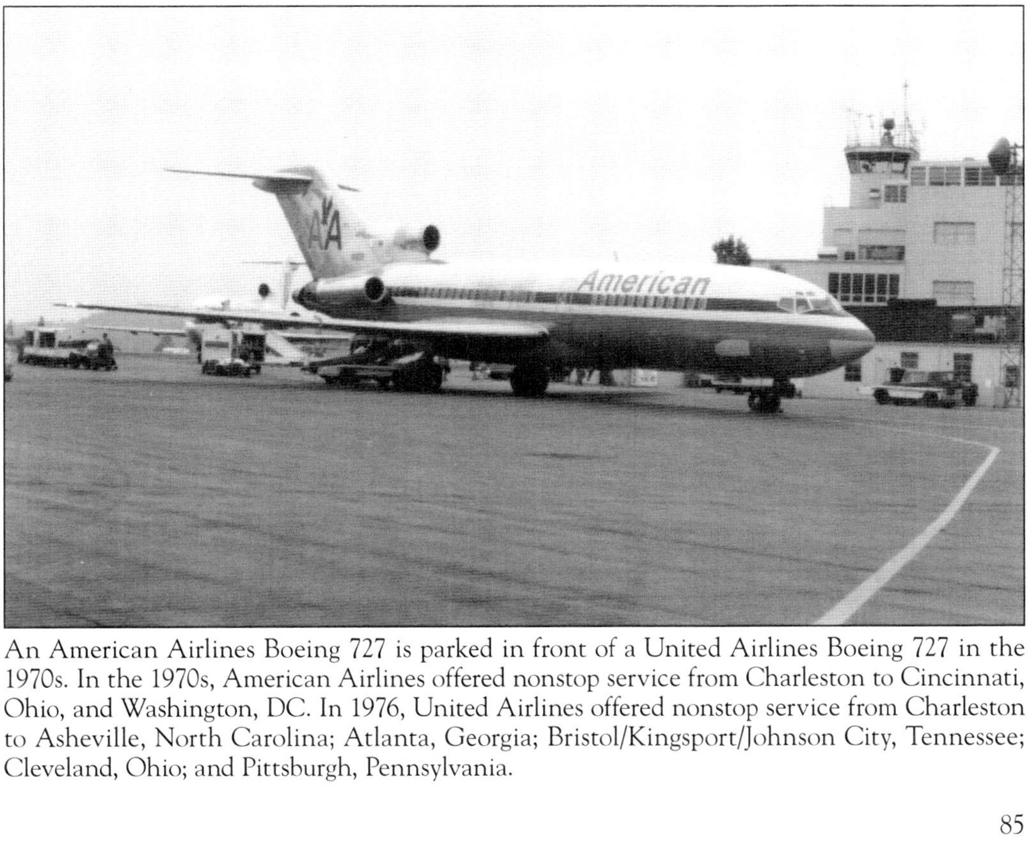

An American Airlines Boeing 727 is parked in front of a United Airlines Boeing 727 in the 1970s. In the 1970s, American Airlines offered nonstop service from Charleston to Cincinnati, Ohio, and Washington, DC. In 1976, United Airlines offered nonstop service from Charleston to Asheville, North Carolina; Atlanta, Georgia; Bristol/Kingsport/Johnson City, Tennessee; Cleveland, Ohio; and Pittsburgh, Pennsylvania.

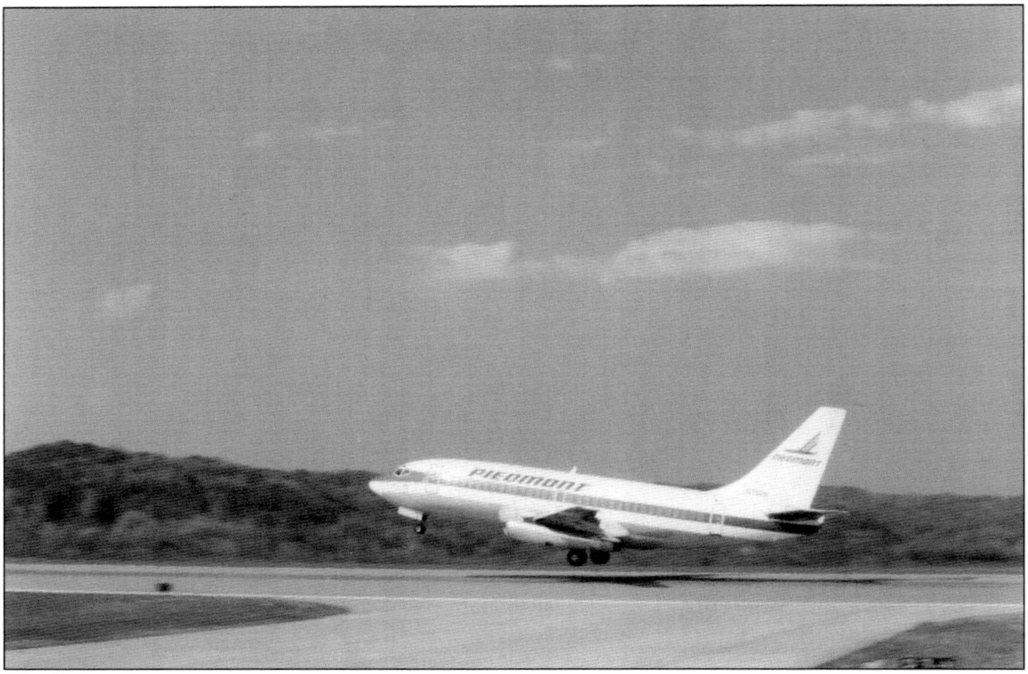

A Piedmont Airlines Boeing 737 takes off in October 1983. In the fall of 1983, Piedmont served the following destinations from Charleston nonstop: Charlotte, North Carolina; Chicago O'Hare, Illinois; Cincinnati, Ohio; Louisville, Kentucky; New York, New York (LaGuardia); Roanoke, Virginia; and Washington, DC (National Airport).

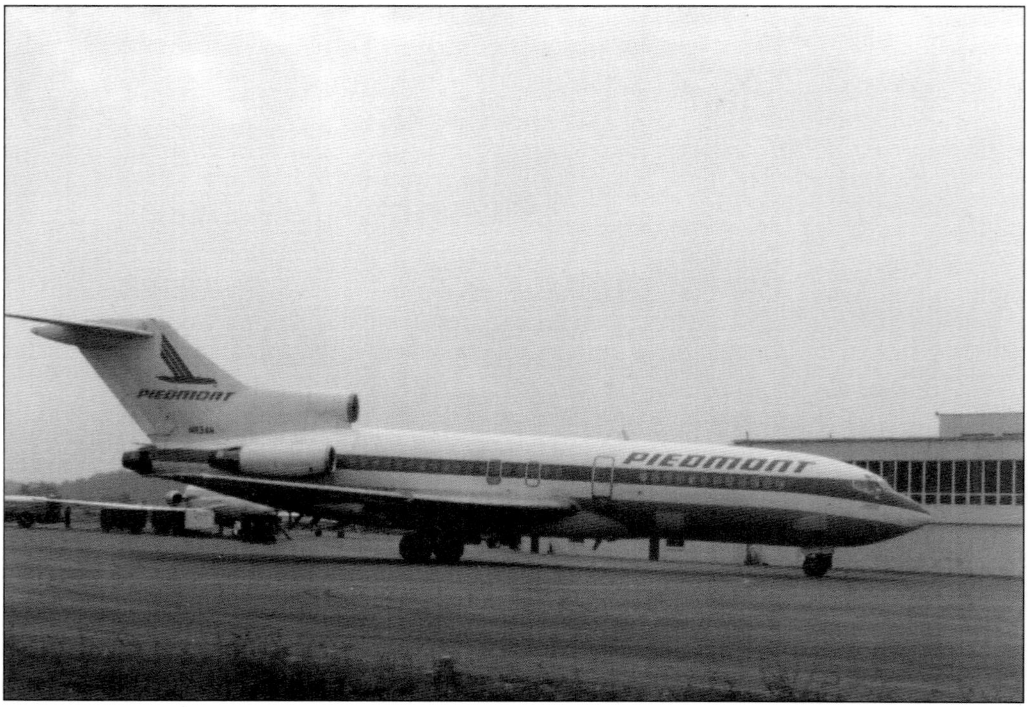

A Piedmont Airlines Boeing 727-100 sits on the ramp in the late 1970s or early 1980s. This particular aircraft was delivered in 1977 and named the *Lindbergh Pacemaker.*

Four

West Virginia Air National Guard

The West Virginia Air National Guard was formed by Lt. Col. J. Kemp McLaughlin in March 1947. The 167th Fighter Squadron was assigned to Kanawha Airport in Charleston, West Virginia, with 10 T-6 Texans. After the airport opened, the P-47 Thunderbolt arrived in November and December 1947 and was quickly replaced by the P-51 Mustang beginning in the summer of 1948. The 167th Fighter Squadron was placed on active duty during the Korean War and returned to Charleston in 1953. In 1955, the 167th moved to Martinsburg, West Virginia, and transitioned to jet fighters.

To replace the 167th Fighter Squadron, the 130th Troop Carrier Squadron was formed at Kanawha Airport. The 130th initially operated the Curtiss C-46, which was soon replaced by the SA-16 seaplane. Later, the C-119 would serve as the unit's main aircraft from 1963 until the arrival of the C-130 Hercules in 1975. The 130th Airlift Wing served in Operation Desert Storm in 1991 and continues to serve the nation and state today, operating missions worldwide.

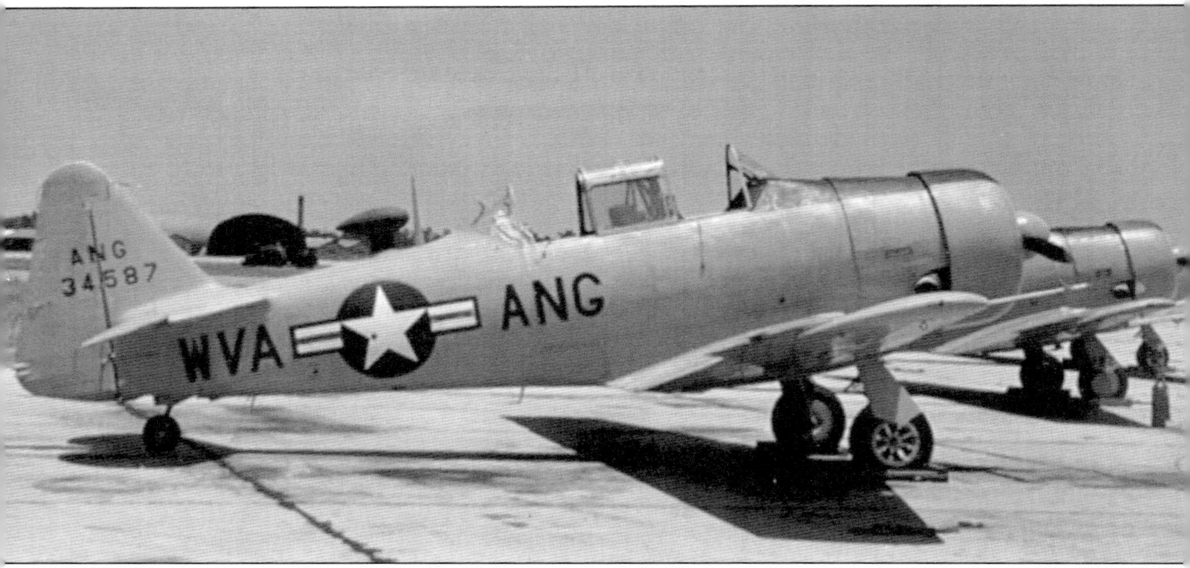

The first aircraft assigned to the West Virginia Air National Guard was the T-6 Texan. Ten Texans were assigned to the 167th Fighter Squadron and were temporarily based at Clark Field near St. Albans, West Virginia, in early 1947 until construction was completed at Kanawha Airport. (Courtesy of the West Virginia Air National Guard.)

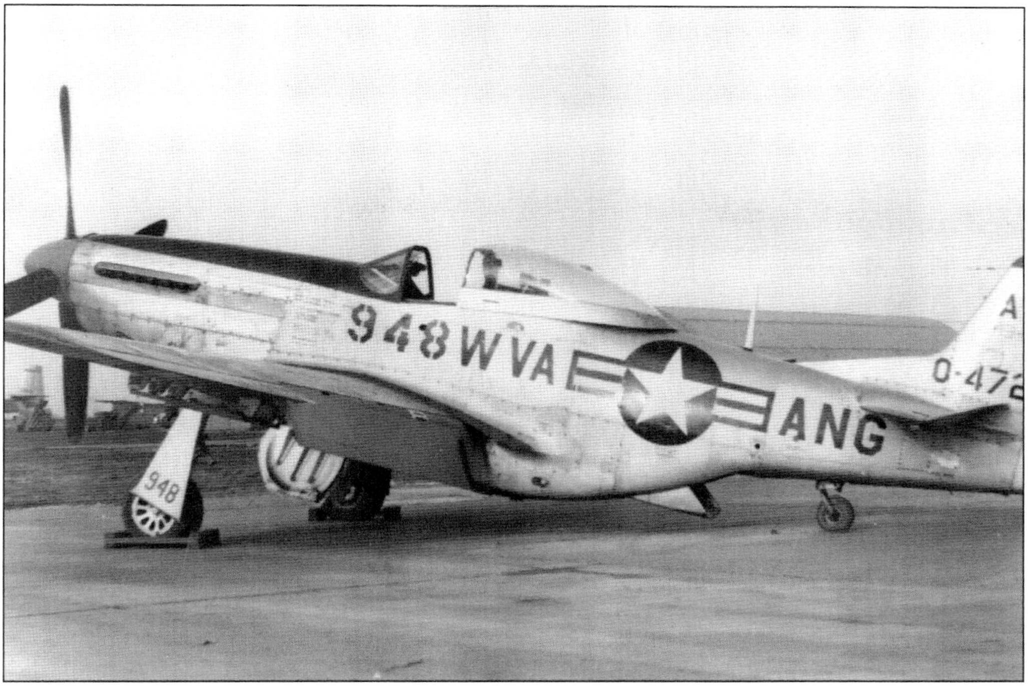

P-51 Mustang No. 948 sits on the West Virginia Air National Guard ramp. After the 167th Fighter Squadron moved to Martinsburg, West Virginia, this aircraft remained in Charleston to be placed on display. By January 1957, the 948 was one of only two P-51s in the Air Force inventory. When repairs and bad weather caused the other P-51 to be delayed, this aircraft was flown from Charleston to Dayton, Ohio, to participate in the official Air Force decommissioning ceremony for the P-51. It was then flown back to Charleston and placed on display at the entrance to Kanawha Airport. Vandalism caused the 130th to reclaim the aircraft to its base, where it remains today. (Courtesy of Bill Peters.)

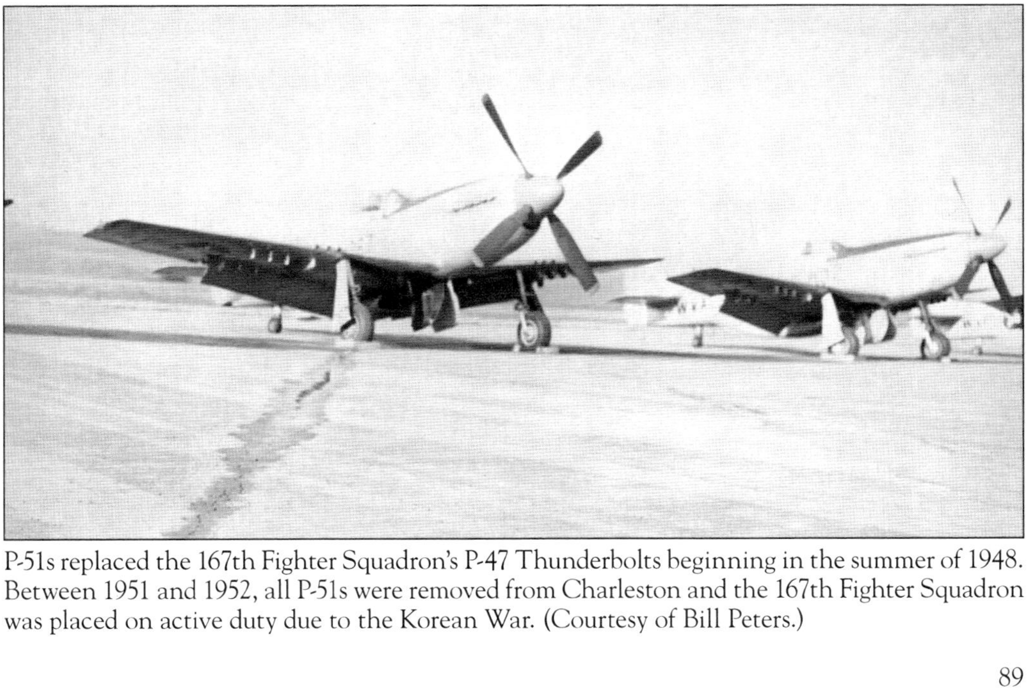

P-51s replaced the 167th Fighter Squadron's P-47 Thunderbolts beginning in the summer of 1948. Between 1951 and 1952, all P-51s were removed from Charleston and the 167th Fighter Squadron was placed on active duty due to the Korean War. (Courtesy of Bill Peters.)

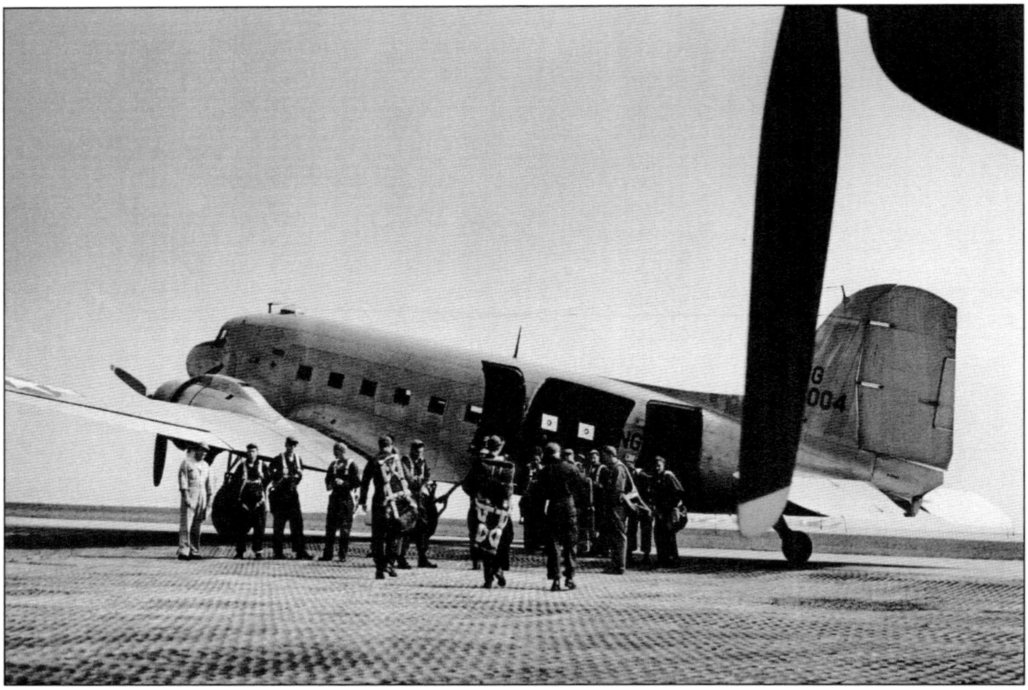

Soldiers with parachutes are next to a West Virginia Air National Guard C-47 at Kanawha Airport in this 1948 photograph. Note the pierced steel planking used to park the airplanes on. The two C-47s assigned were Nos. 004 and 578. One C-47 crew chief was Robert E. Lee Frazier. (Courtesy of the West Virginia State Archives, James Guthrie Collection.)

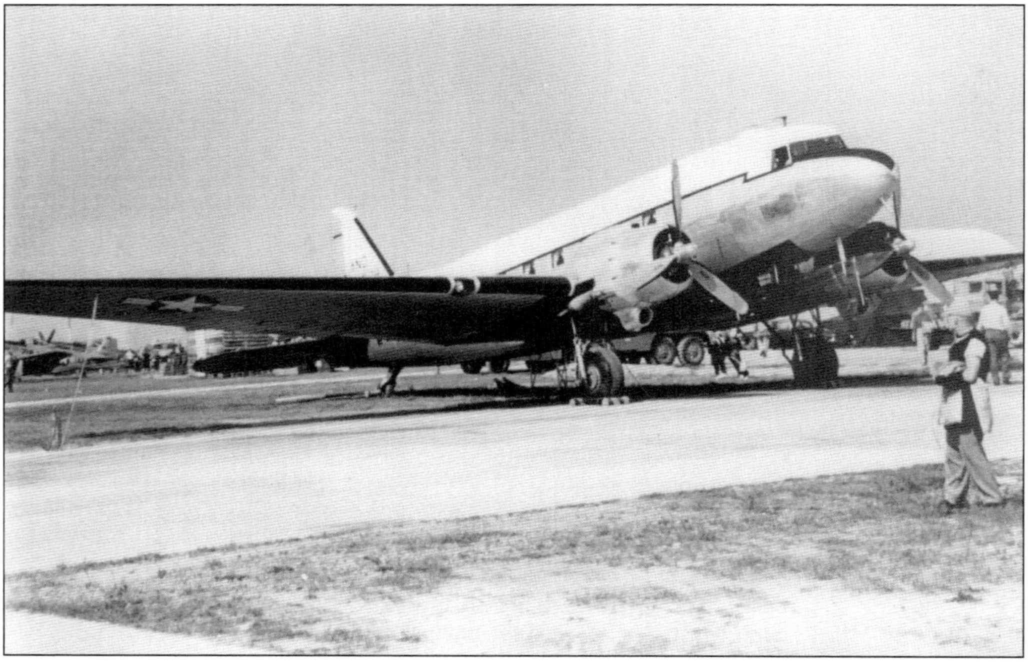

Seen here is a VC-47 assigned to the West Virginia Air National Guard at Kanawha Airport, with a P-51 Mustang sitting in the background. The VC-47 was sometimes used as an aircraft for the governor of West Virginia. (Courtesy of the West Virginia Air National Guard.)

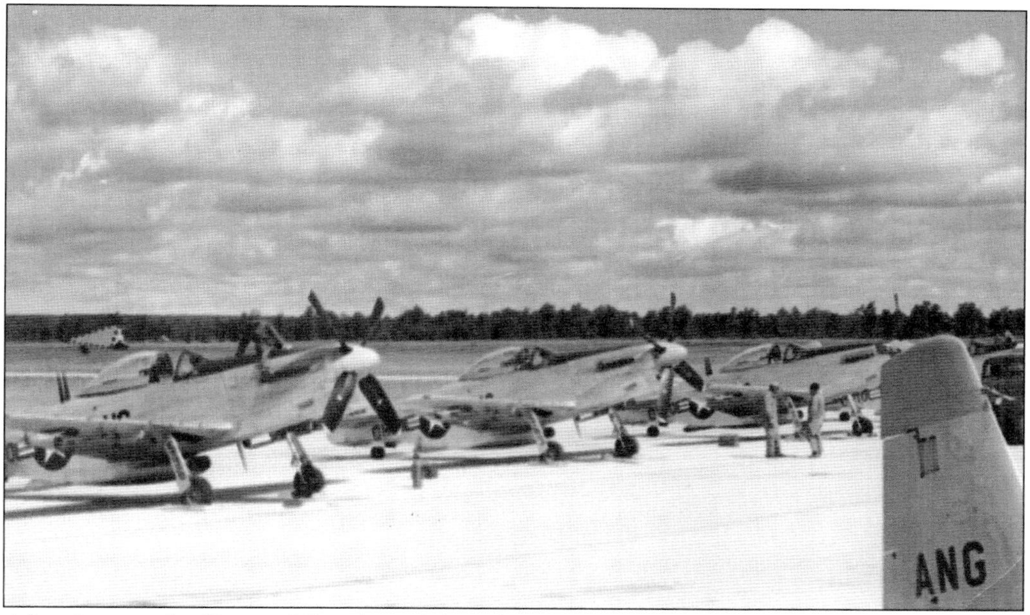

After duty in the Korean War, the 167th Fighter Squadron returned to Kanawha Airport in 1953 with only two P-51H aircraft. The unit was forced to borrow 10 P-51s, some of which are pictured here, from the Ohio Air National Guard to participate in summer training. (Courtesy of Bill Peters.)

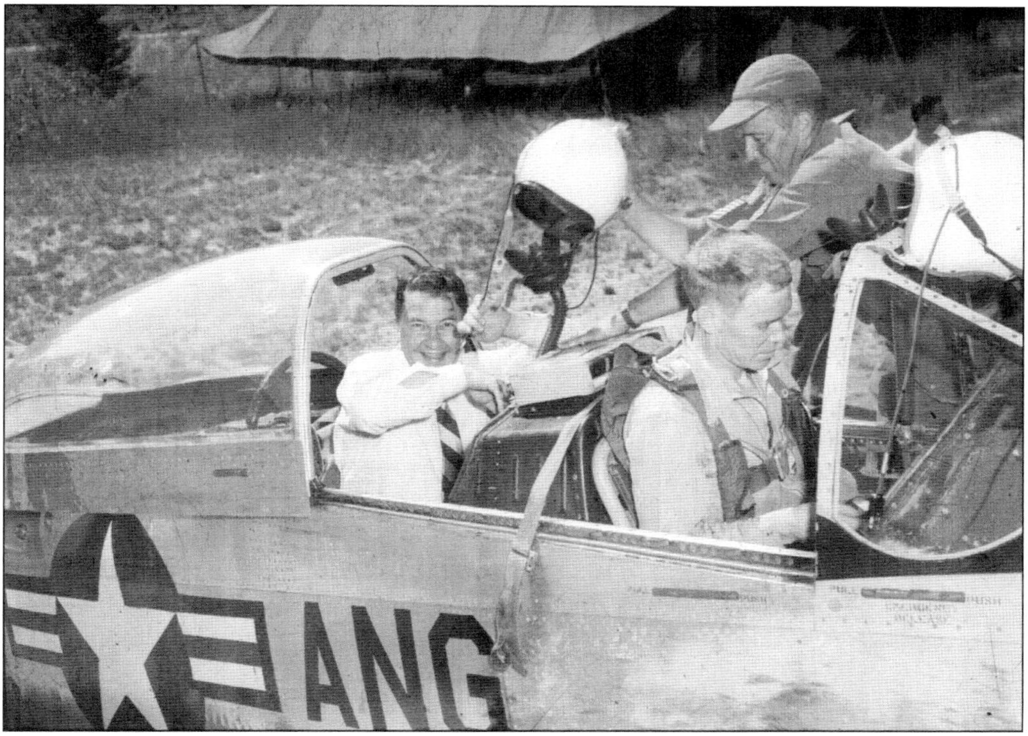

West Virginia governor William Marland smiles after returning from a flight in a 167th Fighter Squadron P-51 Mustang while the unit was at summer training at Camp Grayling, Michigan, in 1953 or 1954. (Courtesy of the West Virginia Air National Guard.)

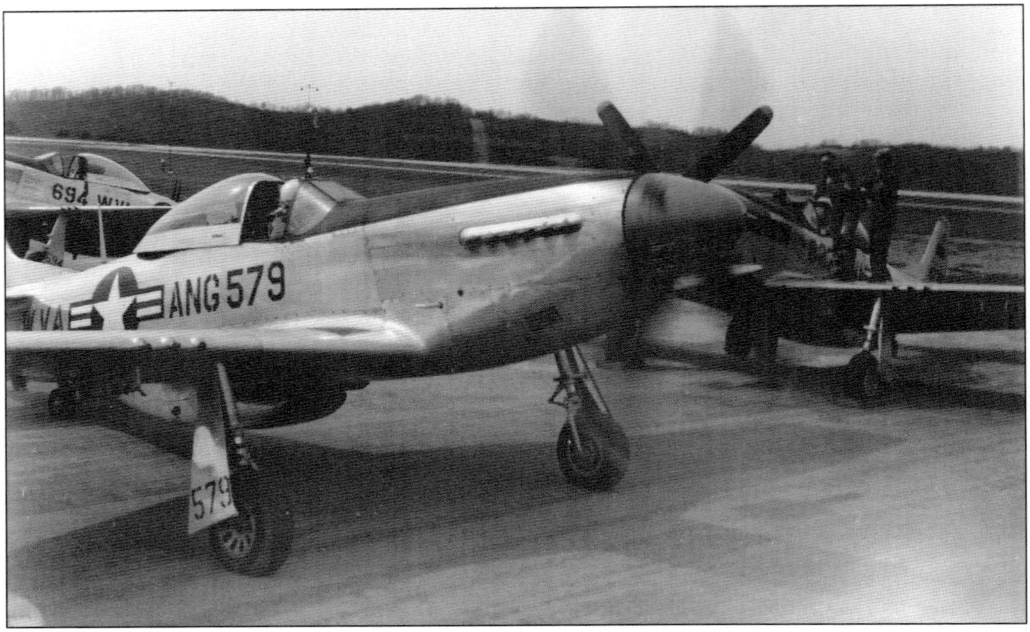

Three P-51D Mustangs are visible here on the ramp at Kanawha Airport. By 1955, it was clear the propeller-driven Mustangs would be replaced by jets that could not operate on the 5,200-foot runway in Charleston. Martinsburg, West Virginia, was selected as the new home for the 167th Fighter Squadron, which transferred in December 1955. (Courtesy of the West Virginia Air National Guard.)

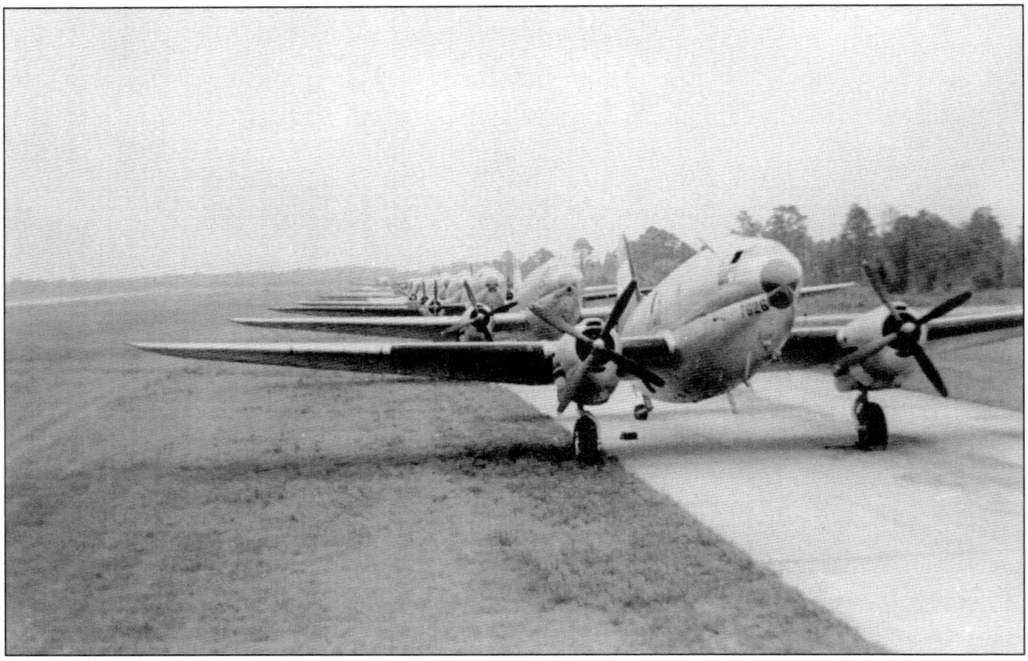

Due to the transfer of the 167th Fighter Squadron, the 130th Troop Carrier Squadron was activated on October 16, 1955, at Kanawha Airport and assigned the C-46 with a mission to fly troops and cargo. In this photograph, a line of Curtiss C-46 Commandos sit at Kanawha Airport. (Courtesy of the West Virginia Air National Guard.)

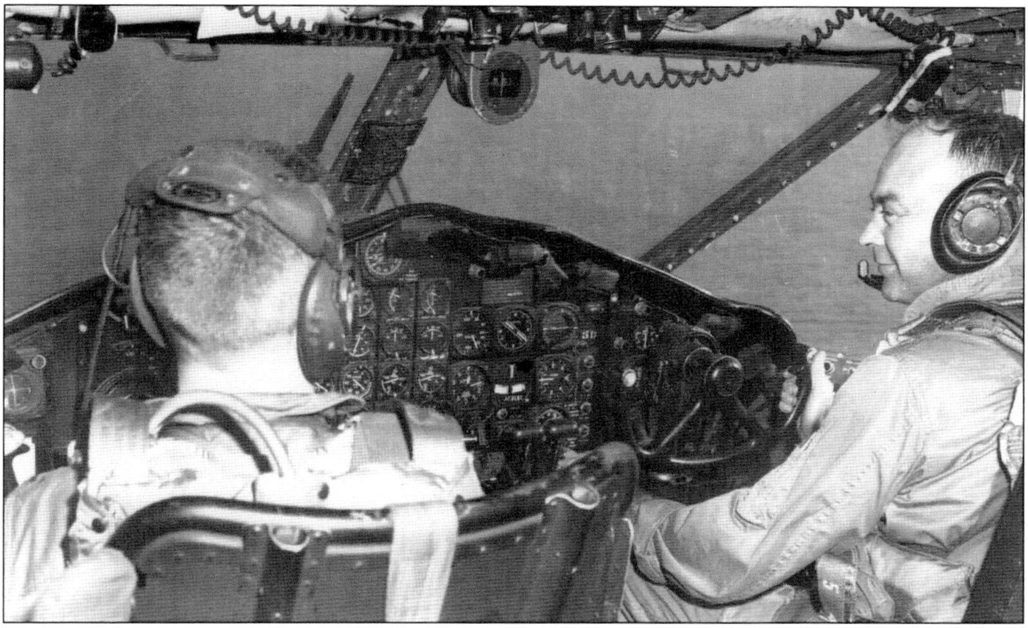

Lyle Carter (left) and Fleetwood Guthrie pilot an SA-16 Albatross. The 130th conducted training landings and takeoffs on the Kanawha River and the Ohio River. The SA-16 was designed to land in oceans and conduct rescue operations in heavy seas. (Courtesy of the West Virginia Air National Guard.)

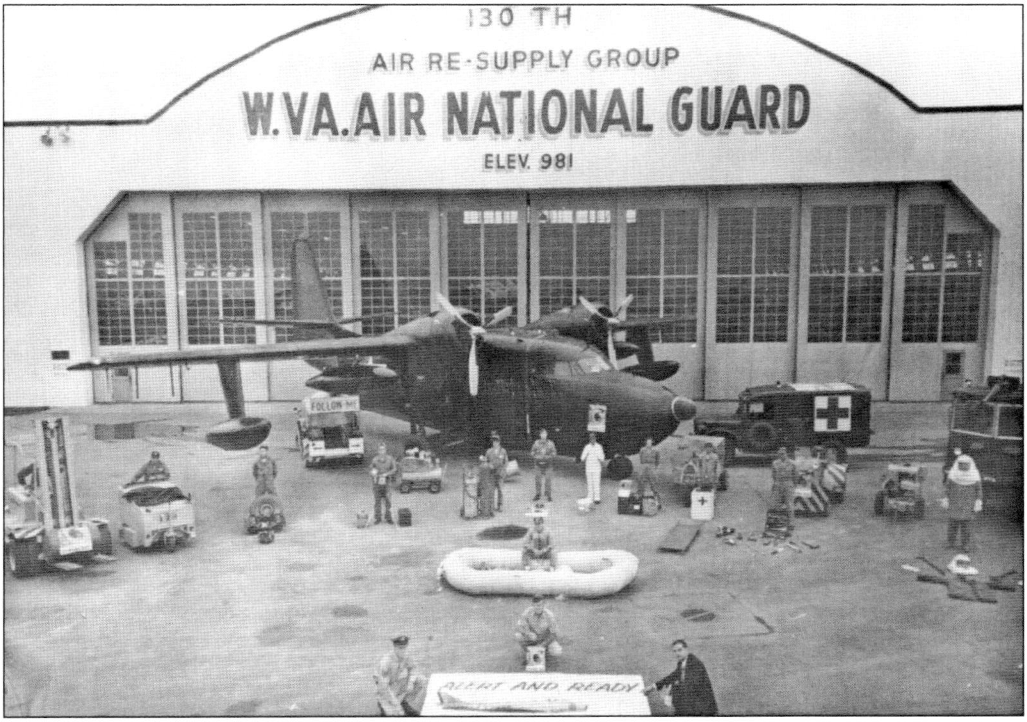

This 1956 photograph shows the 130th Air Resupply Squadron's new aircraft, the SA-16. Also displayed are rescue equipment and other items used by the unit. (Courtesy of the West Virginia Air National Guard.)

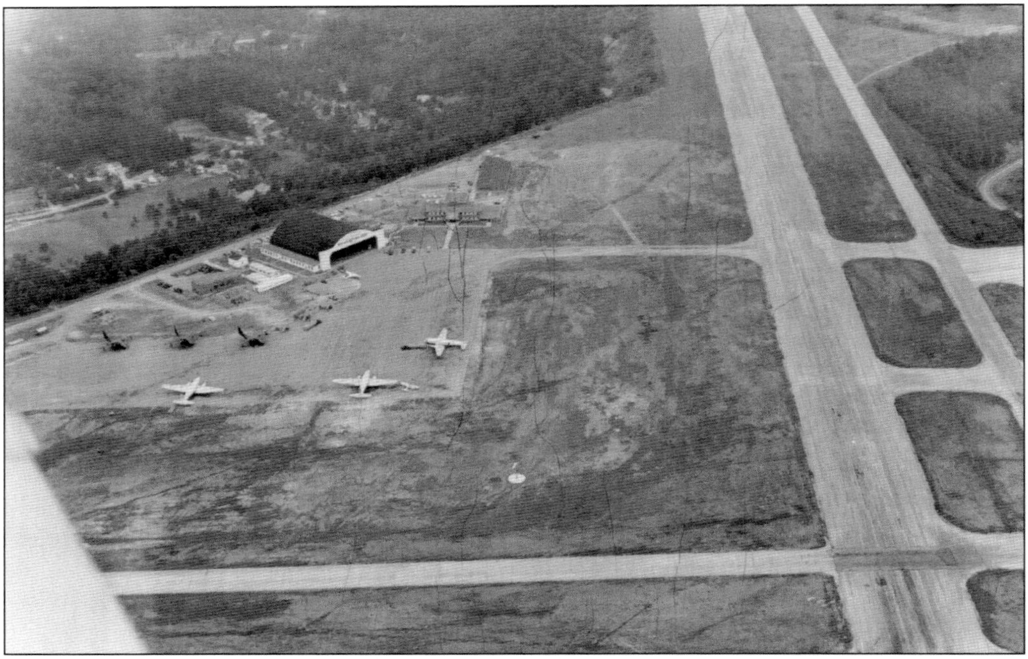

This 1957 view of the West Virginia Air Guard Base shows a time of transition with three SA-16s, three C46s, a P-51 Mustang, and what appears to be the State of West Virginia Aero Commander. The final C-46 was phased out by the 130th in 1958 and replaced with the SA-16. (Courtesy of the West Virginia Air National Guard.)

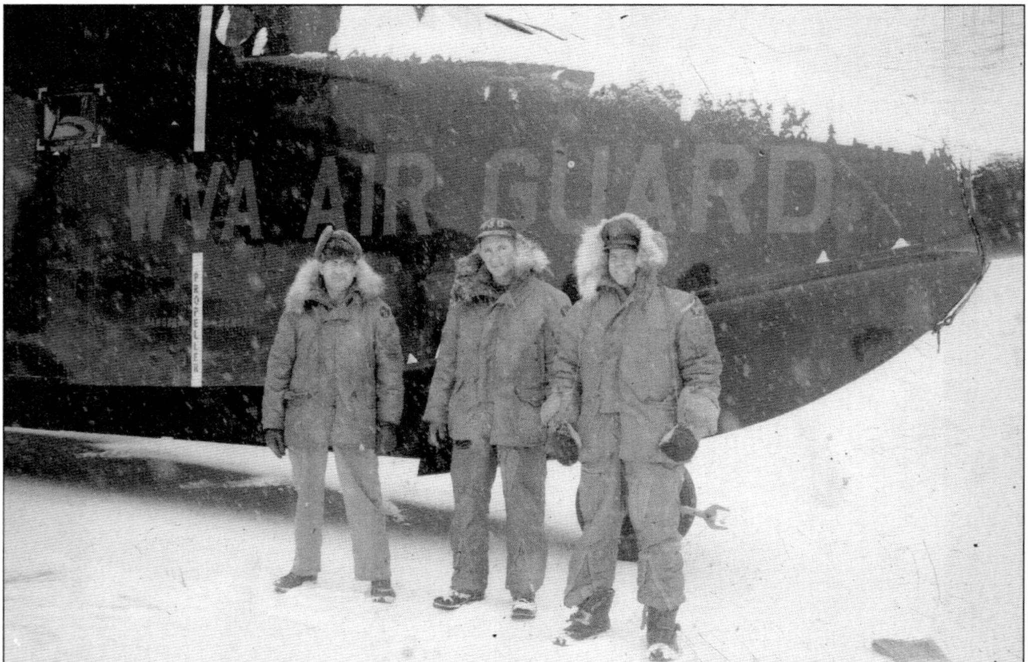

Crew members brave winter weather cleaning the window of an SA-16 Albatross, which was sent to Alaska for cold-weather training. The 130th would end up operating a total of 23 SA-16s between 1956 and 1963. (Courtesy of the West Virginia Air National Guard.)

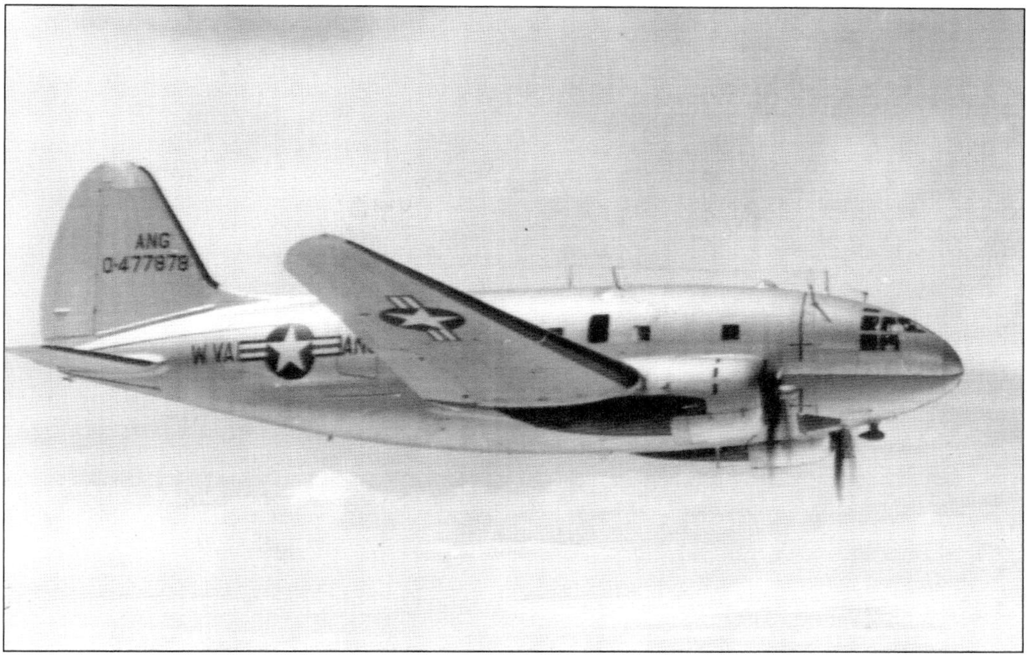

A C-46 from the 130th Troop Carrier Squadron flies over Dunbar, West Virginia, in this undated photograph. The 130th operated five C-46s between 1955 and 1958. The C-46 gained fame in the China-India-Burma theater in World War II flying cargo over the Himalayas. (Courtesy of the West Virginia Air National Guard.)

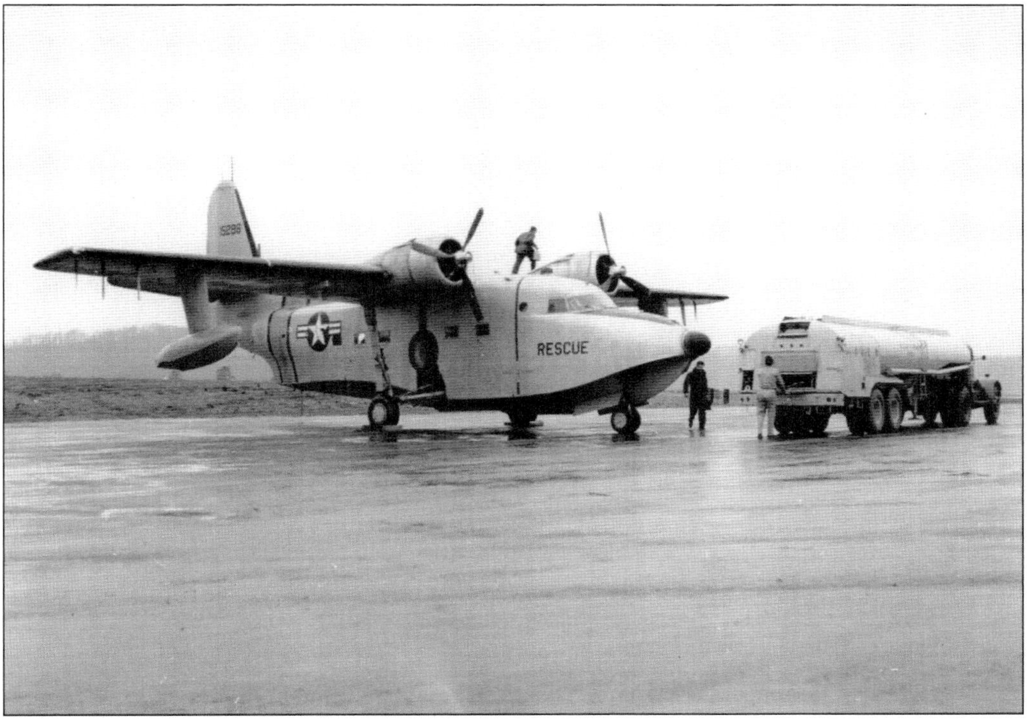

An SA-16 is getting refueled at Kanawha Airport in the late 1950s. The 130th flew aircraft 51-5285 and pictured is sister ship 51-5286. (Courtesy of the West Virginia Air National Guard.)

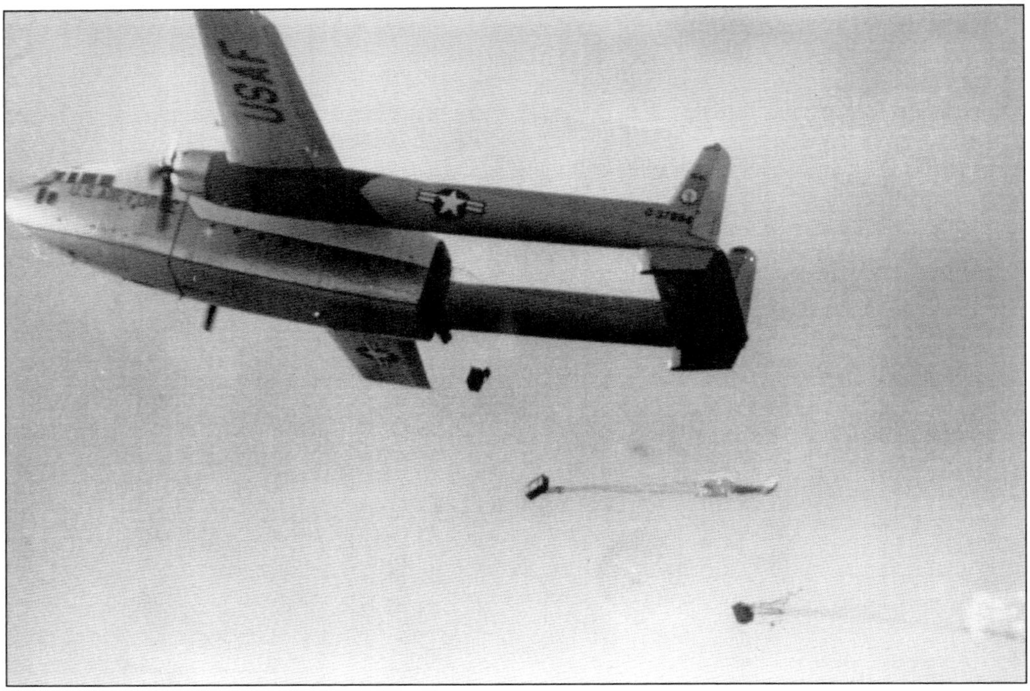

With rear doors removed, a C-119 Flying Boxcar conducts a container delivery airdrop using the supply pallets system. With a maximum range of 2,280 miles, the C-119 carried a payload of 30,000 pounds, 62 troops, or 35 stretchers. (Courtesy of the West Virginia Air National Guard.)

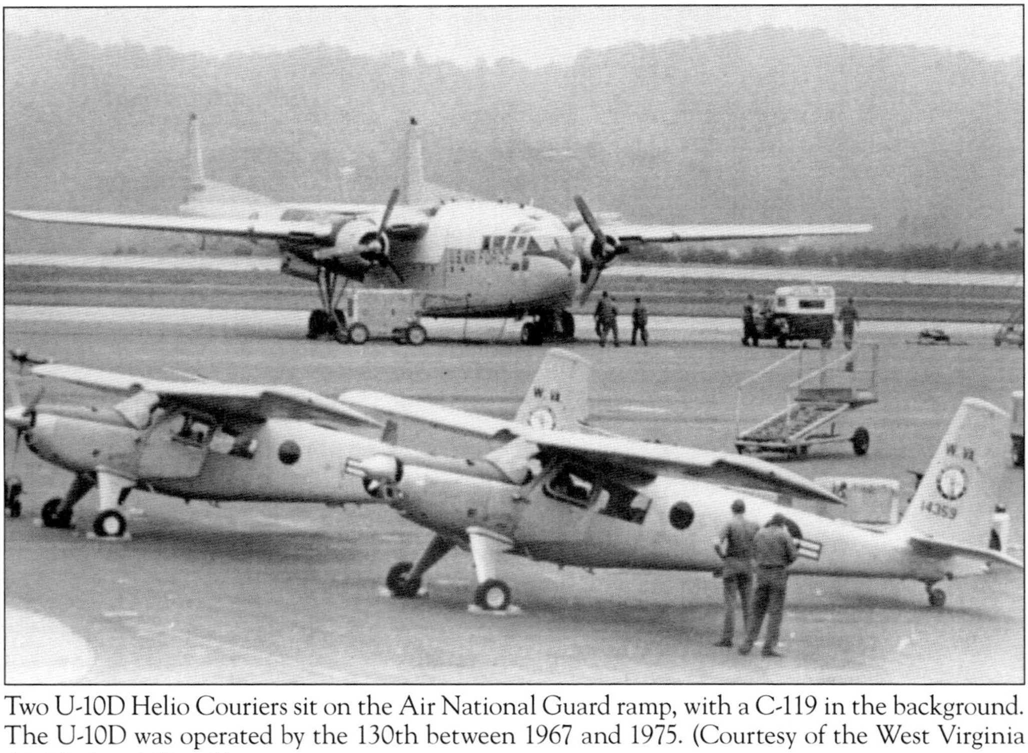

Two U-10D Helio Couriers sit on the Air National Guard ramp, with a C-119 in the background. The U-10D was operated by the 130th between 1967 and 1975. (Courtesy of the West Virginia Air National Guard.)

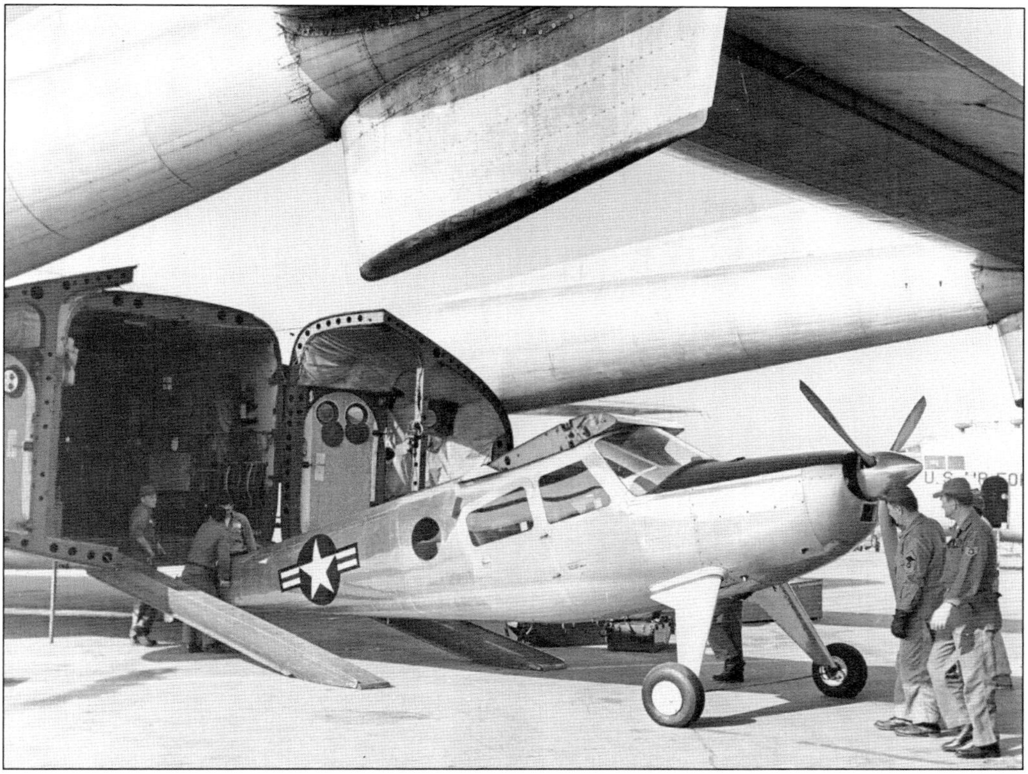

Members of the West Virginia Air Guard load a U-10 aircraft into the cargo bay of a C-119. The aircraft were bound for Howard Air Force Base in the Panama Canal Zone to participate in Operation Higland Fling in 1965. (Courtesy of the West Virginia State Archives, James Guthrie Collection.)

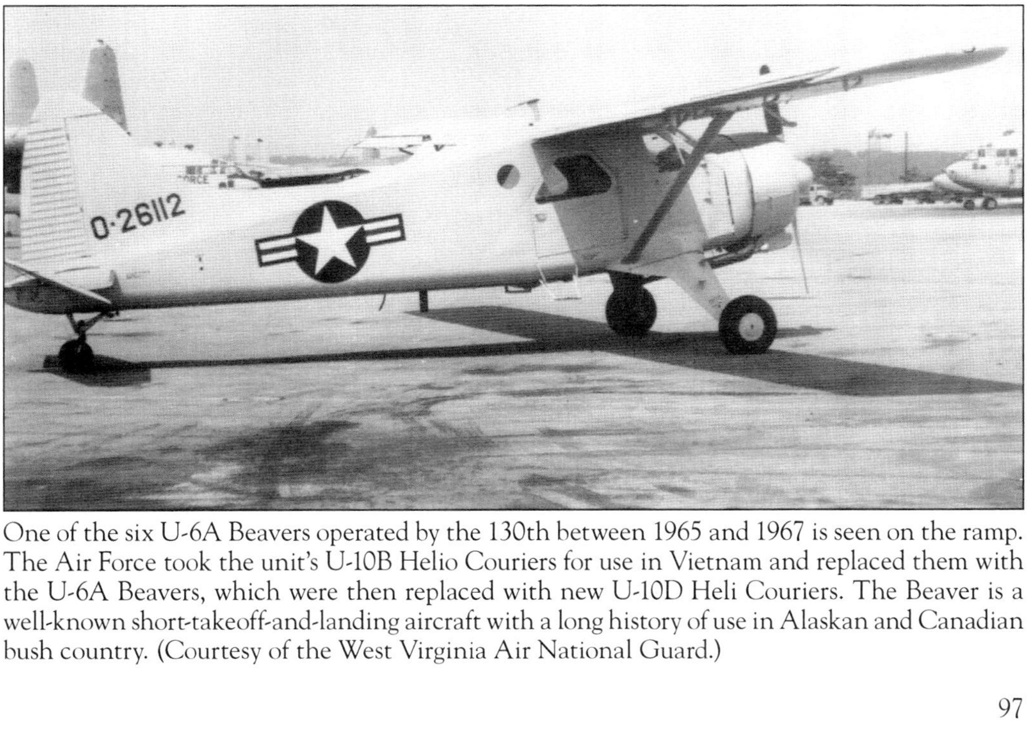

One of the six U-6A Beavers operated by the 130th between 1965 and 1967 is seen on the ramp. The Air Force took the unit's U-10B Helio Couriers for use in Vietnam and replaced them with the U-6A Beavers, which were then replaced with new U-10D Heli Couriers. The Beaver is a well-known short-takeoff-and-landing aircraft with a long history of use in Alaskan and Canadian bush country. (Courtesy of the West Virginia Air National Guard.)

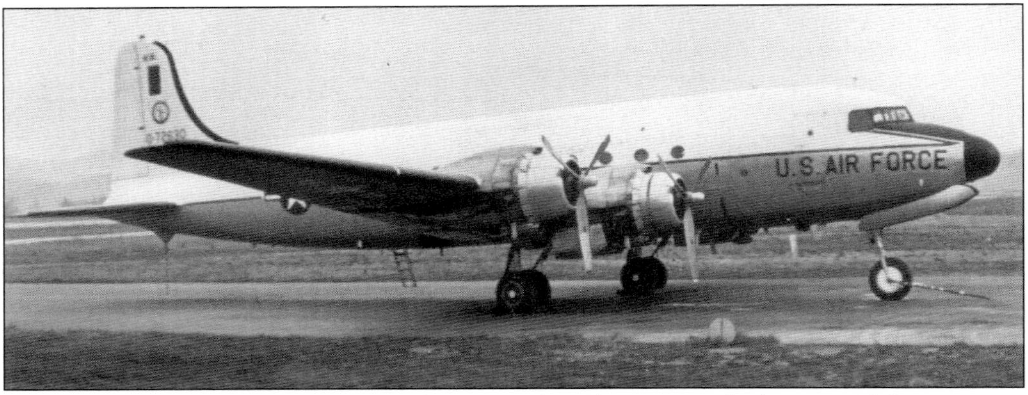

From 1967 to 1971, the 130th operated one VC-54D Skymaster, which was used for executive support missions. This aircraft was configured with executive-style seating. During the Berlin Airlift, this type of aircraft hauled coal and other cargo into Berlin. (Courtesy of the West Virginia Air National Guard.)

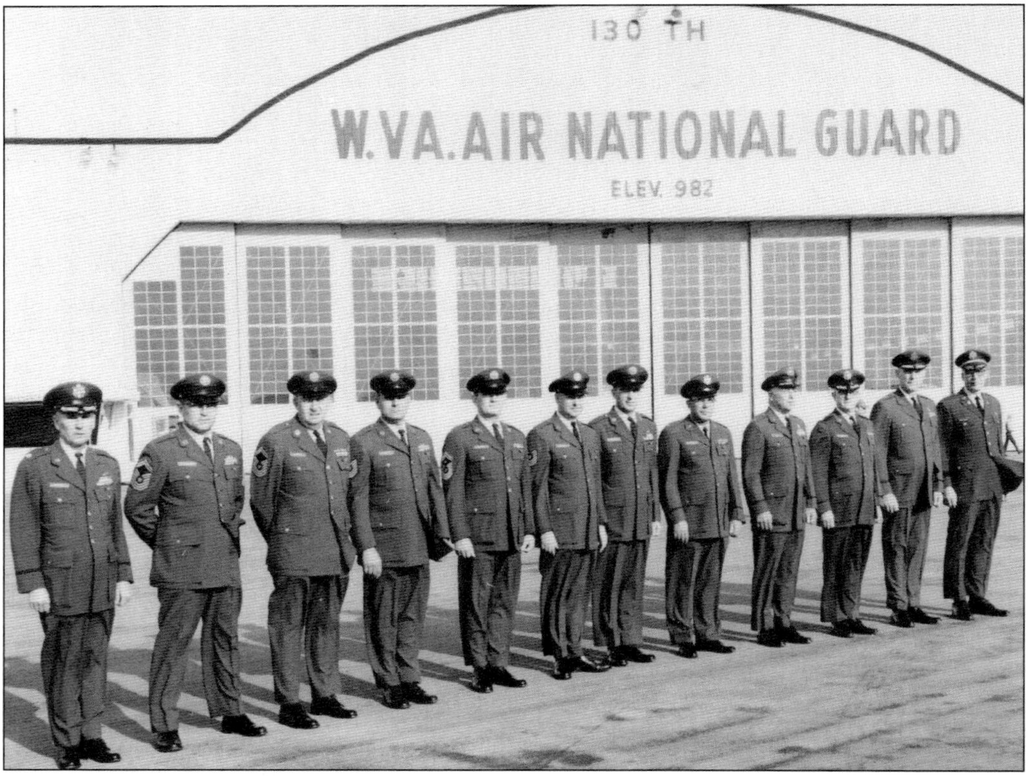

Seen at the West Virginia Air National Guard 20-year celebration in 1967 are, from left to right, Lt. Col. Kenneth C. Hoylman, Maintenance Squadron commanding officer; CMSgt. John B. Shelton, Maintenance; CMSgt. Fredrick K. Dotson, Maintenance; MSgt. Forest W. Chaney, Maintenance; CMSgt. James H. Guthrie, 130th Combat Support Squadron; MSgt. Carl E. Lawson, personnel equipment; SMSgt. Gordon E. Renstrom, Maintenance; W.O. Colvin W. Haddox, Maintenance; Lt. Col. Joseph P. Crane, base commanding officer, Martinsburg; Lt. Col. Roy D. Byrd, state headquarters; Brig. Gen. James K. McLaughlin, chief of staff; and Brig. Gen. Howe Williams, state adjutant general. (Courtesy of the West Virginia State Archives, James Guthrie Collection.)

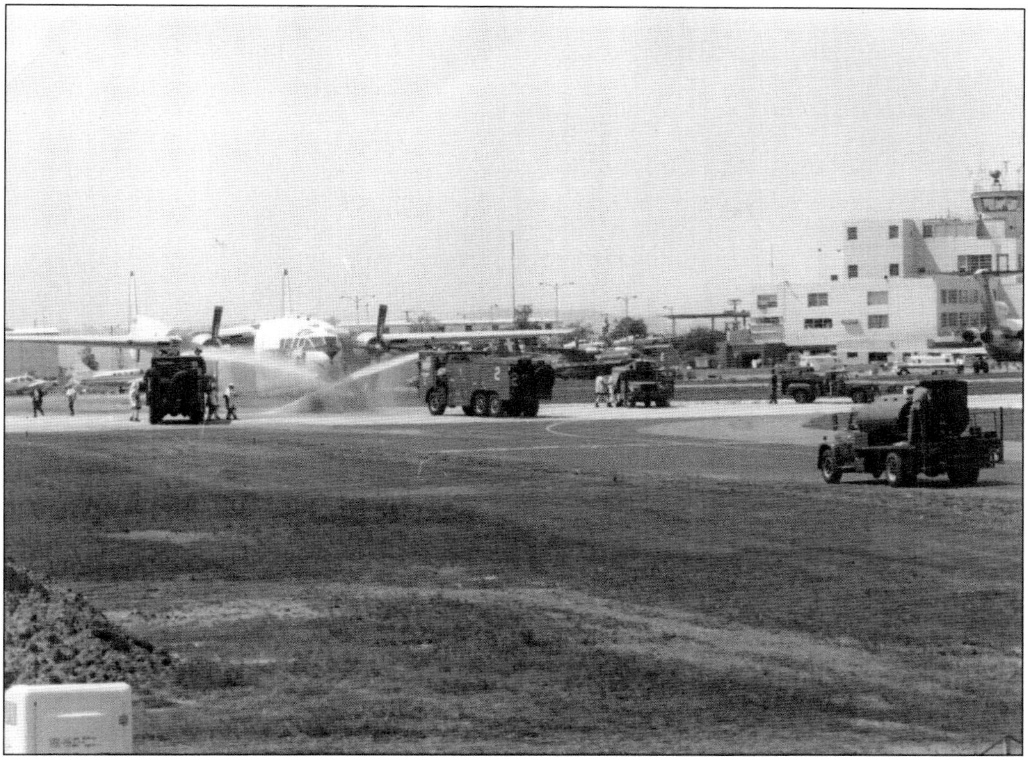

Air Guard fire trucks spray water on the nose gear of a C-119. A Boeing 727 is visible on the right, parked next to the terminal building.

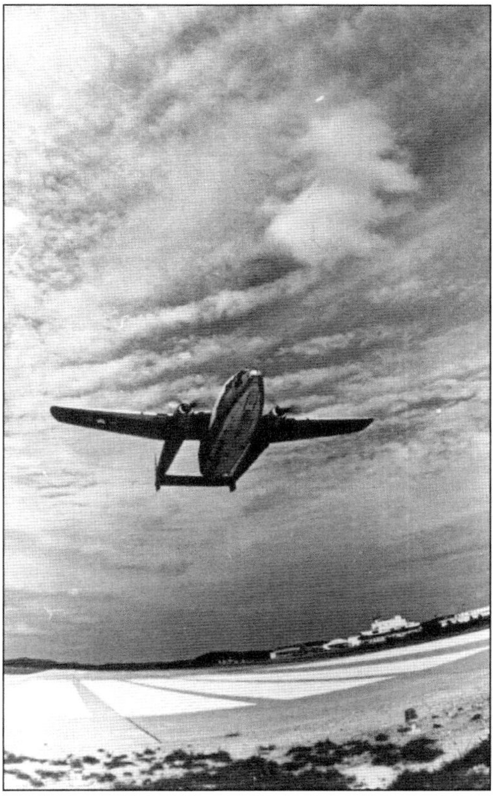

Ralph Cowgill, commander of the 130th, departs Kanawha Airport in the unit's final C-119, which was being replaced by the C-130. Cowgill also served as manager of Kanawha Airport from 1976 to 1981. (Courtesy of the West Virginia Air National Guard.)

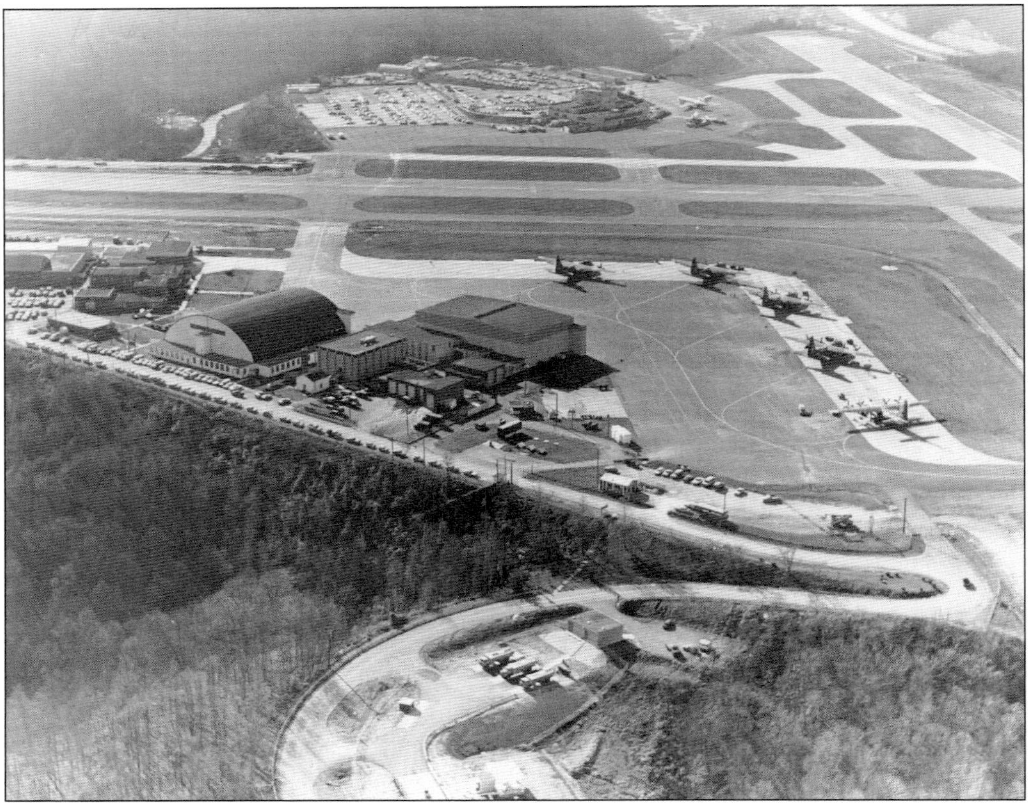

This is a late-1970s aerial view of the West Virginia Air National Guard Base with five C-130s on the ramp. Since this time, the ramp has expanded greatly, allowing ample parking. Next to the terminal building are an American Airlines Boeing 727 and unidentified Boeing 737.

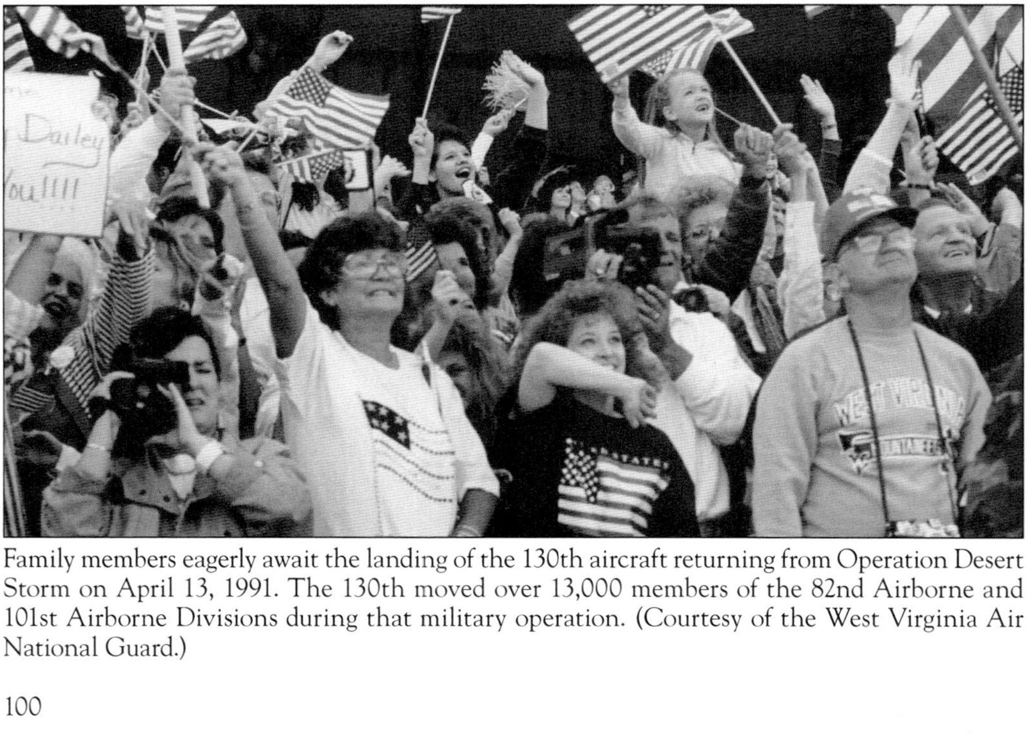

Family members eagerly await the landing of the 130th aircraft returning from Operation Desert Storm on April 13, 1991. The 130th moved over 13,000 members of the 82nd Airborne and 101st Airborne Divisions during that military operation. (Courtesy of the West Virginia Air National Guard.)

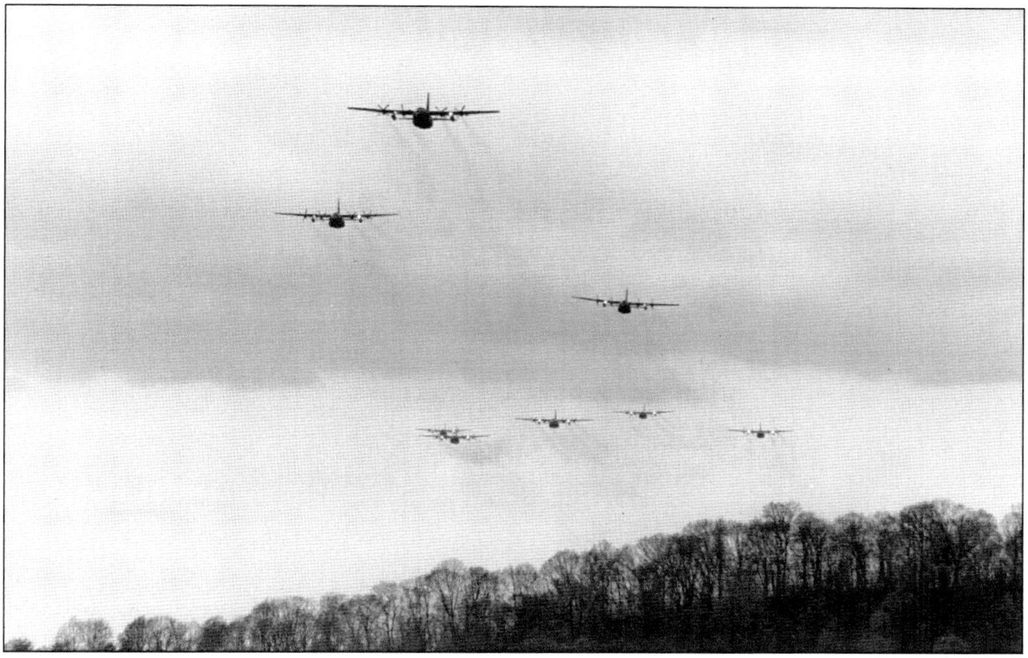

Every C-130 from the 130th Tactical Airlift Group flies in formation while returning to Yeager Airport on April 13, 1991. The 130th was activated by presidential order for Operation Desert Shield in 1990 and placed in command of a group on 16 C-130s from five Air National Guard units. (Courtesy of the West Virginia Air National Guard.)

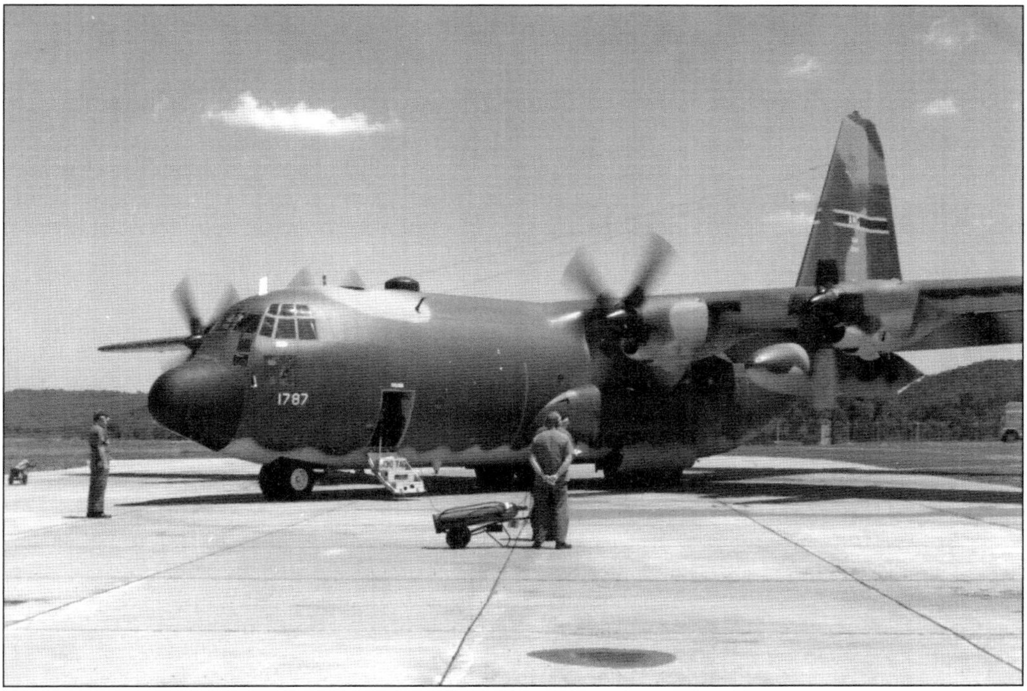

C-130 Nos. 62-1787 was one of the 130th's first C-130E series aircraft delivered from Clark Air Force Base in the Philippines in October 1975. This airplane now resides in the National Museum of the US Air Force in Dayton, Ohio. It served in the 130th until 1986. (Courtesy of Bill Peters.)

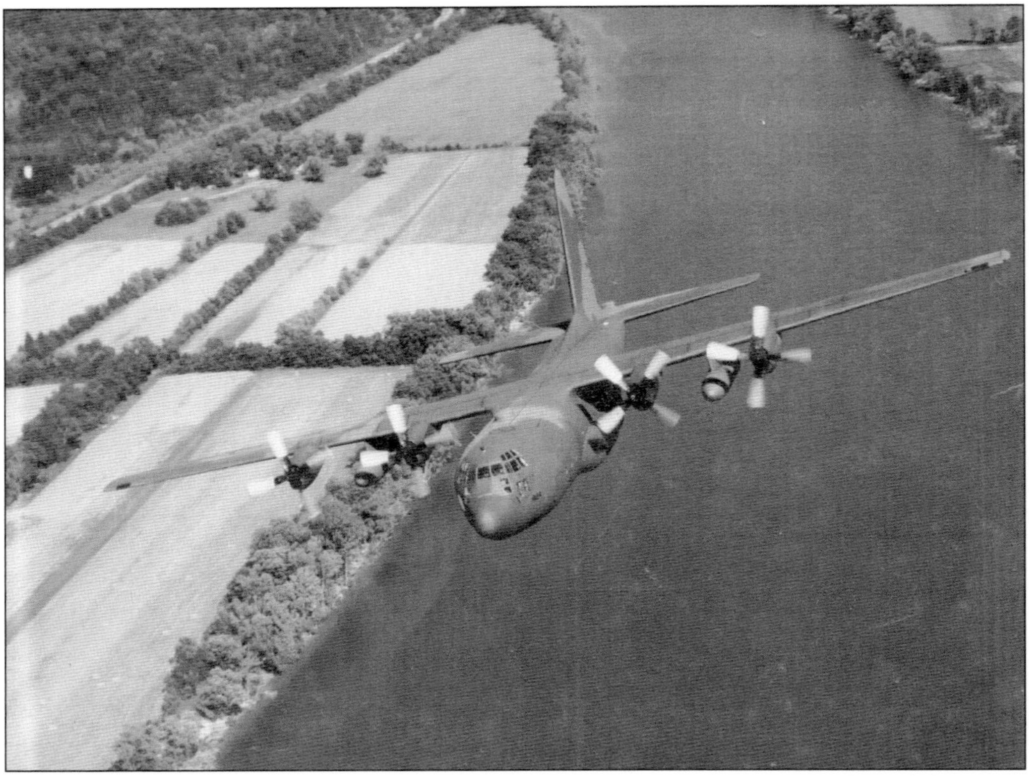

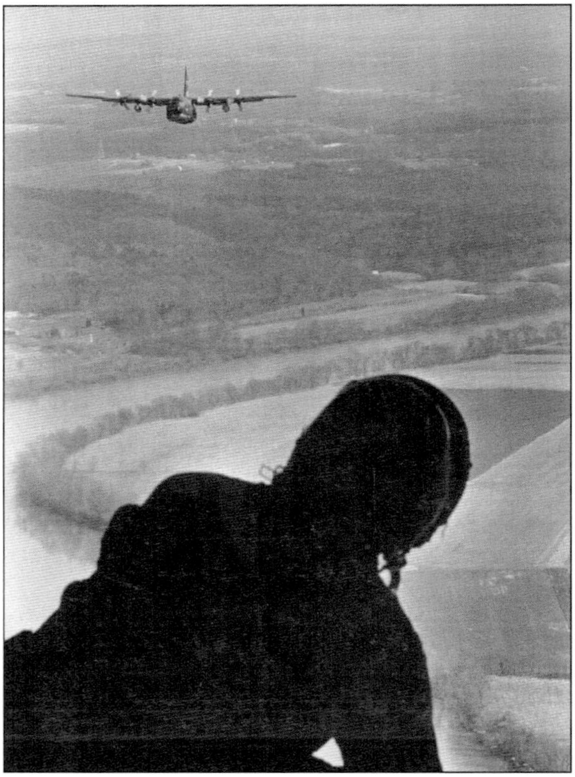

A C-130 from the 130th Airlift Wing is seen flying over the Kanawha River. The C-130 can hold up to 45,000 pounds of cargo, including up to 6 pallets, 2 M113 armored personnel carriers, or 64 paratroopers. (Courtesy of Bill Peters.)

A loadmaster from the 130th Airlift Wing looks from the loading ramp at another C-130. The two aircraft are on an air-drop mission at the Beech Hill, West Virginia, drop zone. (Courtesy of Bill Peters.)

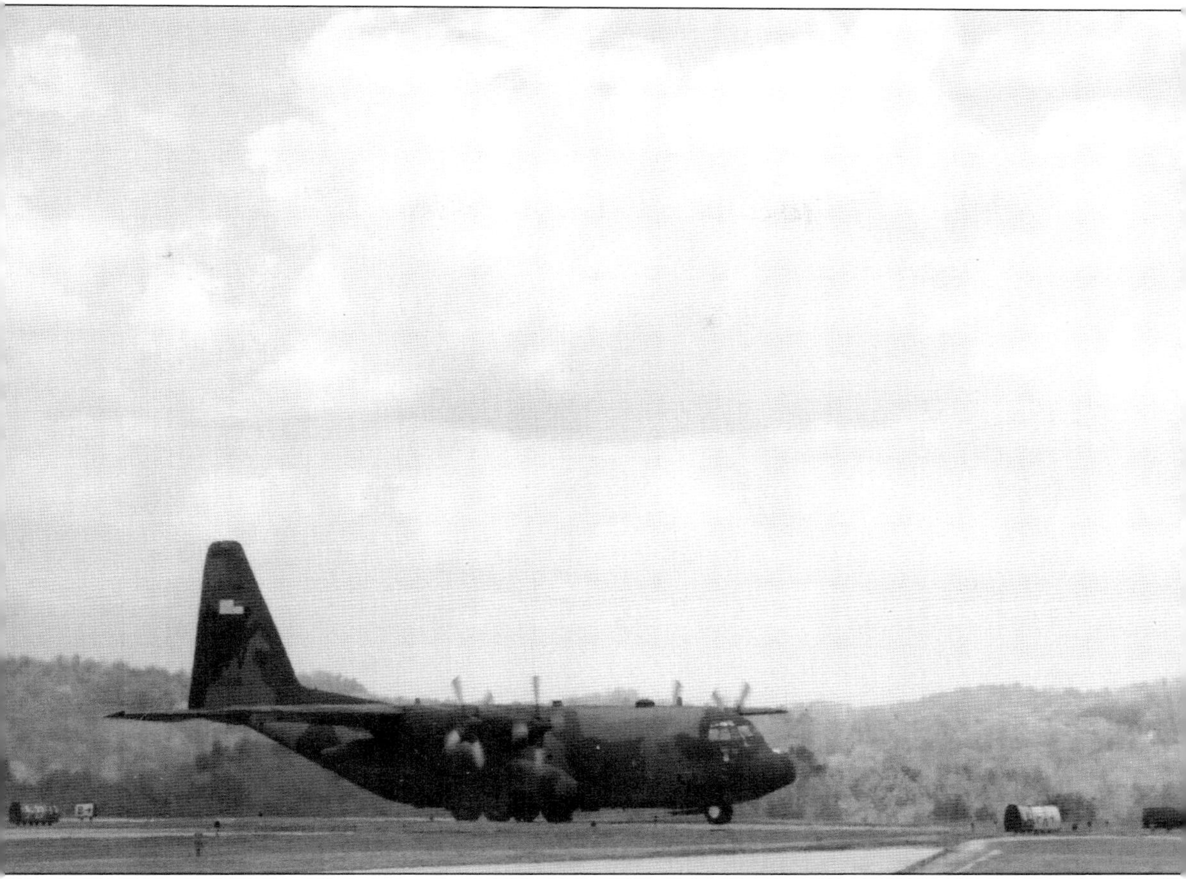

In 1975, the 130th Airlift Wing first received the C-130 Hercules, replacing the C-119. The unit's C-130 fleet was painted in camouflage for over 20 years until being repainted in the current gray scheme.

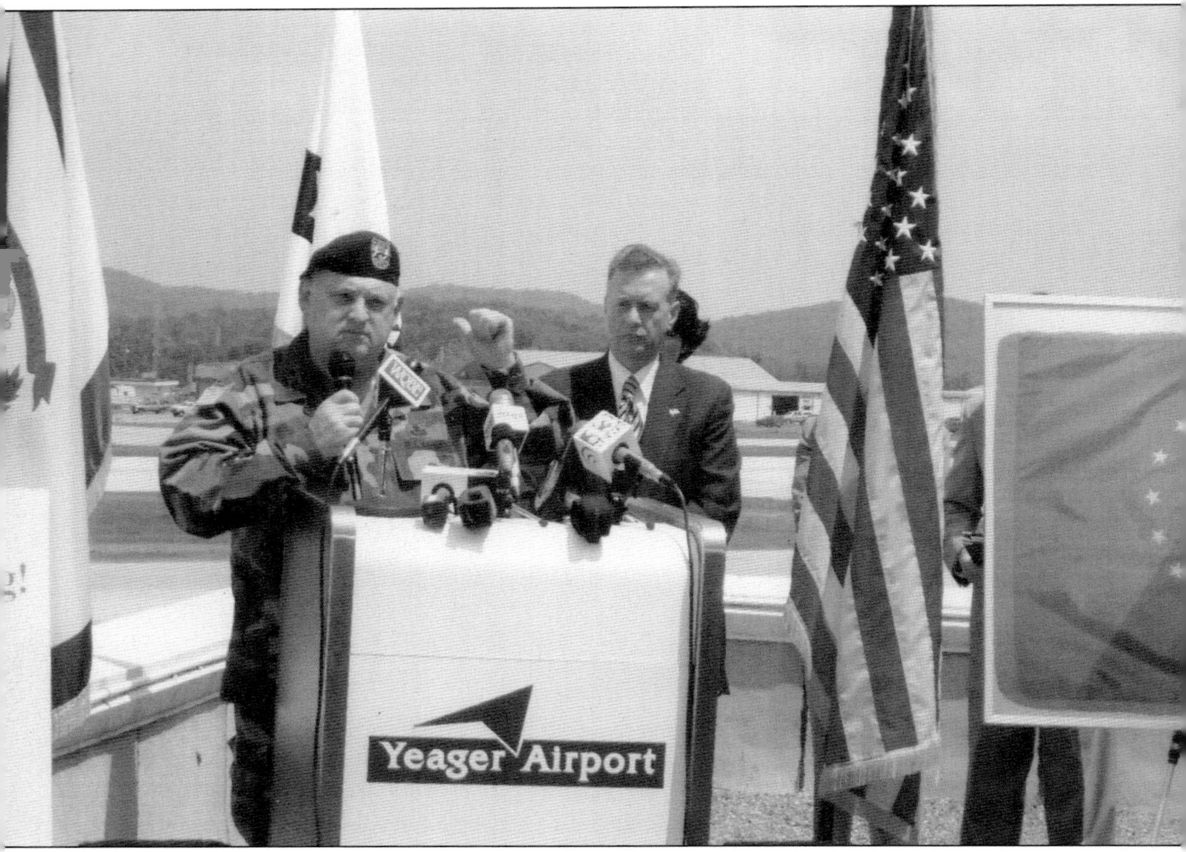

West Virginia National Guard adjutant general Allen Tackett (left) and Kanawha County Commission president W. Kent Carper speak at a press conference in May 2005, announcing the formation of the group Keep the 130th Flying. The group was formed to fight recommendations to remove aircraft from the 130th Airlift Wing during the Base Realignment and Closure (BRAC) process.

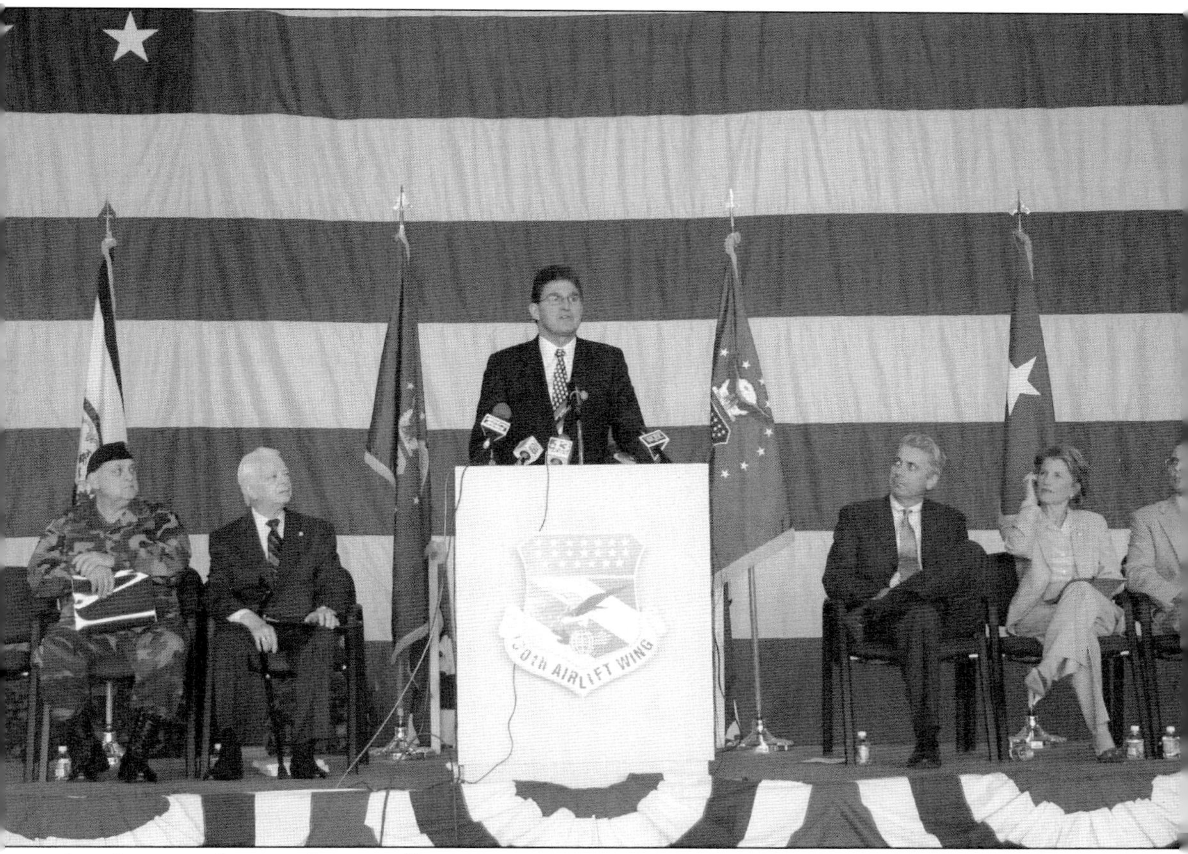

Gov. Joe Manchin speaks at a rally on May 15, 2005, in support of the 130th Airlift Wing after the Department of Defense announced the wing would be realigned and lose its aircraft as part of the BRAC process. A licensed pilot, Manchin is a great support of Yeager Airport and the West Virginia Air National Guard, knowing the importance of both to the community. Also present are, from left to right, Maj. Gen. Allen Tackett, adjutant general of the West Virginia National Guard; Sen. Robert C. Byrd; Kanawha County commissioner David J. Hardy; Rep. Shelley Moore Capito, US House of Representatives; and Wes Holden, office of Sen. John D. Rockefeller IV.

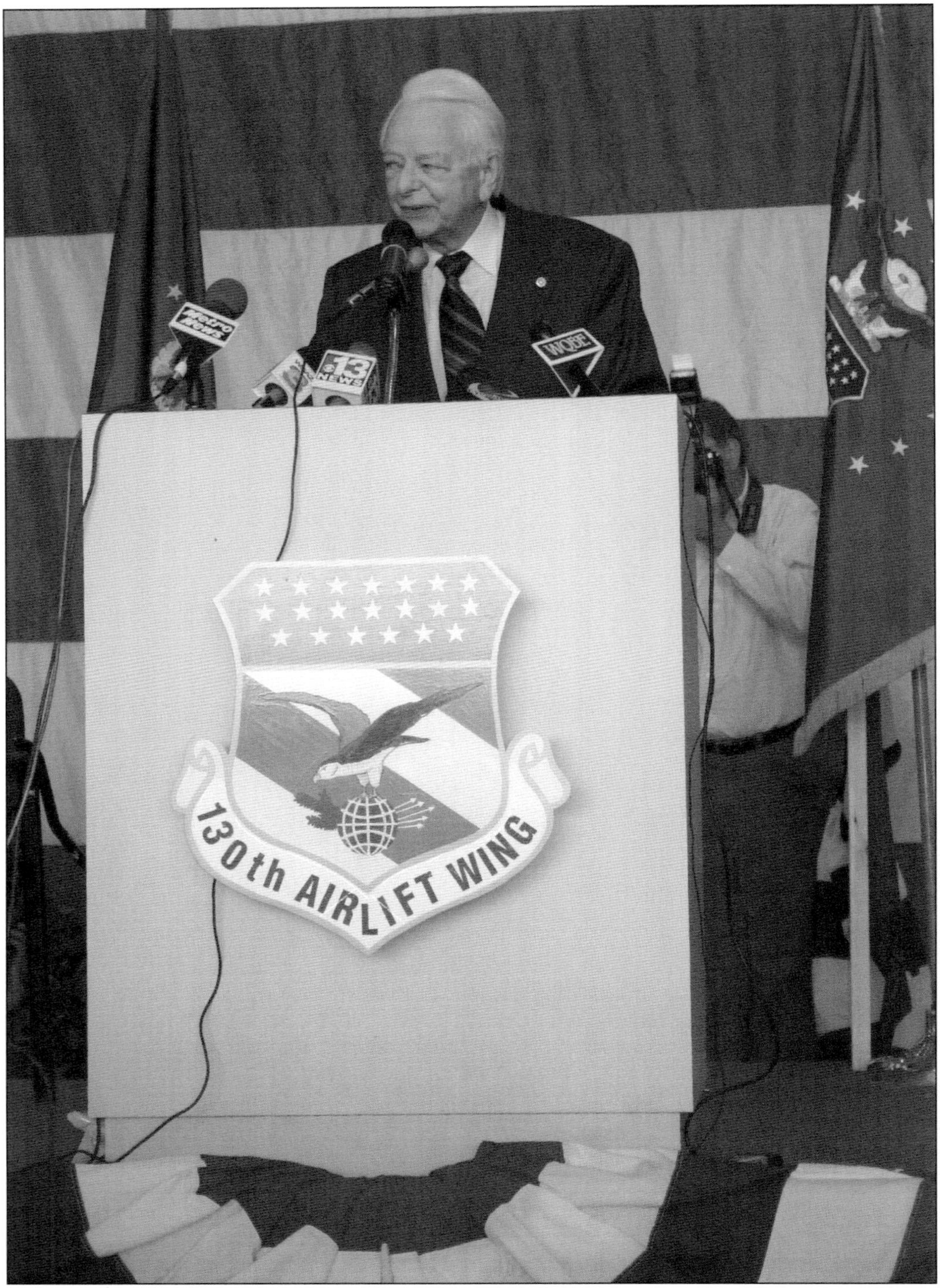

Sen. Robert C. Byrd speaks at the BRAC rally to supporters of the 130th Airlift Wing. Senator Byrd played a crucial role in saving the unit from realignment. After the BRAC report was released, a community effort known as Keep the 130th Flying began to enlist support and appeal to the BRAC Commission, who held the decision-making power as to whether the unit would be realigned.

Five

Yeager Airport

In October 1985, Kanawha Airport became Yeager Airport, renamed in honor of West Virginia native Brig. Gen. Charles "Chuck" Yeager. The 1980s saw changes in air service to Charleston, as airlines were free to choose their routes and fares after deregulation in 1978. Piedmont Airlines greatly expanded its presence until being acquired by USAir in 1989. Throughout the 1990s, USAir was the largest carrier serving Charleston, operating primarily to Pittsburgh, Pennsylvania, with larger main line jets. Various construction projects would occur to enhance the airport, including the first long-term parking garage in 1991, addition of the C concourse, expansion of the A gates, a rental car service facility, a rental car parking garage, the second long-term parking garage, expanded runway safety areas, the addition of several jet bridges, and the construction of a café in the passenger boarding gate area. Yeager Airport became the first airport in West Virginia to receive low-fare airline service when Independence Air began operations in 2004. Later, AirTran Airways and Spirit Airlines would begin low-fare service to Charleston. Today, Yeager Airport offers convenience and a variety of air service to key airline hubs, making it West Virginia's gateway to the world.

YEAGER AIRPORT
DEDICATION CEREMONY

Monday, October 14, 1985

2:00 PM

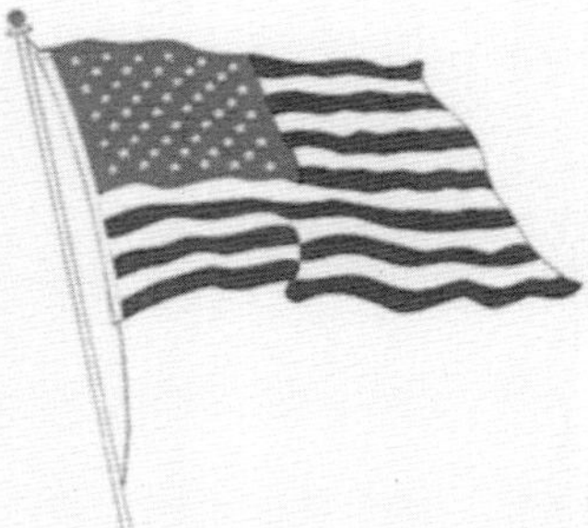

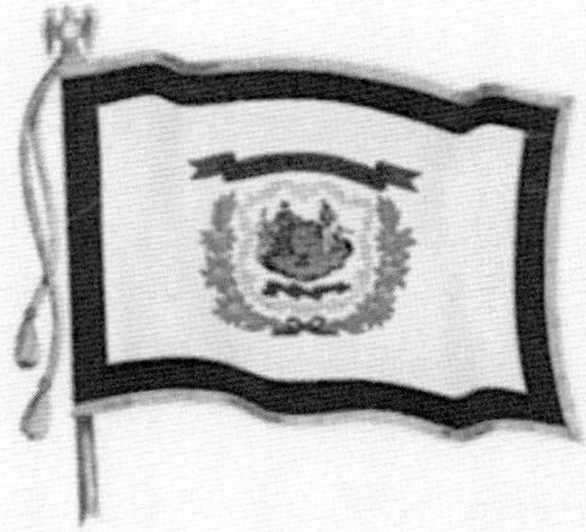

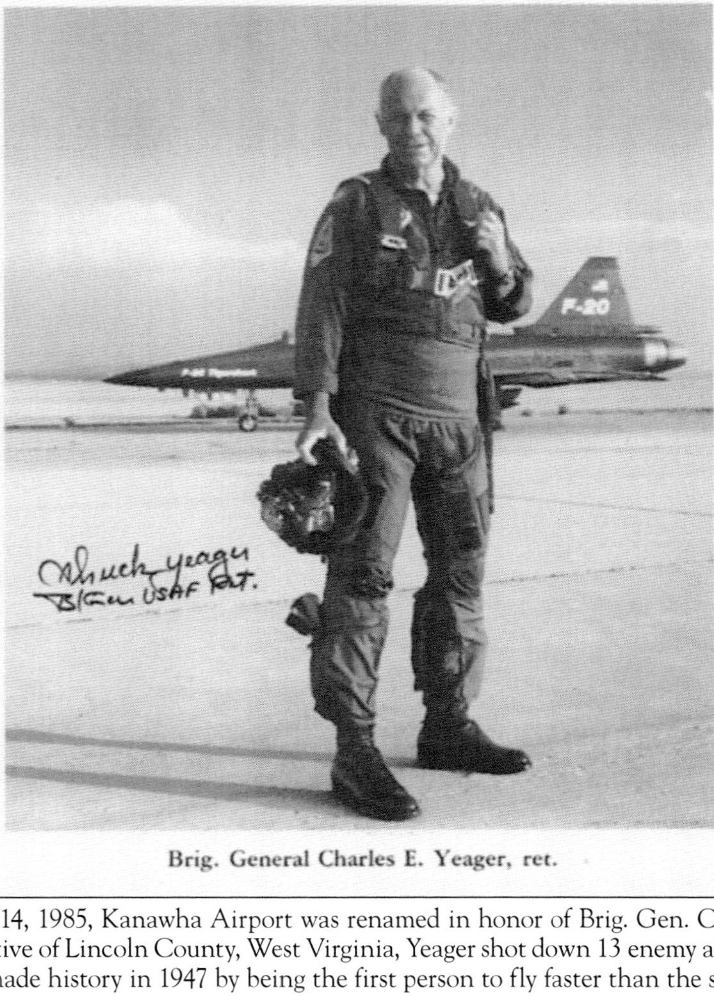

Brig. General Charles E. Yeager, ret.

On October 14, 1985, Kanawha Airport was renamed in honor of Brig. Gen. Charles "Chuck" Yeager. A native of Lincoln County, West Virginia, Yeager shot down 13 enemy aircraft in World War II and made history in 1947 by being the first person to fly faster than the speed of sound.

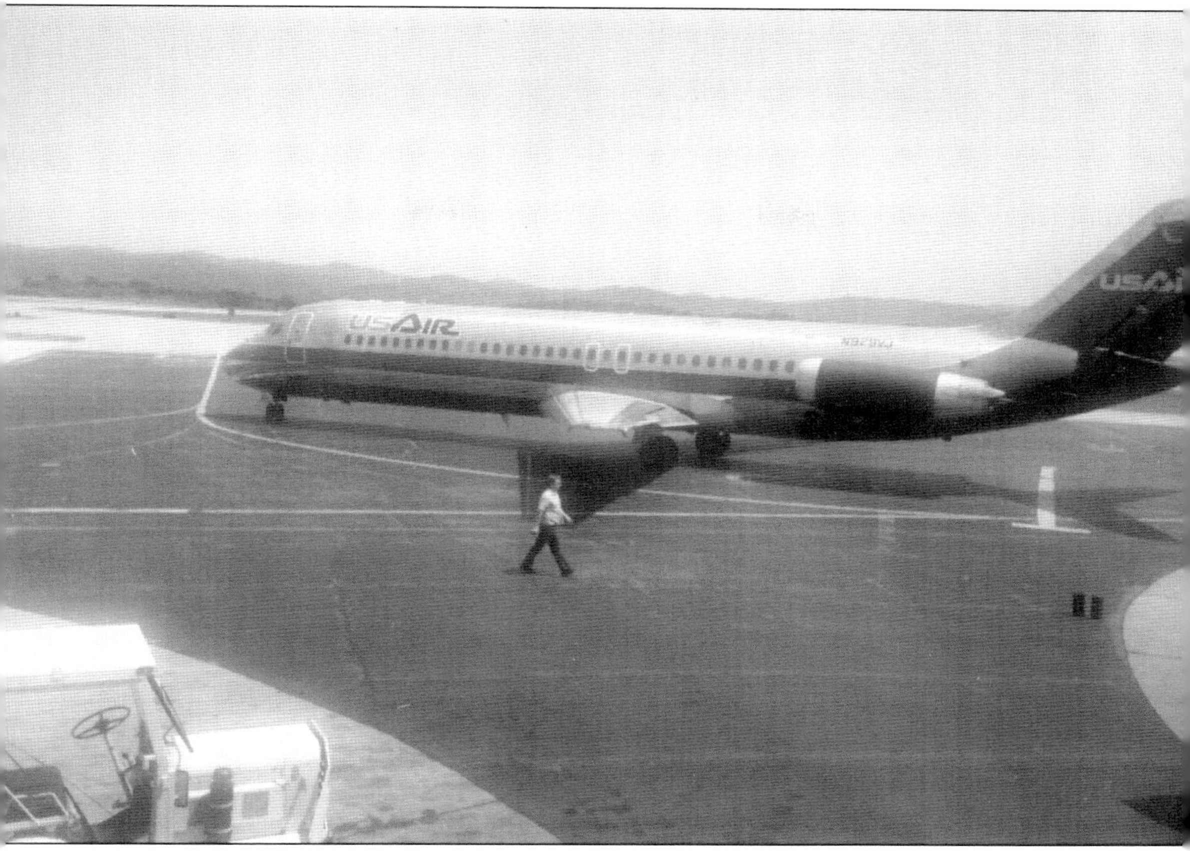

A USAir DC-9 taxis away from the gate in 1986 bound for Pittsburgh, Pennsylvania. The DC-9 was once a common sight at Yeager Airport flying for Eastern, Allegheny, and USAir. (Courtesy of Kathy Keller.)

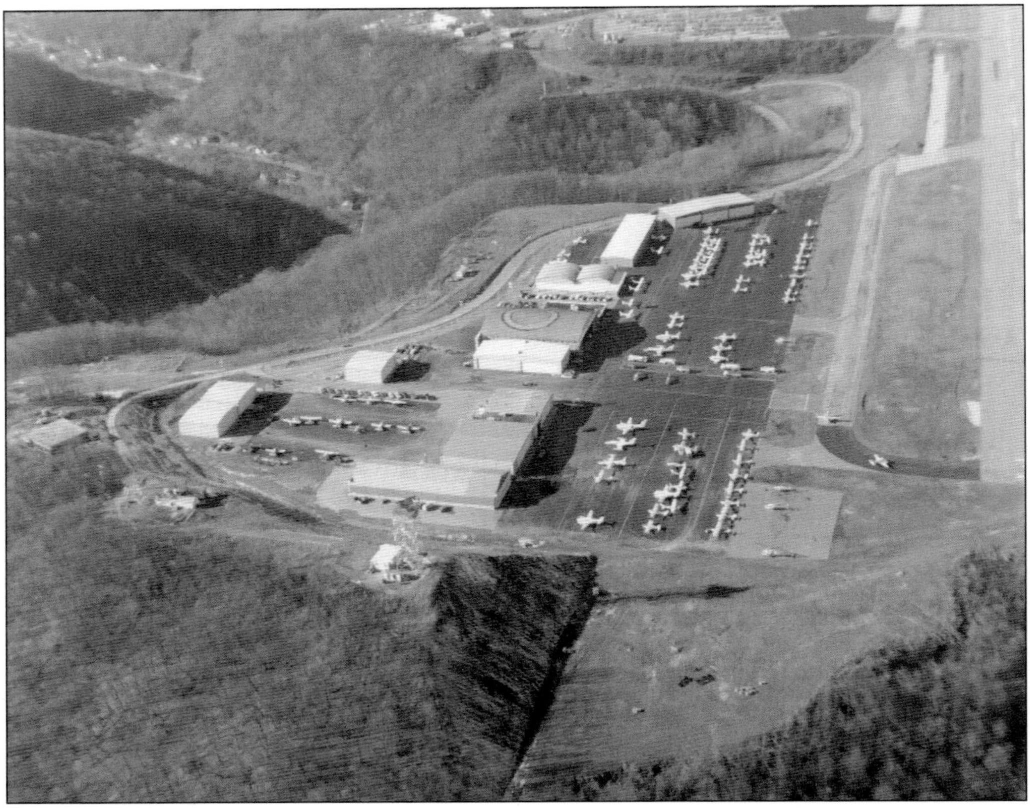

A view of the general aviation ramp shows a large number of aircraft present. Runway 33 is seen on the right and Taxiway B parallels the runway. When Eagle Mountain Road was constructed, dirt was removed from the hillside, causing Taxiway B to be shifted to the right in one section.

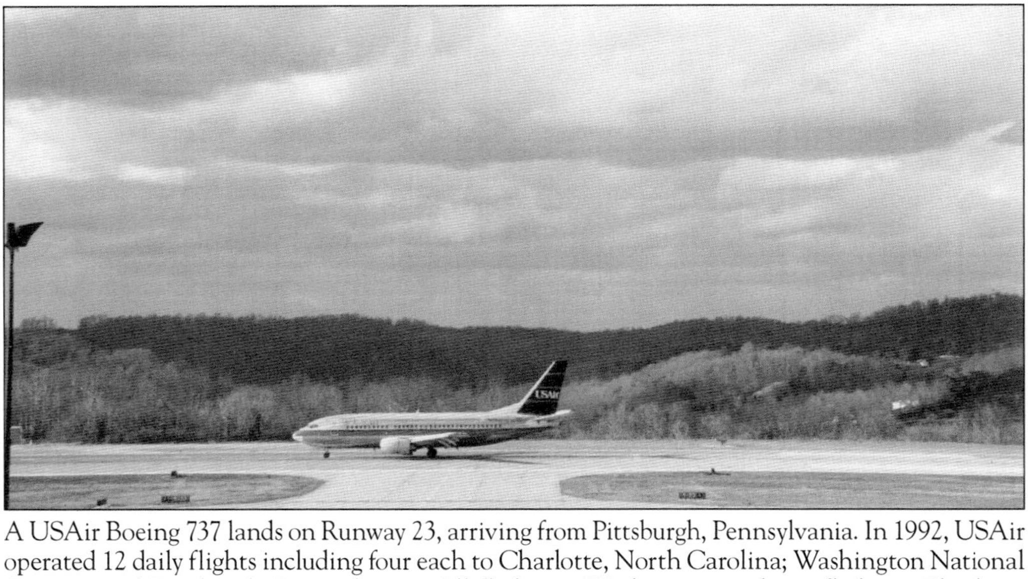

A USAir Boeing 737 lands on Runway 23, arriving from Pittsburgh, Pennsylvania. In 1992, USAir operated 12 daily flights including four each to Charlotte, North Carolina; Washington National Airport; and Pittsburgh, Pennsylvania. All flights to Washington and one flight to Charlotte utilized smaller USAir Express propeller aircraft. The remainder of the flights were on USAir main line jets such as the Boeing 737 or Douglas DC-9.

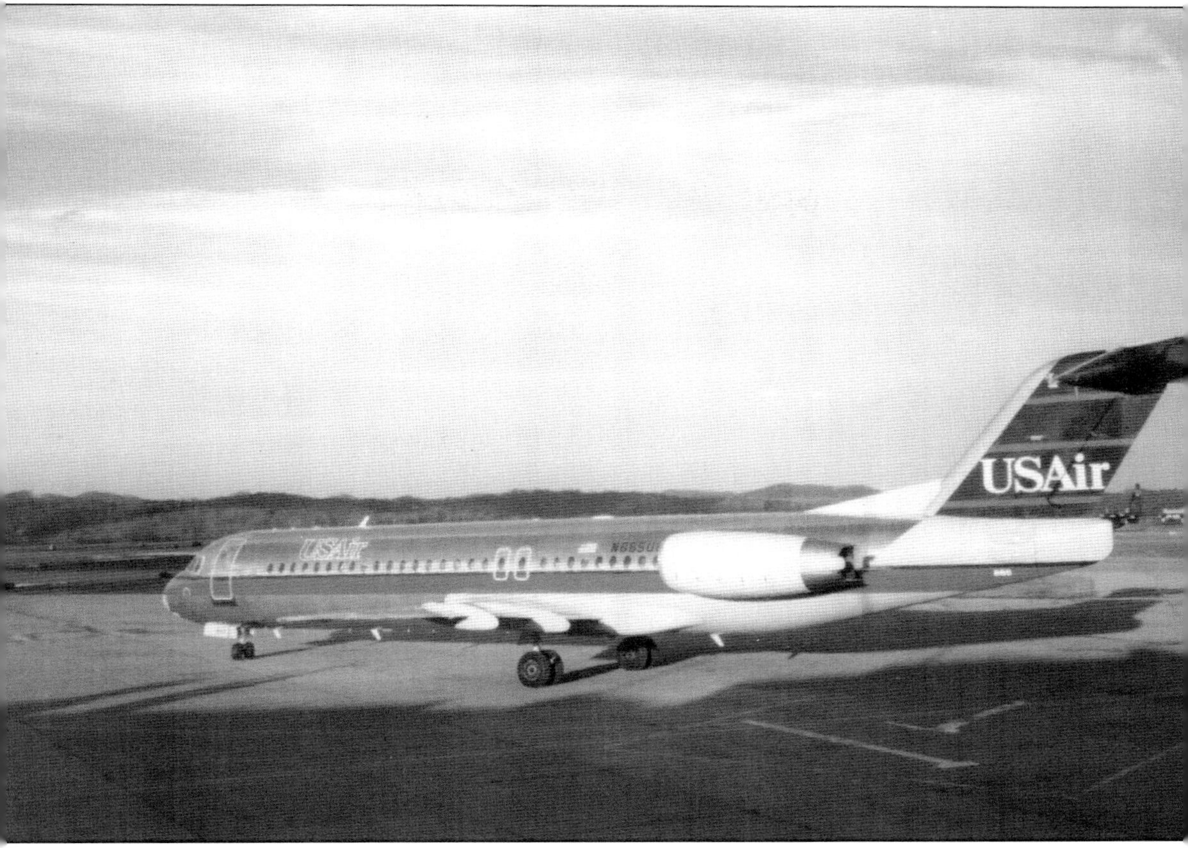

A US Airways Fokker 100 still in USAir paint taxis away from the gate in 1999. In December 1999, US Airways operated five nonstop flights from Charleston to Pittsburgh, Pennsylvania. Three of the flights were operated with Fokker 100s; the other two were handled by a Douglas DC-9 and a Dash-8 turboprop. (Author's collection.)

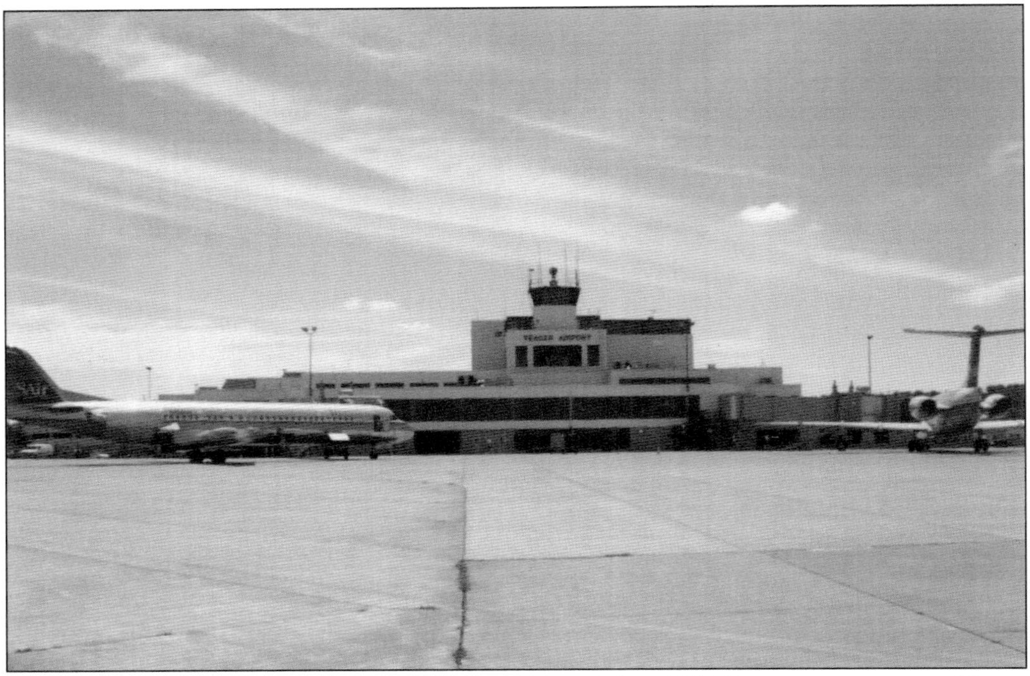

Two USAir Fokker 100s sit at what is now known as gates B1 and B2. This gate area was an addition to the terminal building, which opened in approximately 1971. The upper floor of the addition featured floor-to-ceiling windows, allowing uninterrupted views of the airfield with seating for 149. The bottom floor was a lobby for arriving passengers that seated 75.

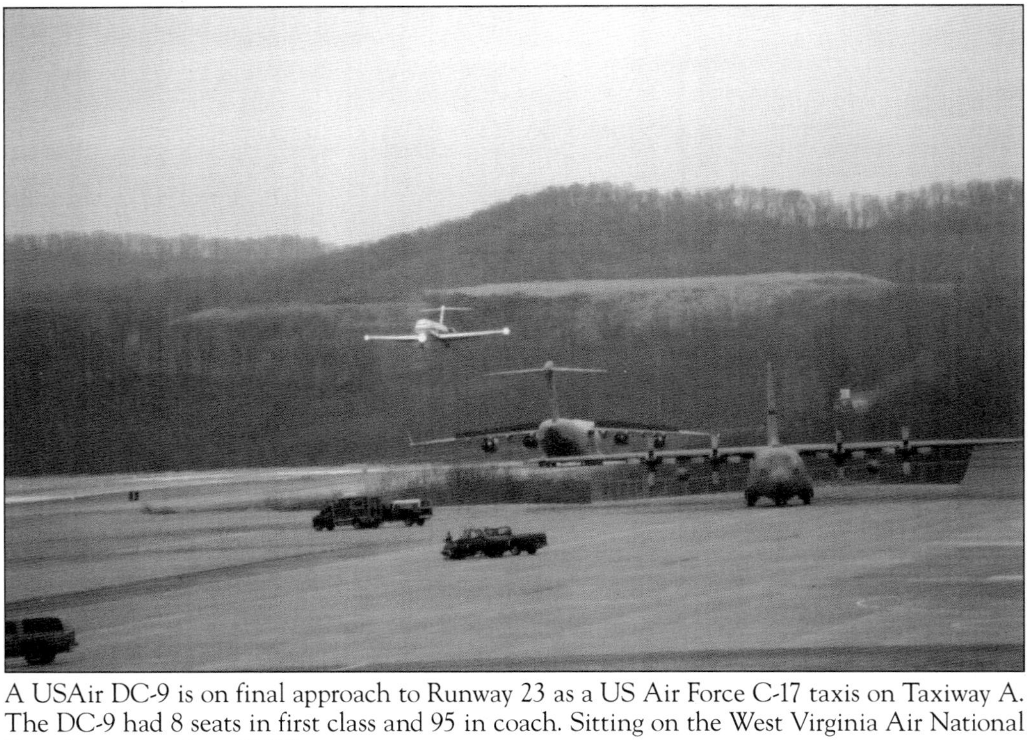

A USAir DC-9 is on final approach to Runway 23 as a US Air Force C-17 taxis on Taxiway A. The DC-9 had 8 seats in first class and 95 in coach. Sitting on the West Virginia Air National Guard ramp is a lone C-130.

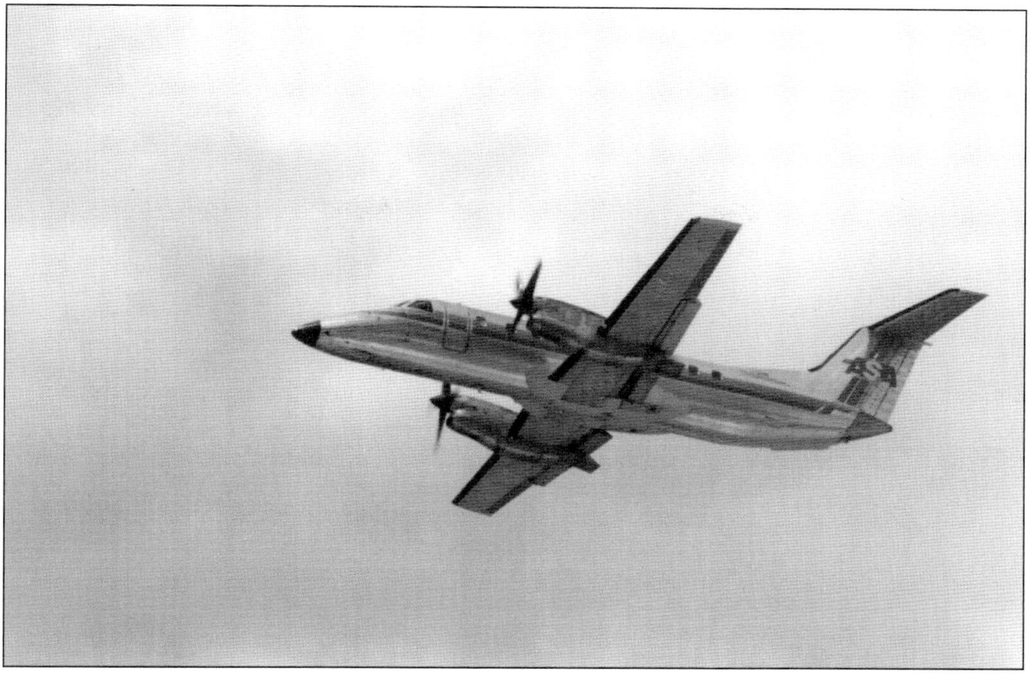

An Atlantic Southeast Airlines (Delta Connection) Embraer 120 Brasilia takes off for Atlanta, Georgia. The Embraer 120 seats 30 passengers and has a cruise speed of 340 miles per hour.

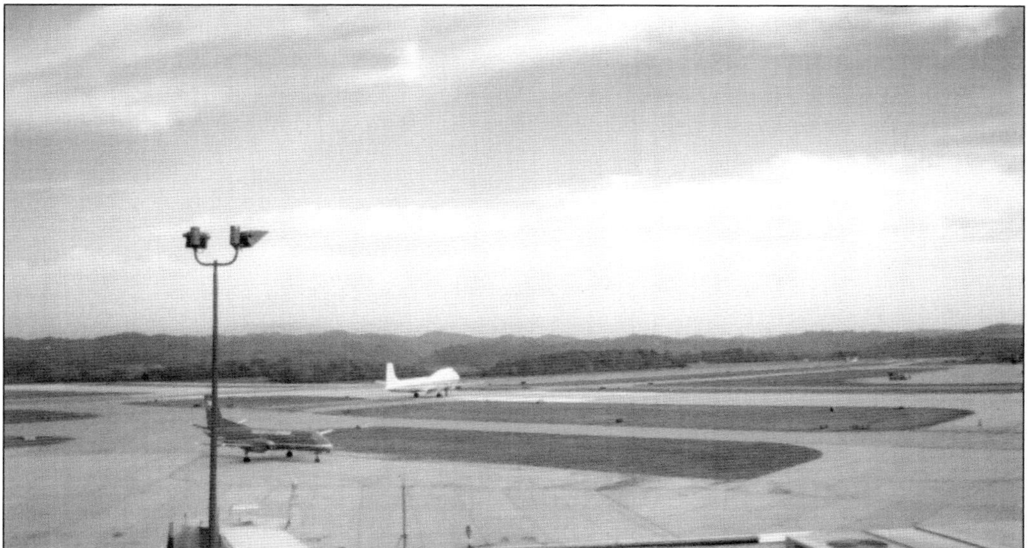

Seen here is a Northwest Airlink Saab 340 (foreground) with a rare visitor in the background. An Aviation Traders Carvair is seen taxiing toward Runway 23. The Carvair was able to carry 21 passengers in the cabin and five cars in a cargo area. Only 21 of these unique aircraft were built.

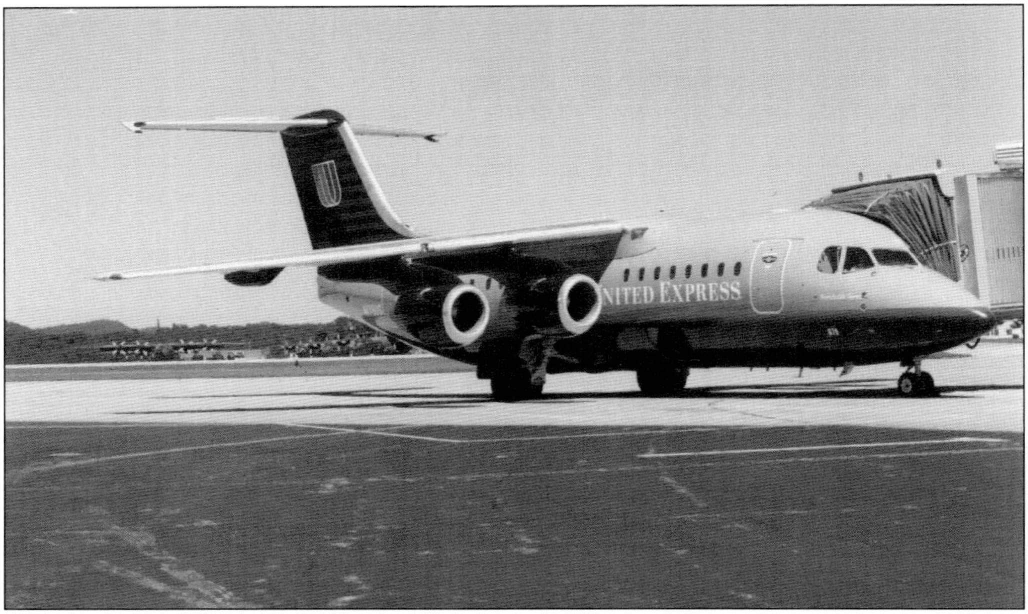

Air Wisconsin operated these BAE-146 four-engine jets on behalf of United Express from Charleston to Chicago's O'Hare International Airport with a stop in Lexington, Kentucky. By 1999, these aircraft and the stop in Lexington were replaced with Canadair Regional Jets nonstop to Chicago, Illinois.

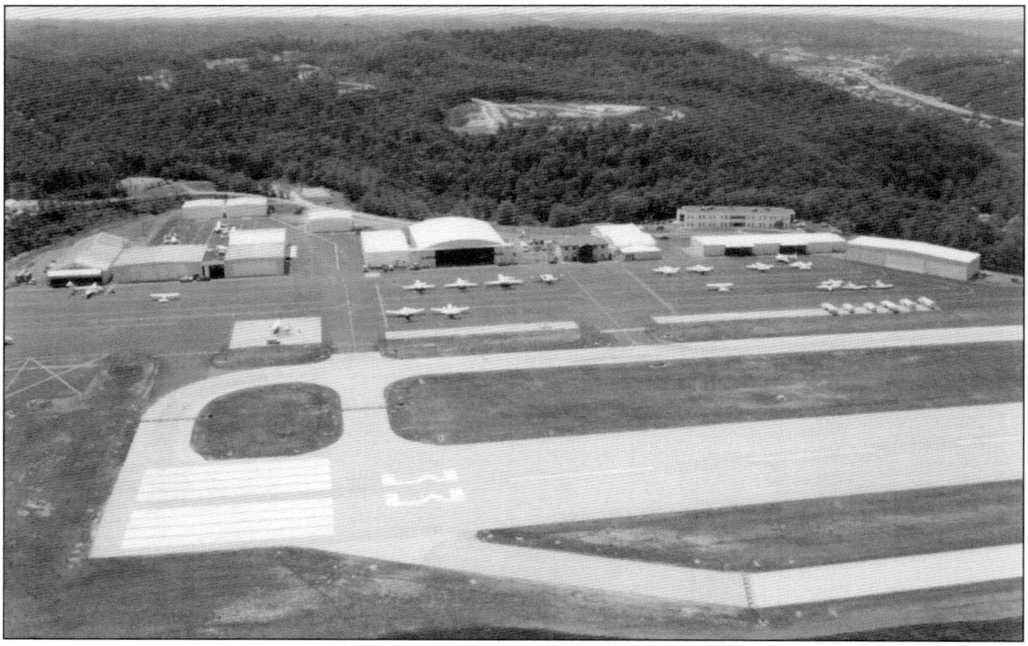

Many private aircraft sit on the general aviation ramp, with Runway 33 in the foreground. The general aviation area is where all civil aircraft go— other than scheduled airlines. The airport grants one or more organizations the right to be a fixed-base operator, selling aviation fuel, aircraft servicing, parking, and other aeronautical services. Military aircraft also commonly use general aviation facilities to obtain fuel from the fixed-base operator. Executive Air is the current fixed-base operator at Yeager Airport.

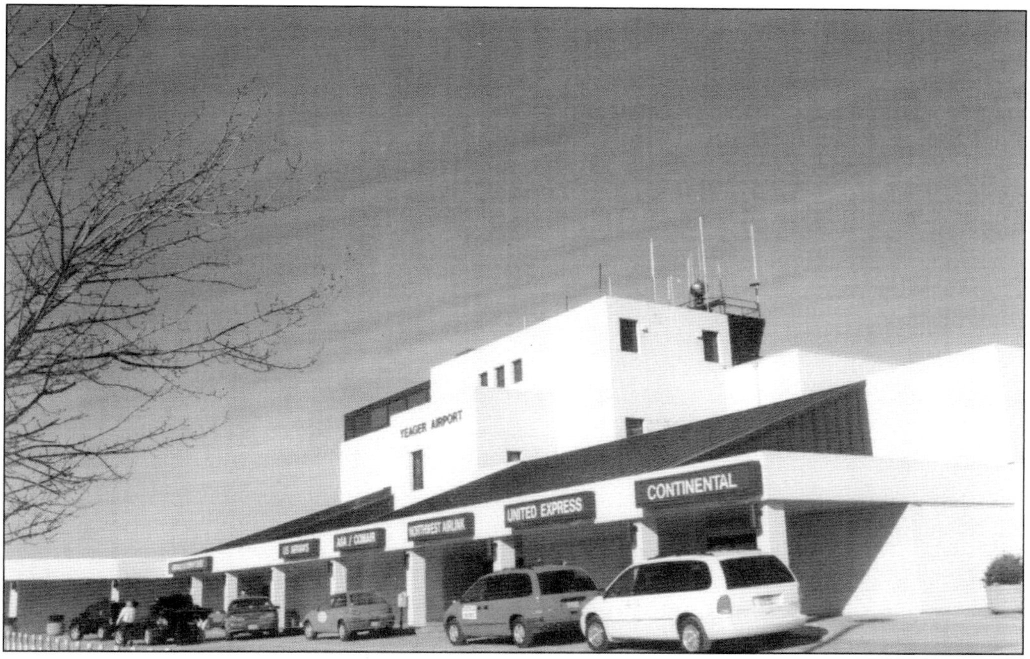

This late-1990s view shows the terminal building with the names of each airline displayed on the front. An awning now covers the first lane of the road to make drop-off and pickup more convenient in inclement weather conditions.

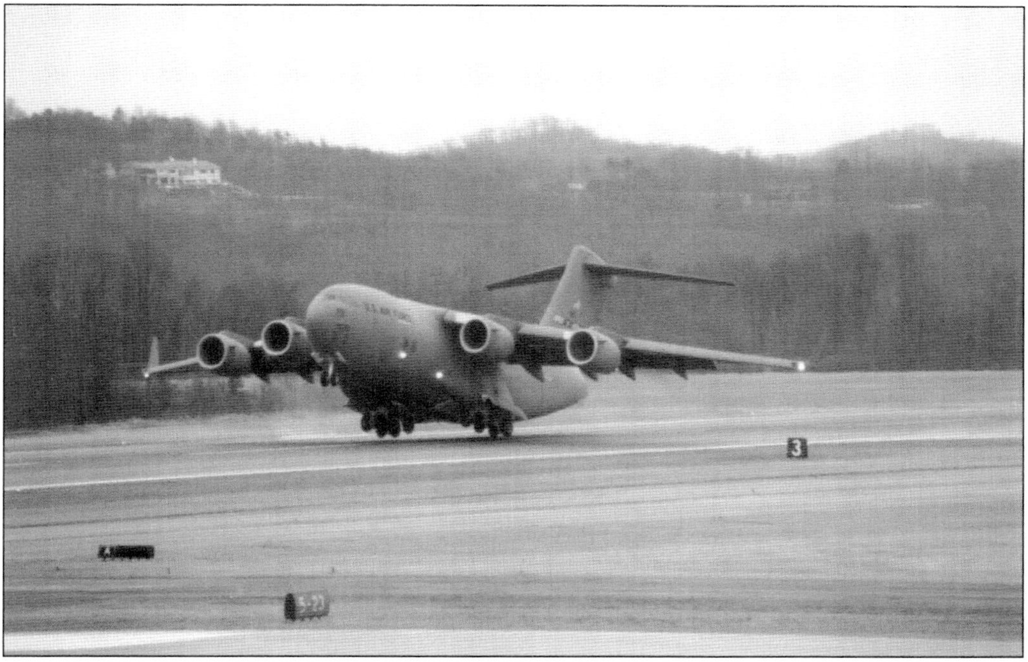

A US Air Force C-17 Globemaster III taking off from Runway 23. These cargo aircraft have a wingspan of 169 feet 10 inches. The 167th Airlift Wing of the West Virginia Air National Guard currently flies the C-17 out of Martinsburg, West Virginia, and is commonly seen at Yeager Airport. The large block box with the 3 is a distance remaining sign and indicates 3,000 feet of runway remaining.

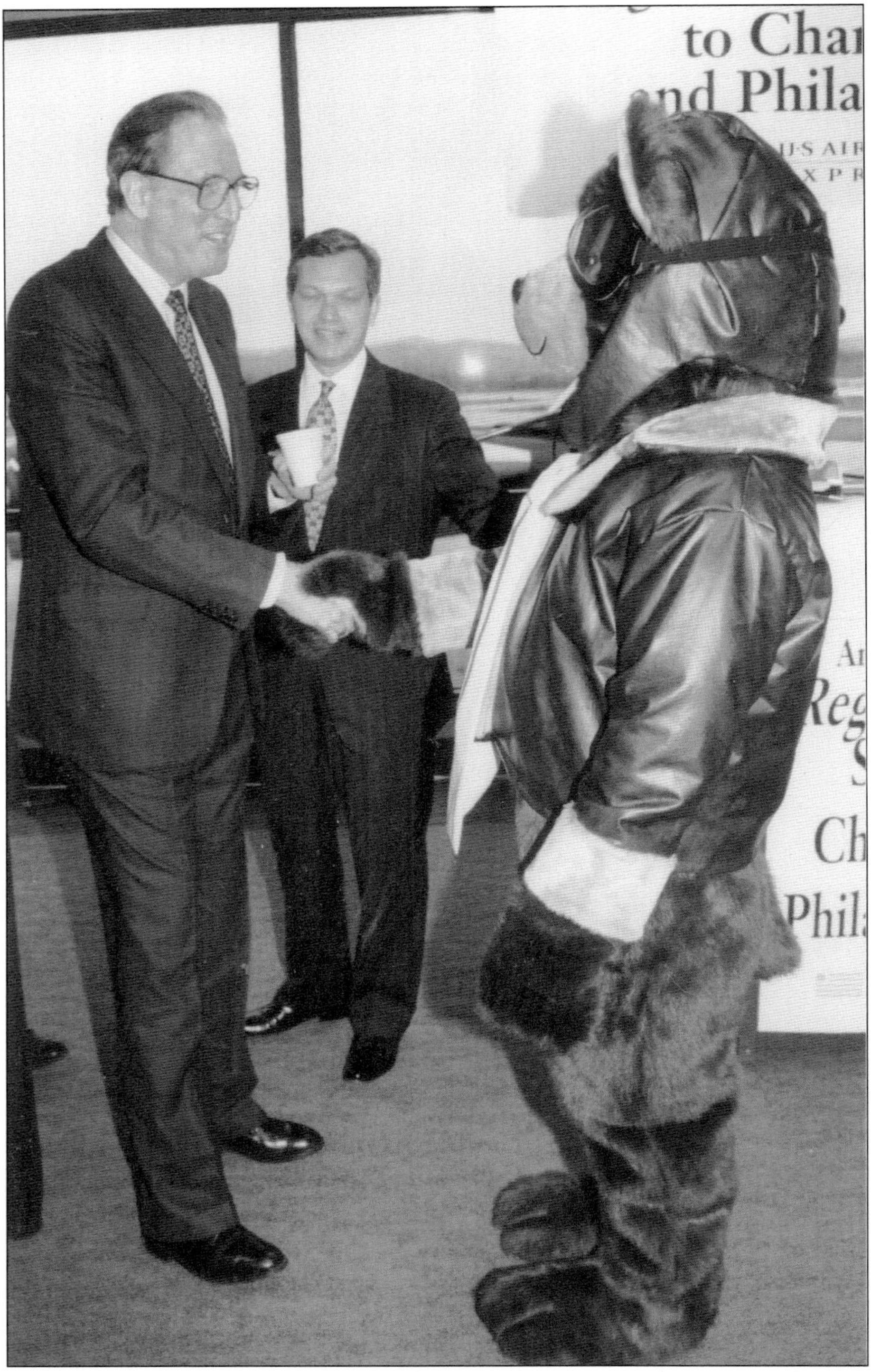

Sen. John D. Rockefeller IV (left) and Central West Virginia Regional Airport Authority Board chairman R. Edison Hill (center) talk with airport mascot Yeagie Bear. On May 27, 2003, the Board of Members of the Central West Virginia Regional Airport Authority named the terminal building in honor of Senator Rockefeller for his leadership on aviation issues.

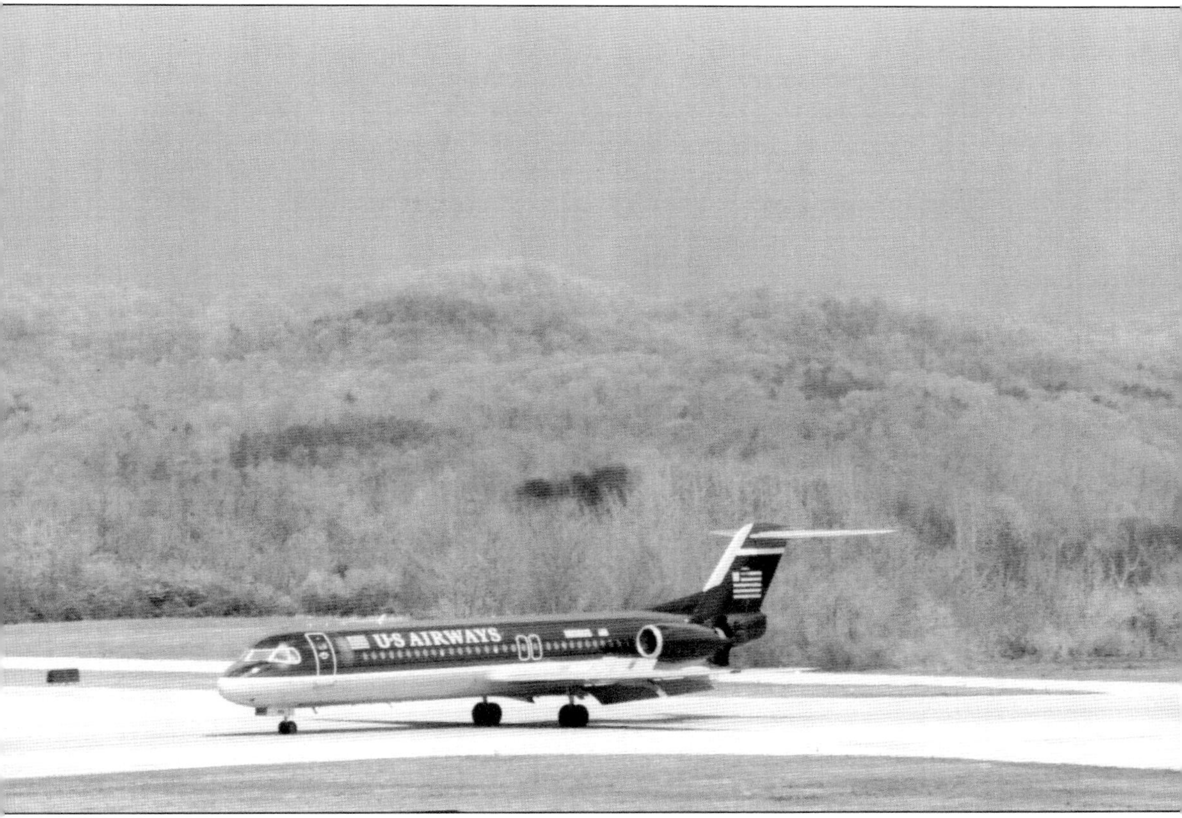

A US Airways Fokker 100 lands on Runway 23. In 1997, USAir changed its name to US Airways and eventually merged with American Airlines.

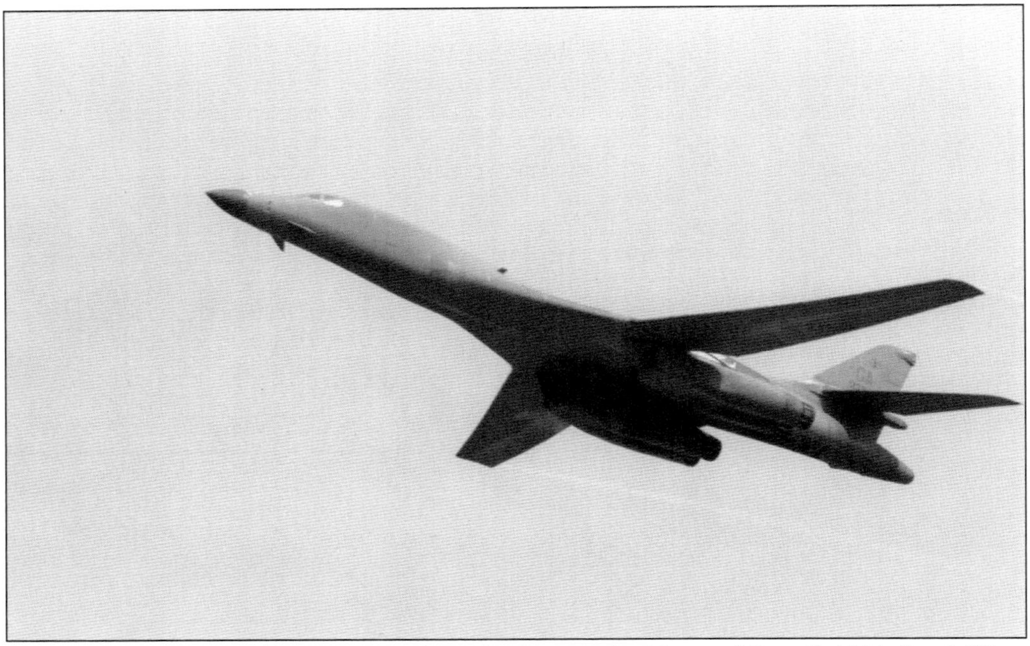

A US Air Force Rockwell B-1B Lancer from the Georgia Air National Guard's 116th Bomb Wing flies over Yeager Airport in the late 1990s. The B-1B is a supersonic four-engine jet bomber first introduced in 1986.

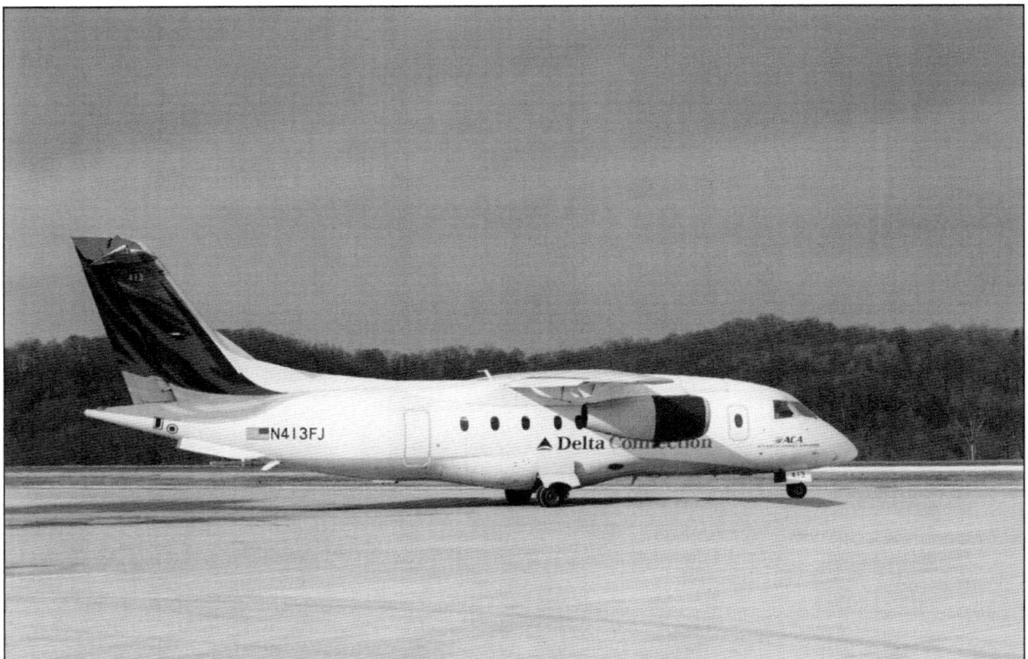

Seen here is a Dornier 328Jet, operated by Atlantic Coast Airlines on behalf of Delta Connection. These 32-seat aircraft operated nonstop to Atlanta, Georgia, replacing turboprop aircraft previously operated on the route.

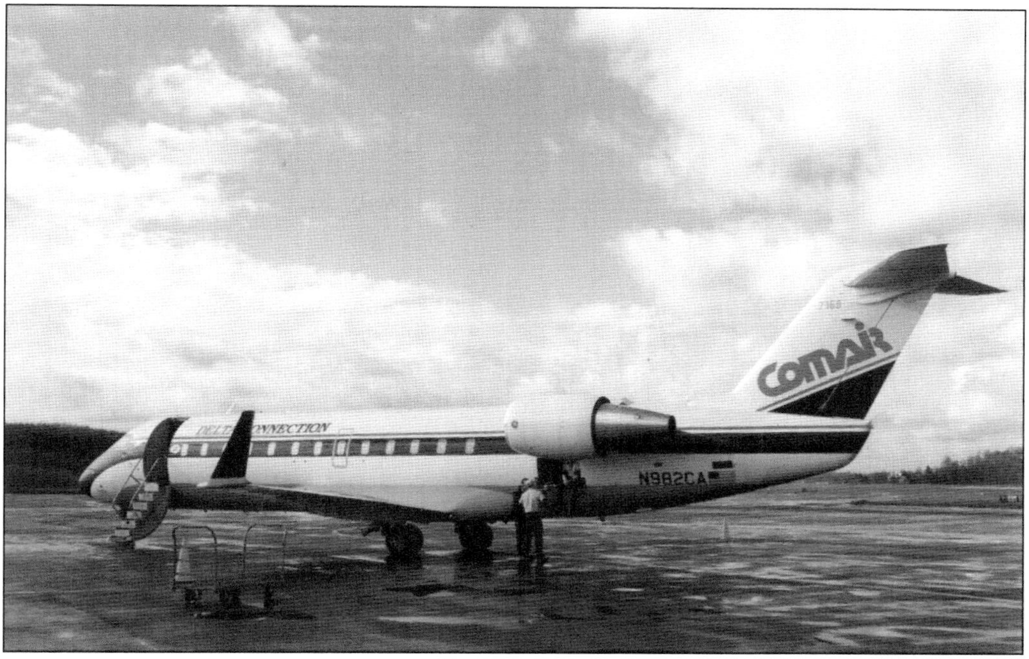

Comair operated the 50-seat Canadair CRJ-100 on behalf of Delta Connection with nonstop service to Cincinnati/Northern Kentucky International Airport. The CRJ was a popular aircraft that proliferated in the early 2000s, replacing many slower turboprop aircraft.

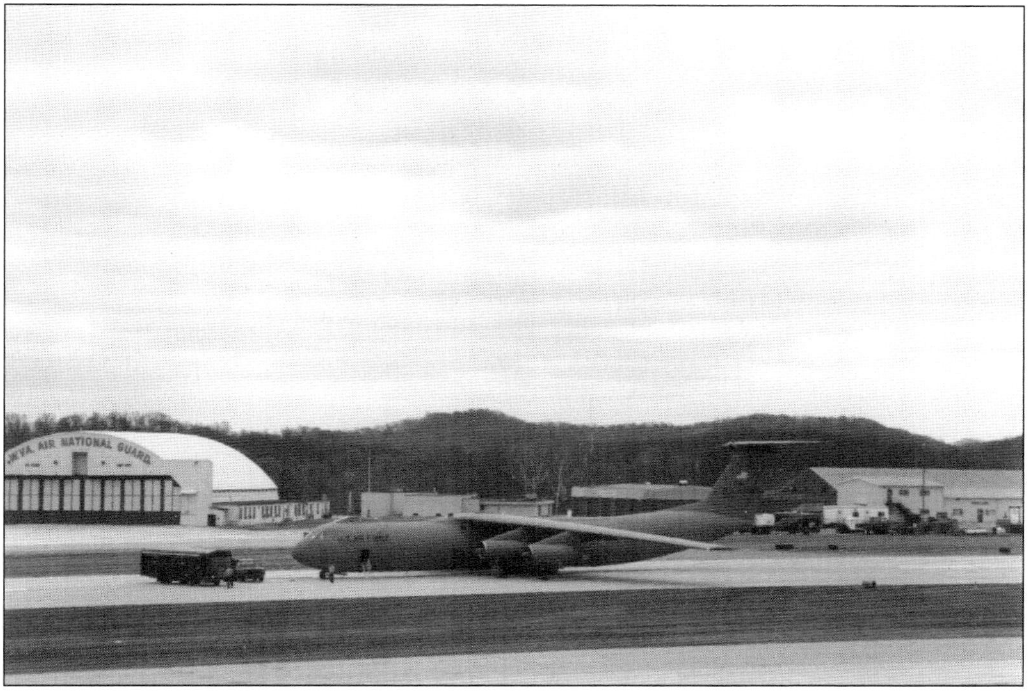

A US Air Force C-141 Starlifter is parked on Runway 15/33 in the 1990s. The C-141 was a long-range transport introduced in 1965 as a replacement for slower propeller-driven transports. The final C-141 was retired by the US Air Force in 2006 and replaced by the C-17.

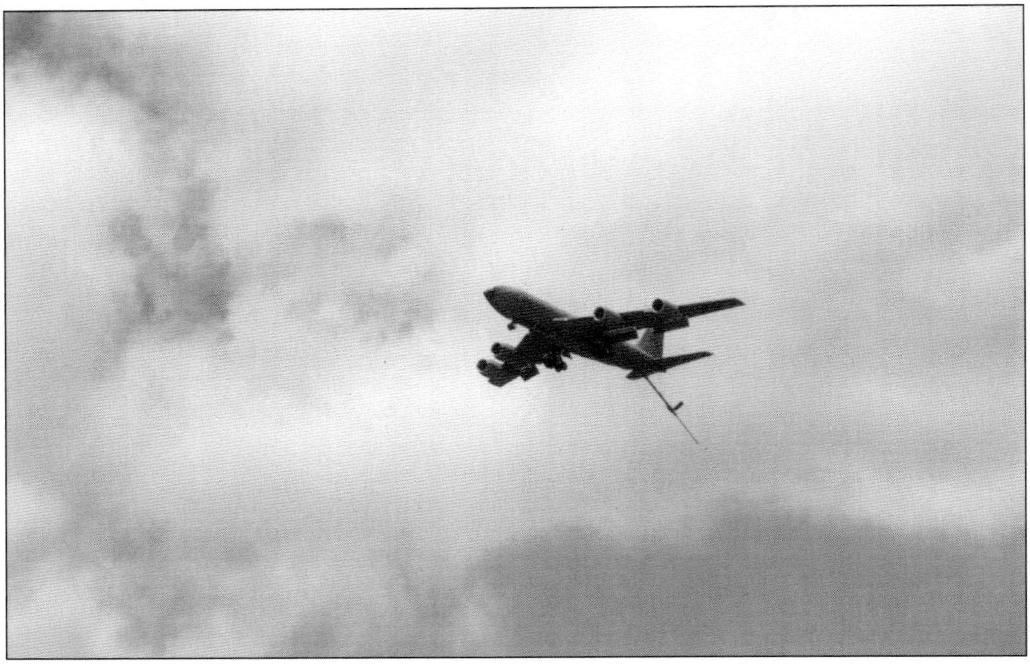

A US Air Force KC-135 aerial refueling tanker conducts a flyby with its aerial refueling boom extended during the 2000 air show. The KC-135 was introduced in 1956 and holds a maximum transfer fuel load of 200,000 pounds.

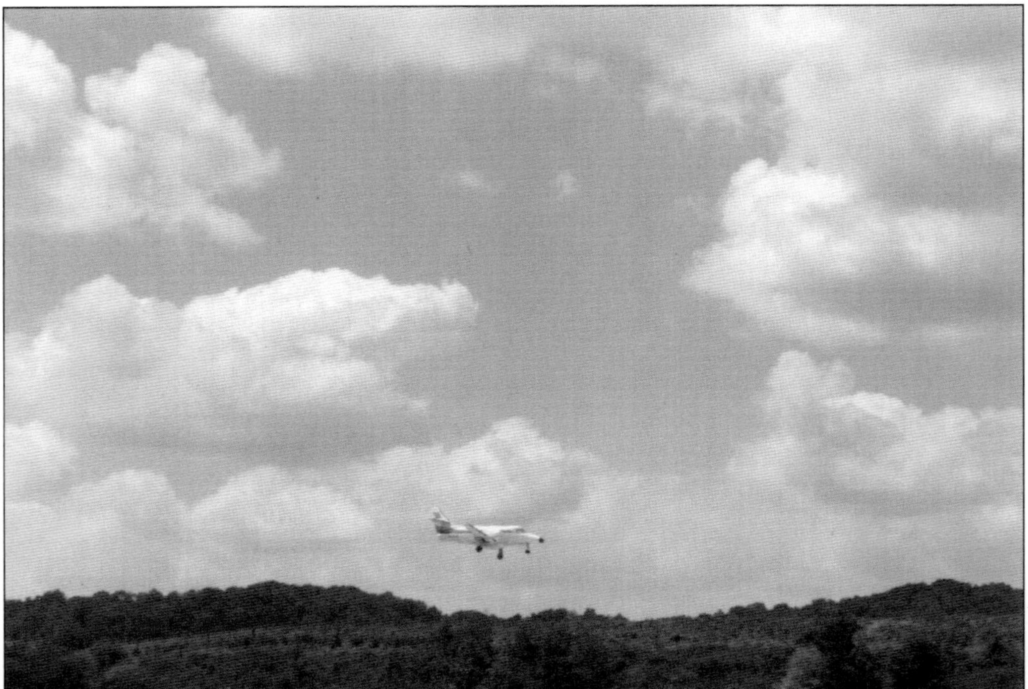

A United Express Jetstream 31 comes in for a landing on Runway 5 in the late 1990s. These aircraft operated on nonstop flights from Charleston to Washington Dulles International Airport in one hour and ten minutes. (Author's collection.)

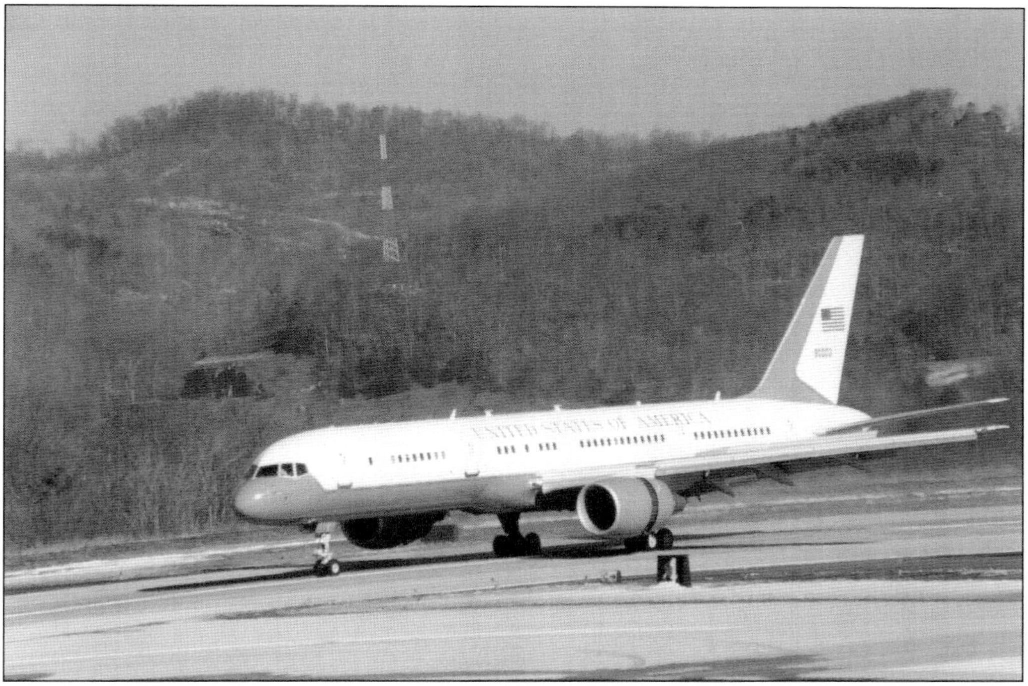

A common visitor since the 1990s, the US Air Force C-32 (Boeing 757-200) conducts a touch-and-go landing. These aircraft appear in the presidential paint scheme and are operated by the 89th Airlift Wing and used primarily for the vice president, cabinet members, and members of Congress. If the president is on board this or any other Air Force aircraft, it is known as Air Force One.

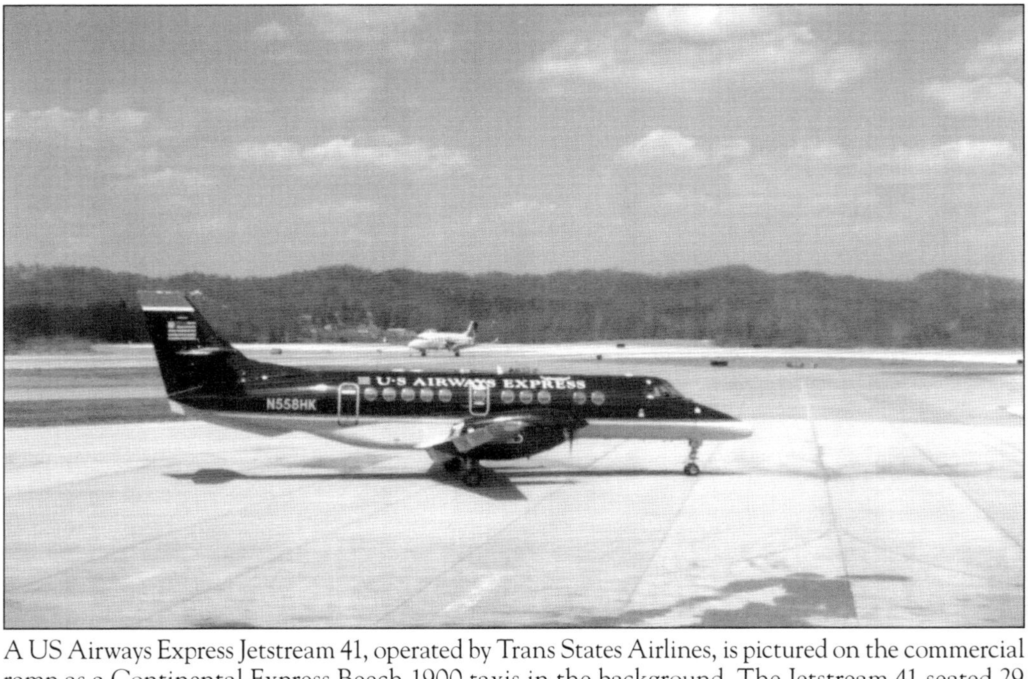

A US Airways Express Jetstream 41, operated by Trans States Airlines, is pictured on the commercial ramp as a Continental Express Beech 1900 taxis in the background. The Jetstream 41 seated 29 passengers and had a cruising speed of 299 miles per hour.

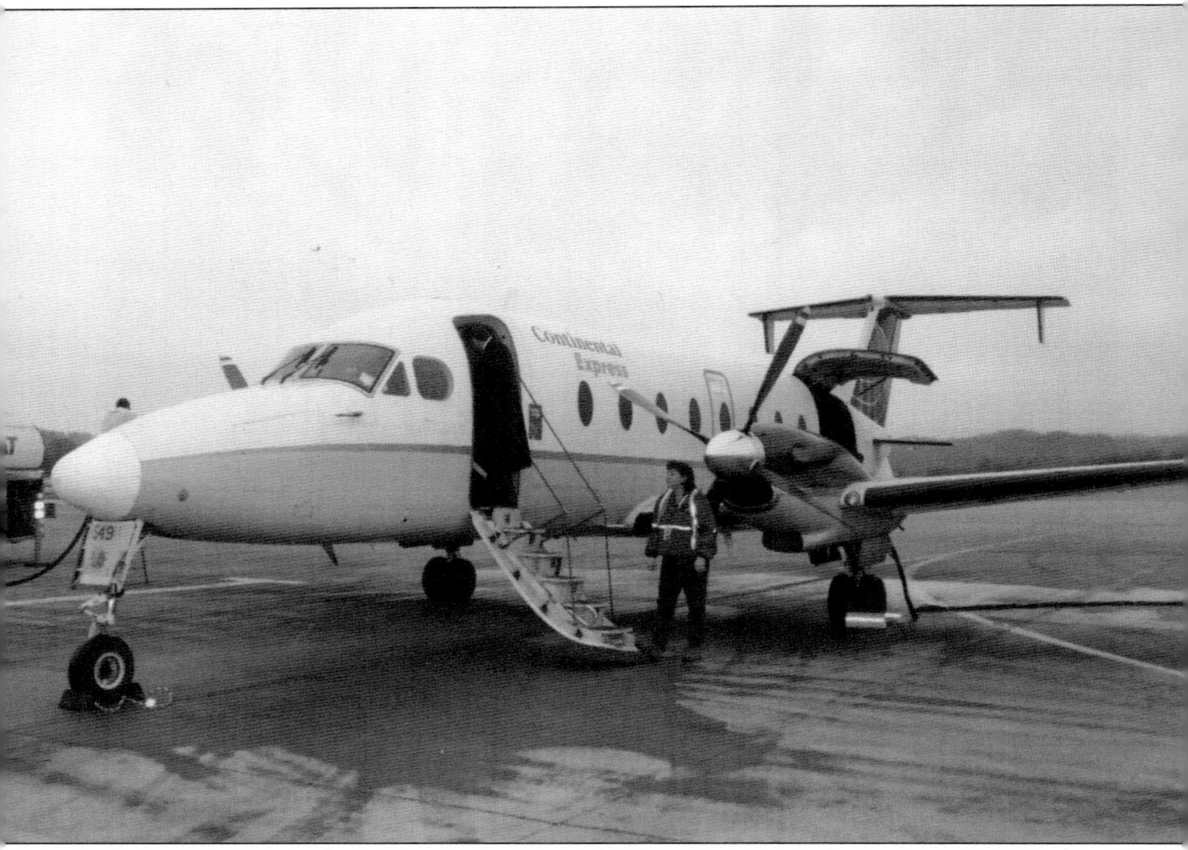

A passenger enters the cabin of a Continental Express Beech 1900D operated by CommutAir as an employee watches from the ramp. CommutAir flew from Charleston to Continental's hub at Cleveland, Ohio. The Beech 1900D seated 19 passengers and did not have a flight attendant, lavatory, or cockpit door.

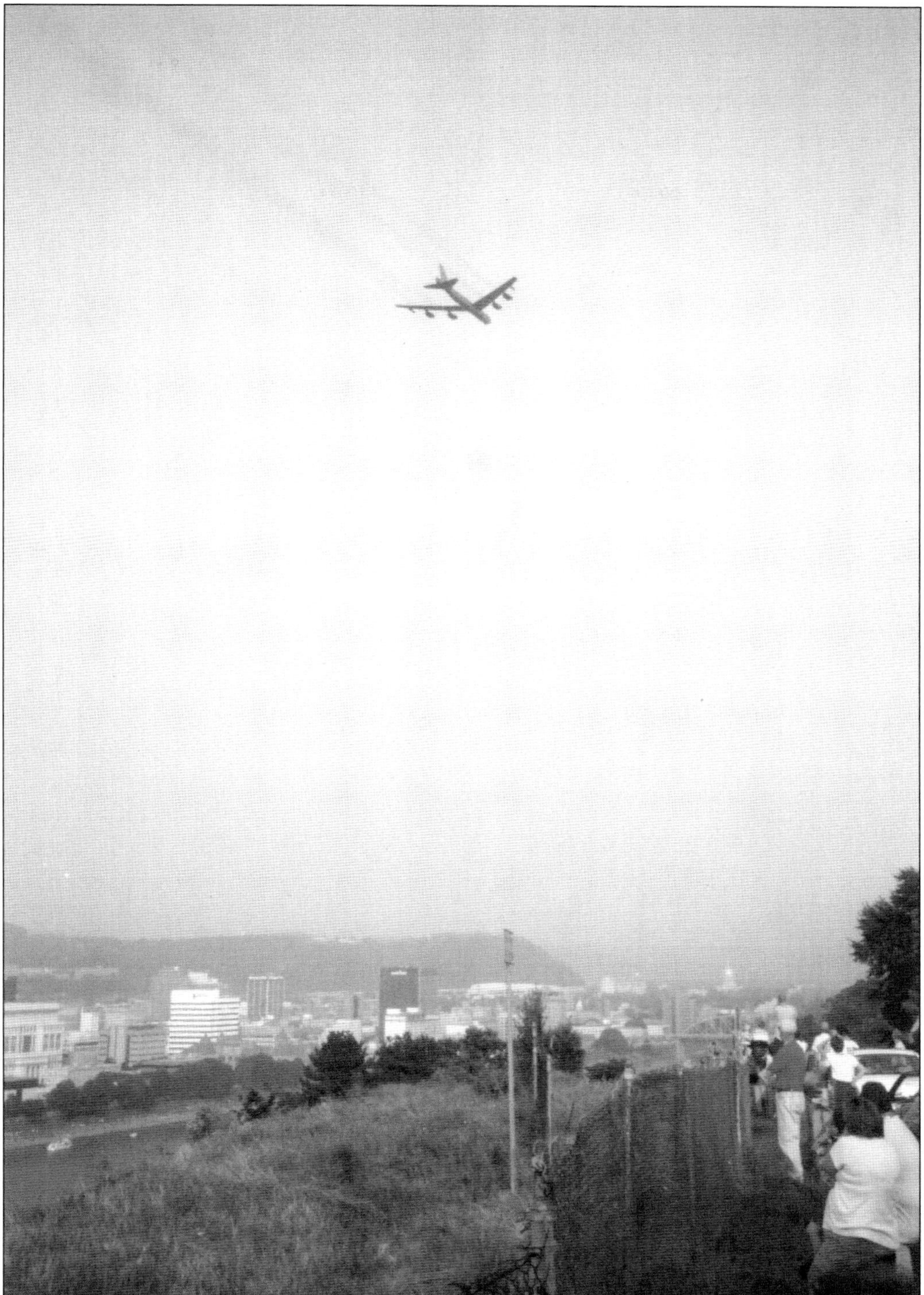

On July 4, 2003, a US Air Force B-52 bomber conducted a flyover of Fourth of July celebrations in downtown Charleston, West Virginia. This is likely the only time a B-52 has flown over Charleston. (Author's collection.)

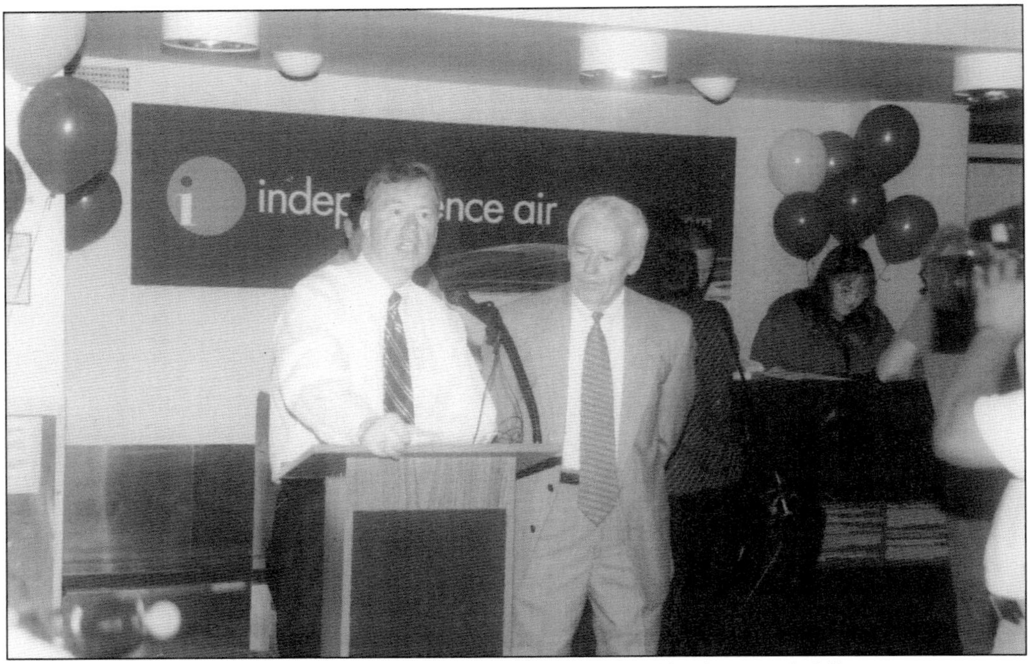

Kanawha County Commission president W. Kent Carper (left), along with fellow commissioner Henry C. "Hoppy" Shores, speaks at a ceremony celebrating West Virginia's first low-fare airline, Independence Air. The airline initially offered six nonstop flights per day to Washington Dulles International Airport from Charleston.

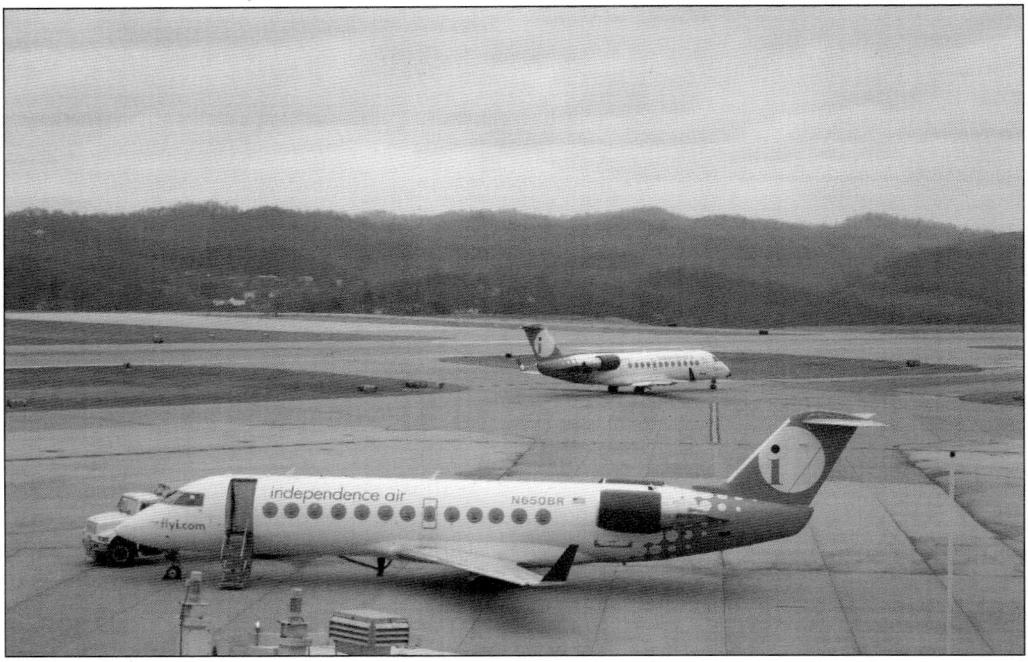

Two Independence Air Bombardier CRJ-200 fifty-seat regional jets are pictured on the commercial ramp. Based at Washington Dulles International Airport, Independence Air operated from June 2004 until January 2006, after declaring bankruptcy in November 2005. The airline offered six flights per day from Charleston to Washington Dulles and advertised one-way fares as low as $39.

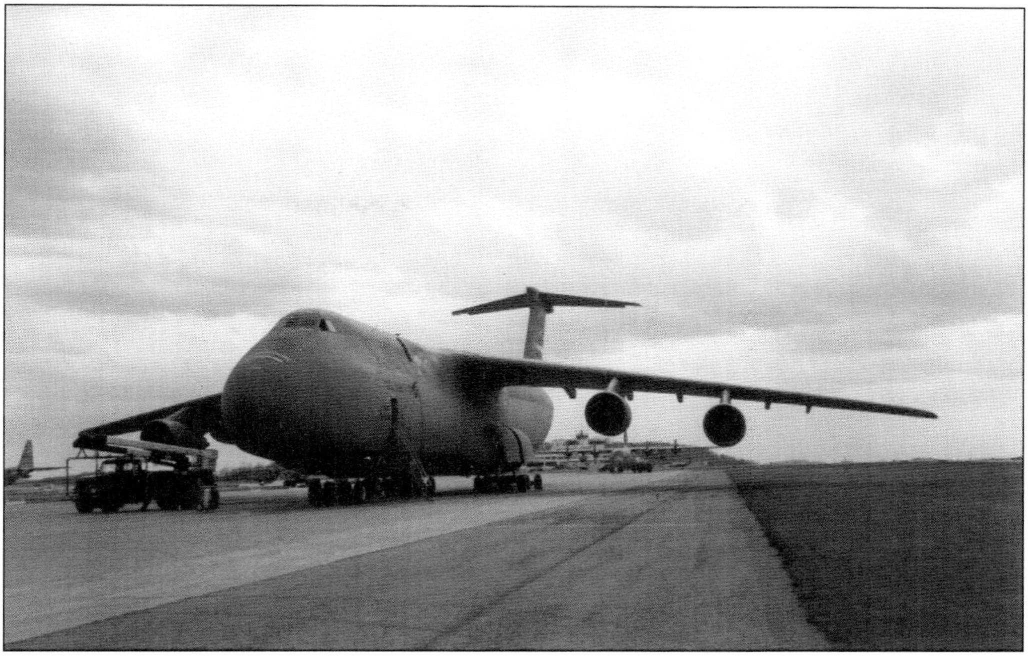

A gigantic Lockheed C-5 Galaxy sits on the West Virginia Air National Guard ramp on June 29, 2009. The C-5 is one of the largest aircraft in the world and has five sets of landing gear with a total of 28 wheels. The C-5 was a frequent visitor to Yeager Airport when the aircraft was operated by the 167th Airlift Wing in Martinsburg, West Virginia.

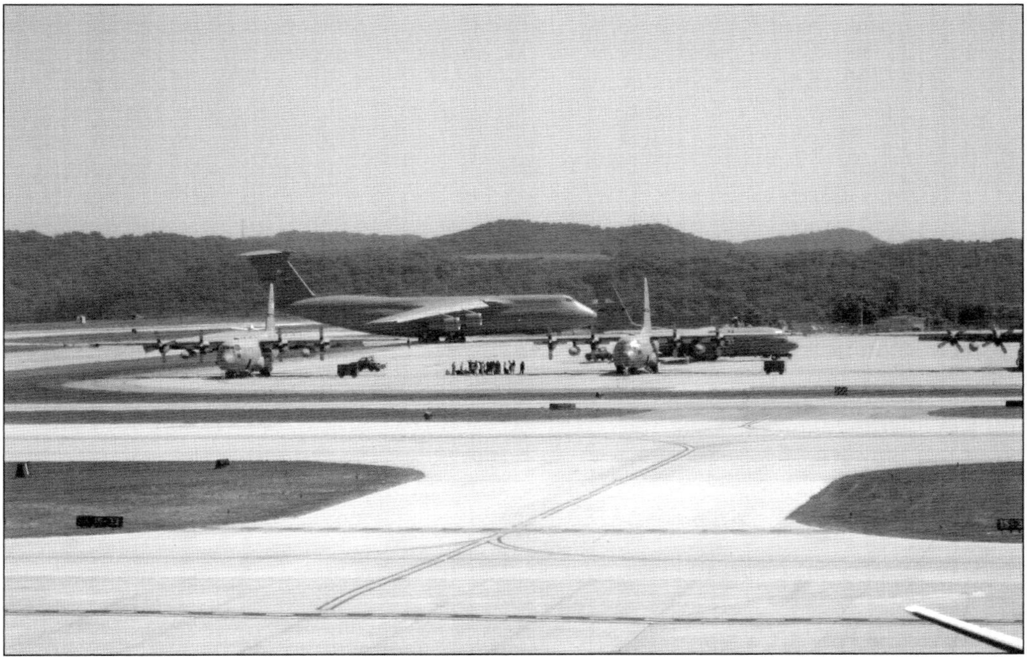

A C-5 Galaxy from the West Virginia Air National Guard's 167th Airlift Wing in Martinsburg, West Virginia, dwarfs the 130th Airlift Wing's C-130 Hercules. The C-5 is 65 feet 1 inch-tall, is 247 feet 1 inch in length, and has a wingspan of 222 feet 9 inches. The C-130 is 38 feet 9 inches tall, has 97 feet 9 inches in length, and a wingspan of 132 feet 7 inches.

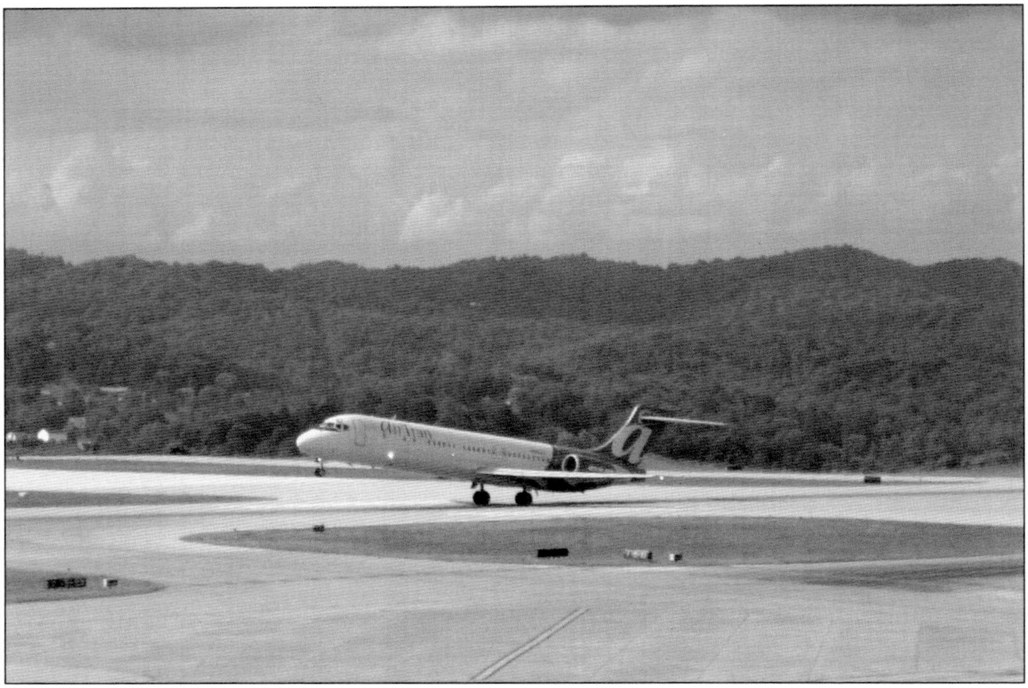

An AirTran Airways flight from Charleston takes off on June 30, 2009, bound for Orlando, Florida. AirTran operated successfully three days per week primarily using the Boeing 717 and ceased operating at Yeager Airport on June 3, 2012, after being acquired by Southwest Airlines.

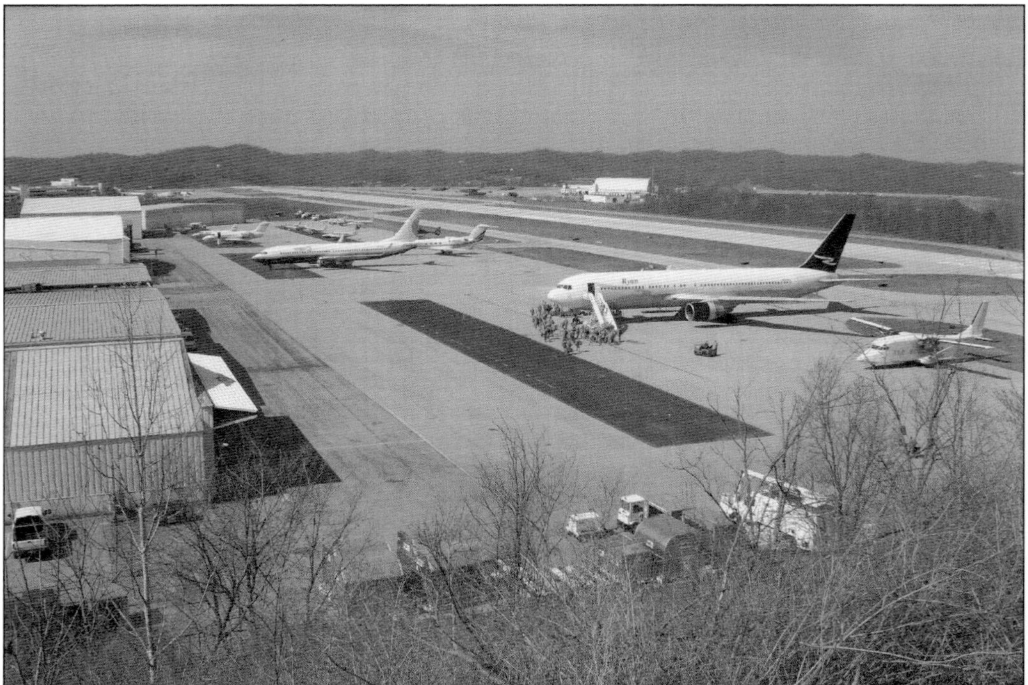

A busy general ramp on June 30, 2009, includes a Miami Air Boeing 737 and Ryan Boeing 767. Both aircraft arrived in Charleston bringing soldiers home on charter flights.

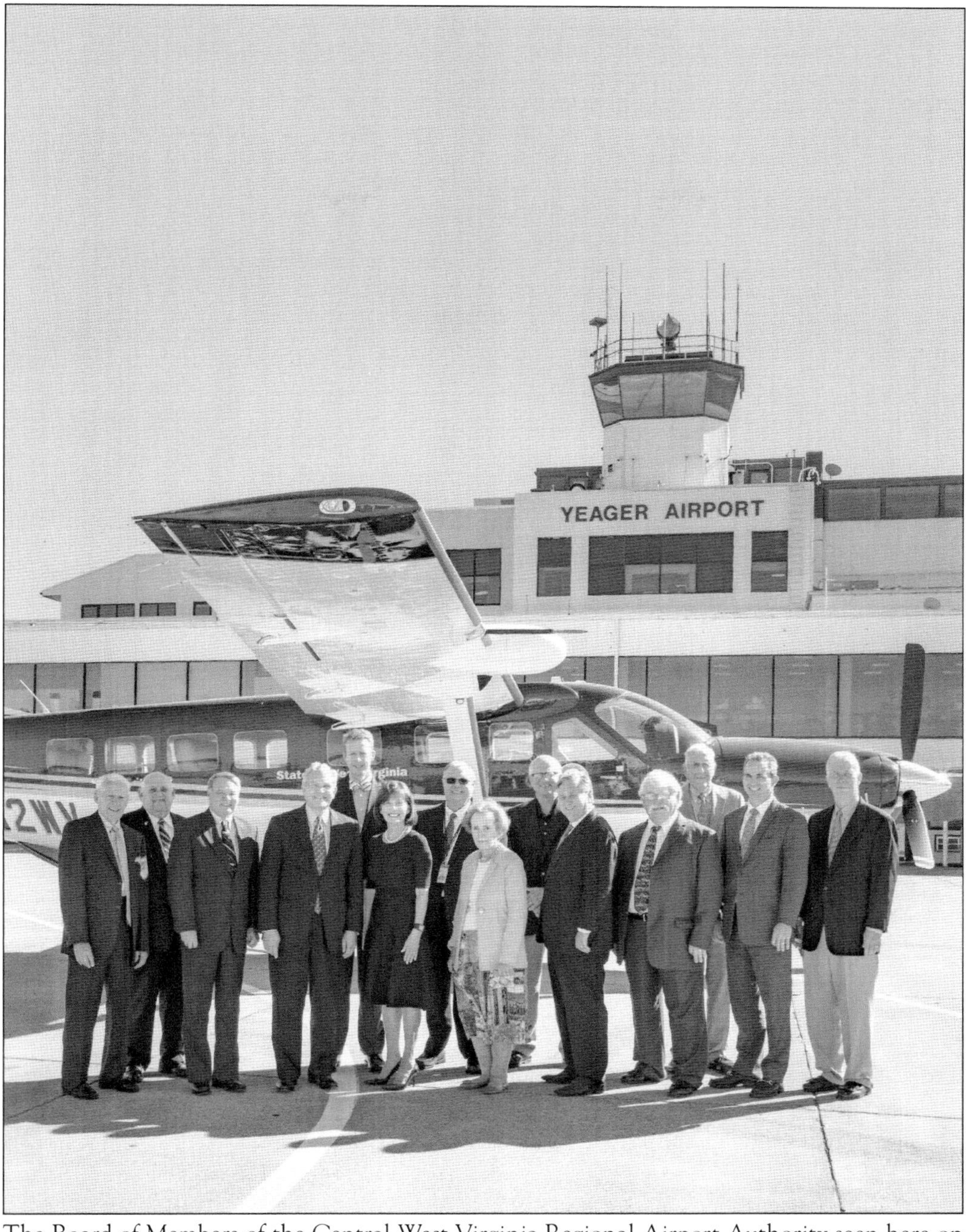

The Board of Members of the Central West Virginia Regional Airport Authority seen here on September 28, 2016, includes, from left to right, Henry C. "Hoppy" Shores; Maj. Gen. Allen Tackett (Ret.); Col. Bill Peters (Ret.); R. Edison Hill, chairman; Todd Goldman; Karen Haddad; Terry Sayre, airport director; Priscilla Haden; Brad Reed; Charles Bailey, general counsel; Jim Caruthers; Charles Jones; Norman "Trip" Shumate; and H.B. Wehrle. Not pictured are Charles Dusic, David Hill, and Allen Holder.